The Family Cult Paradox

Copyright © 2024 by Kenogi Gigagei Latham

All rights reserved. No part of this book may be reproduced or transmitted in any form or by any means, electronic or mechanical, including photocopying, recording, or by any information storage and retrieval system, without the prior written permission of the publisher, except where permitted by law.

Published by NLH Publishing, LLC
200 University Blvd
Ste 225-420
Round Rock, TX 76537
https://www.nlhpublishing.com

ISBN: 979-8-9918702-0-7
Second Edition

Printed in the United States of America

For permissions or licensing inquiries, contact:
info@nlhpublishing.com

About the Author

Kenogi Gigagei Latham is a courageous familial cult survivor who has spent more than three decades trapped in a closed, fundamentalist Christian family cult. Born into a tightly controlled environment, Kenogi's formative years were marked by isolation within a homeschooling Christian community, where the influence of narcissistic, enmeshed parents—who were also the cult's leaders—dominated every aspect of their life. Despite the psychological and emotional toll, Kenogi's determination to escape and find freedom has been nothing short of transformative.

In their book, *The Family Cult Paradox*, Kenogi offers a deeply personal and practical guide for survivors of cults, with a focus on those born into the oppressive structures of familial fundamentalist Christian cults. The book is not only an exploration of their own harrowing journey but also a roadmap for those who are still struggling to break free. Through a blend of insight, research, and healing, *The Family Cult Paradox* addresses the unique challenges of surviving and thriving after such profound trauma, including religious abuse and coercive control.

After escaping their family's grip, Kenogi embarked on a path of healing and self-discovery. Along the way, they found troubling gaps in the therapeutic community's understanding of cult survivors, particularly those who grew up in isolated, religiously controlled environments. With the wisdom gained from their own experience, Kenogi set out to bridge these gaps by combining psychological, spiritual, and emotional healing strategies. Their mission is to offer both survivors and therapists the tools needed to understand and heal from religious trauma and cultic influence.

Kenogi's personal journey, which includes finding safety, freedom, and a sense of self, inspired their profound message: "No Longer Hushed." Through their book and advocacy, they encourage all cult survivors, whether from familial or other cultic backgrounds, to find their voice, reclaim their lives, and begin their healing process.

Kenogi's work has already made a significant impact in the lives of many cult survivors, providing a sense of solidarity, understanding, and practical guidance. Their vision is to ensure that no survivor feels alone or unheard, as they continue to build a network of support for those who have suffered religious and psychological trauma.

In addition to writing, Kenogi is a passionate advocate for the closing of therapeutic gaps related to cult recovery and regularly speaks on platforms that support healing from religious trauma. They continue to build bridges of understanding, one survivor at a time.

To learn more, connect with Kenogi on social media or visit their website at https://www.nolongerhushed.com.

ACKNOWLEDGEMENTS

I would like to take a moment to acknowledge all of those that have both knowingly and unknowingly taken part in my journey and left a lasting impact.

First, to Moon Child, you are the most beautiful person I will ever know. I am forever in your debt. Thank you for ALWAYS protecting me, even when I hated you. I am so sorry. I love you more than you will ever know, and my appreciation will never have an end.

To my Edoda and Itsi, I love you both more than words could ever express. You have shown me love and acceptance that I never expected. I am proud to call you both my parents and family. You have exceeded in every way imaginable to show me what real parenting and love looks and feels like. Thank you for… everything.

To Thomas, thank you for helping me remember my smile and being ever present. You are my brother.

To Terrence McGee, you are my muse and inspiration. You ignited and continue to ignite the very fiber of my creativity. You are such an inspiration to me, and an incredible human. I feel truly privileged and honored to call you my friend. Your books and words have and always will be food for my soul. Thank you for the countless hours you spent with me, you have no idea how your presence pulled me out of the depths of despair.

To Kelsey, thank you for teaching me how to embrace my inner child. You have inspired me so much to embrace my true self by your life example. You have taught me so much about acceptance and how to accommodate people around me. You are such a truly beautiful person inside and out. I truly love you, and thank you for all that you are, do, and have been in my life.

To Jalice, thank you for not leaving my side. You are such an amazing person… You have taught me to embrace the true nature of, "F*** that s***!". Never stop what you are doing!

To Noodle, thank you for reigniting my love of art. Your gifts and friendship were integral to my healing and therapy. You are such an amazing and talented person. Thank you for always being yourself, and for having the difficult conversations with me. I love and respect you so much for that.

To my beautiful partner, I don't even know where to begin. Instead of listing all the ways I am thankful for you, and how deep my love is for you... I would rather say this:

"I have a strange feeling with regard to you. As if I had a string somewhere under my left ribs, tightly knotted to a similar string in you. And if you were to leave I'm afraid that cord of communion would snap. And I have a notion that I'd take to bleeding inwardly." – Charlotte Brontë, Jane Eyre

Bug…

If I could teach you one thing, it is the wisdom I have learned by observing these tiny creatures…

Be like the cricket that sings a sweet song every night…

Learn from the bumblebee… they understand the true meaning of community, support, and survival…

Understand, you like the ant, might be small… but you are the strongest on the planet…

Don't be afraid to leap for your dreams like a grasshopper, and make the big jumps…

Lay still and learn to listen to nature…a ladybug will always find you…

Some day you will realize…we really do follow the cycle of the caterpillar to a butterfly in our life… embrace it…

Try to discover and understand why the moth is drawn to the flame and ultimately gets burned…it will be a key part of your entire life's journey…

Don't forget to light up every sky, like a firefly…let your soul glow…

This is what I too hope you can observe of this tiny world, and respect the lessons they can teach you.

To everyone I have not mentioned by name, you know who you are. I love you and I wouldn't be here without you. Thank you for being here with me throughout this incredibly painful and acclimating time. I would not be who I am now without each and every one of you.

Kenogi

FROM THE AUTHOR

I'M NOT A DOCTOR, I'M A SURVIVOR

Dear Reader,

I want to emphasize that I am not a doctor, psychologist, or any kind of expert or authority on this matter. My insights come from personal experience as a survivor of a Christian fundamentalist family cult. The information I share is based on my own journey and observations, and it may not be applicable to everyone's experiences.

Surviving and recovering from such an environment can be an intricate and challenging process, and seeking professional support is crucial. If you or someone you know is dealing with the aftermath of a family cult or any form of trauma, I strongly encourage reaching out to mental health professionals, counselors, or support organizations that specialize in cult recovery.

Remember, you are not alone, and there is help available. Everyone's path to healing is unique, and seeking guidance from those with expertise in trauma and recovery can make a significant difference.

PREFACE

A family cult refers to a closed, insular group within a family unit that revolves around a particular set of beliefs, practices, or ideologies. In such a dynamic, the family members often follow a charismatic leader, typically one of their own, who holds significant influence and control over the group.

This leader may dictate the family's values, rules, and lifestyle, creating an environment where dissent is discouraged, and conformity to the established belief system is enforced. Family cults can have profound psychological and emotional effects on members, impacting their autonomy and sense of individual identity.

Being born into a family cult and being homeschooled can be a challenging and isolating experience. In such situations, the boundaries between family life and ideological adherence often blur, with education becoming a tool for indoctrination rather than a means of holistic development. Homeschooling, under the influence of the family cult, may prioritize the teachings of the group's beliefs over a well-rounded education, limiting exposure to diverse perspectives.

The isolation inherent in this environment can hinder social development, restricting interaction with peers outside the cult and impeding the development of critical thinking skills. The pressure to conform to the cult's ideologies may overshadow the child's natural curiosity and desire for independent thought.

Breaking free from this cycle can be an arduous journey, requiring resilience, self-discovery, and often external support. Recovery involves not only escaping the immediate influence of the cult but also navigating the challenges of adapting to mainstream society and, in some cases, overcoming educational gaps.

Escaping a family cult with enmeshed parents is a complex and emotionally charged process. Enmeshment, characterized by blurred emotional boundaries and over-dependence within the family, intensifies the difficulty of breaking away. The first step often involves recognizing the need for independence and understanding the impact of the cult's influence on personal autonomy.

Leaving such an environment requires careful planning, as the cult may exert significant control over its members. Support networks, whether friends, other family members, or professionals, become crucial allies in providing emotional and practical assistance during this challenging transition.

Breaking free from enmeshed parents involves establishing clear boundaries and reclaiming one's identity (This may include going completely no contact). Emotional support, counseling, and, in some cases, legal assistance may be necessary to navigate the complexities of separating from the cult and establishing a new, healthier life. Rebuilding self-esteem and learning to trust one's judgment are integral components of the recovery process.

Ultimately, escaping a family cult with enmeshed parents requires courage, resilience, and a commitment to personal growth and independence. It is a journey towards reclaiming one's life and forging connections outside the confines of the cult's influence.

The journey after leaving a family cult is a profound process of rediscovery and adaptation. Emerging from the controlled environment of the cult into mainstream society often brings about a significant culture shock. Individuals may find themselves grappling with unfamiliar norms, beliefs, and social dynamics that starkly contrast with the insular world they left behind.

Recovery involves unlearning the conditioned behaviors and thought patterns instilled by the cult, fostering independent thinking, and rebuilding shattered self-esteem. Establishing a support network becomes crucial, connecting with individuals who understand the complexities of cult recovery and can provide emotional encouragement.

Navigating the cultural shift may involve seeking therapy or counseling to address the psychological aftermath of cult life. Learning to trust others, rebuilding relationships, and finding a sense of belonging in a wider community are integral aspects of this journey. Educational gaps from limited exposure during homeschooling may also present challenges, requiring dedication and resilience to bridge.

Coping with the culture shock during the recovery process is a transformative experience that demands patience and self-compassion. Over time, individuals can gradually adapt to and embrace the diversity of the outside world, carving out a new, authentic identity beyond the constraints of the family cult.

The breakthrough of finding and establishing one's identity after leaving a family cult is a liberating and transformative moment. It marks the culmination of a challenging journey towards self-discovery and independence. Breaking free from the confines of the cult allows individuals to explore their own beliefs, values, and aspirations, unencumbered by the controlling influences of the past.

This breakthrough often involves embracing a sense of agency and reclaiming personal autonomy. It may include rediscovering suppressed interests, passions, and talents that were stifled within the confines of the cult. Establishing a clear sense of identity involves shedding the imposed roles and expectations, allowing for authentic self-expression.

Building a support network of understanding friends, mentors, or mental health professionals becomes crucial during this process. These allies provide encouragement and guidance as individuals navigate the challenges of forming new connections and integrating into a broader community.

Ultimately, the breakthrough of finding and establishing one's identity after leaving a family cult represents a triumph over adversity. It symbolizes the resilience to overcome past conditioning, embrace personal authenticity, and forge a path towards a fulfilling and self-directed life.

CHAPTER 1
Understanding Family Cult Dynamics — 1

CHAPTER 2
Abuse And Sexual Assault — 44

CHAPTER 3
Victim Experience — 77

CHAPTER 4
Other Victim Experiences — 131

CHAPTER 5
Leaving — 181

CHAPTER 6
The Support System — 208

CHAPTER 7
Recovery — 241

CHAPTER 8
Processing Trauma And Therapy — 290

CHAPTER 9
Healing and Forgiveness — 311

CHAPTER 1

UNDERSTANDING FAMILY CULT DYNAMICS

Trigger Warning: Sensitive Content

This content may contain information or discussions that could be distressing or triggering for some individuals. Topics may include but are not limited to trauma, abuse, violence, or other potentially upsetting subject matter. Reader discretion is advised. If you find that you are emotionally impacted by such content, it is recommended to seek support or refrain from reading further. Your well-being is important.

A family cult, while sharing some characteristics with organized cults, is distinct in its structure and dynamics. Unlike organized cults that often involve charismatic leaders attracting a broader following, family cults are insular groups centered around a familial hierarchy. These groups are characterized by a patriarchal or matriarchal figure who assumes a god-like status within the family, wielding significant control over members' lives.

In a family cult, the leader, typically a parent, establishes and enforces a set of rigid beliefs, rituals, and practices, often rooted in a distorted interpretation of religious or spiritual doctrines. This tight-knit structure creates an environment where the leader's authority is unquestioned, and dissent or deviation from established norms is met with severe consequences.

The family cult dynamic often extends beyond immediate family members, with the cult leader exerting influence over extended family members or close associates. The group's isolationist tendencies may lead to a lack of exposure to external perspectives, reinforcing the leader's control and shaping a unique worldview within the cult.

While organized cults can have a broader influence and outreach, family cults primarily revolve around the internal dynamics of a single family unit.

The manipulation, control, and indoctrination within a family cult are deeply ingrained, creating an atmosphere where individuals may face challenges in breaking free from the influence of the cult leader.

FREQUENTLY ASKED QUESTIONS AND ANSWERS

WHAT IS THE DIFFERENCE BETWEEN AN ORGANIZED CULT AND A FAMILY CULT?

Understanding the distinctions and differences between family cults and organized cults is crucial for recognizing the specific challenges faced by those within such familial structures and tailoring support and recovery strategies accordingly. The terms "organized cult" and "family cult" refer to different types of cultic structures, each characterized by its own dynamics and characteristics.

Here is a brief overview of the distinctions between an organized cult and a family cult:

Organized Cult:

Size and Scope: Organized cults are typically larger in scale, often consisting of numerous members who may not necessarily be connected by familial ties.

Centralized Leadership: There is usually a single charismatic leader or a small group of leaders who hold significant authority and influence over the entire organization.

Doctrine and Beliefs: Organized cults often have a specific set of doctrines or beliefs that all members are expected to adhere to. These beliefs may be unconventional or extremist in nature.

Recruitment Strategies: Organized cults may employ systematic recruitment strategies, targeting individuals from various backgrounds and demographics. Recruitment often involves charismatic appeals and the promise of spiritual or personal fulfillment.

Control Mechanisms: There are established control mechanisms within organized cults, including strict hierarchies, surveillance, and often, isolation from external influences.

Isolation from Society: Members may be encouraged to isolate themselves from mainstream society to strengthen their commitment to the cult's ideology.

Rituals and Practices: Organized cults often have specific rituals, practices, and ceremonies that serve to reinforce group cohesion and adherence to the cult's belief system.

Economic Exploitation: Some organized cults engage in economic exploitation, requiring members to contribute financially to the organization or its leaders.

Family Cult:

Family Ties: Family cults are characterized by a familial structure, where the leader is often a family member, such as a parent or grandparent. The cult may include extended family members.

Less Formalized Structure: Family cults may have a less formalized organizational structure compared to larger cults. Decision-making may be more centralized within the family unit.

Inheritance of Leadership: Leadership in family cults may be inherited within the family, passing from one generation to the next.

Intimate Control: The control exerted in family cults can be more intimate, with leaders having direct influence over family members' personal lives and decisions.

Isolation from Extended Family: Family cults may isolate members from extended family who are not part of the cult, fostering a sense of exclusivity.

Education and Upbringing: The indoctrination of beliefs often starts at an early age within family cults, with children raised to embrace the family's specific ideology.

Religious or Ideological Focus: Family cults may have a strong focus on religious or ideological beliefs, often tying them closely to the family's identity.

Control Through Emotional Bonds: Control mechanisms in family cults can involve emotional bonds, dependence, and a sense of obligation within the family structure.

While both types of cults share some characteristics, such as manipulation and control, the primary distinction lies in the scale, organizational structure, and leadership dynamics. Both can have significant psychological and social impacts on their members, necessitating understanding and support for those seeking to leave such environments.

WHAT SHOULD PEOPLE UNDERSTAND ABOUT BEING BORN INTO A FUNDAMENTAL CHRISTIAN FAMILY CULT?

Being born into a fundamental Christian family cult can have profound and lasting effects on an individual's life and worldview. Here are some key points to understand:

Indoctrination: Children born into cults are often subjected to intense indoctrination from a young age, being taught strict beliefs, values, and practices that may be oppressive or harmful. This indoctrination can shape their entire worldview and identity, making it difficult to question or challenge the teachings of the cult.

Isolation: Cults often isolate their members from mainstream society, limiting their exposure to outside influences and alternative perspectives. This isolation can make it challenging for individuals to develop critical thinking skills, form independent beliefs, or access support networks outside of the cult.

Control: Cults typically exert strict control over their members' behavior, thoughts, and actions, enforcing obedience and conformity through manipulation tactics, fear-based teachings, and authoritarian leadership. This control can undermine individuals' autonomy, self-esteem, and ability to make independent decisions.

Trauma: Growing up in a cult environment can be traumatic, with children experiencing emotional, psychological, and sometimes physical abuse or neglect. The trauma of leaving a cult or questioning one's beliefs can also be profound, leading to feelings of guilt, shame, confusion, and isolation.

Recovery: Leaving a fundamentalist Christian family cult can be a challenging and complex journey, requiring support, understanding, and resources. Recovery may involve deprogramming from cult indoctrination, healing from trauma, rebuilding one's identity and beliefs, and establishing connections with supportive communities outside of the cult.

Overall, it's important to recognize the unique challenges faced by individuals born into fundamentalist Christian family cults and to offer compassion, empathy, and support to those who are navigating their journey of leaving the cult and reclaiming their lives.

WHAT DOES A TYPICAL FAMILY CULT POWER STRUCTURE LOOK LIKE?

In a Christian patriarchal hierarchy within a family cult, the ranks typically follow a structure that emphasizes male authority. Here's a general outline:

Patriarch/Leader: The head of the family and often the spiritual leader of the cult. This individual holds ultimate authority, making decisions related to both family and religious matters.

Matriarch/Supportive Role: While the patriarch holds the primary authority, the matriarch may play a supporting role, particularly in managing domestic affairs. Her role is often subordinate to the patriarch's leadership.

Eldest Son (if applicable): In some cases, the eldest son may hold a special status and be groomed to eventually assume leadership responsibilities. This role emphasizes lineage and the continuation of patriarchal authority.

Other Sons: Younger sons may hold varying degrees of authority based on their age and the patriarch's preferences. They are typically expected to follow in their father's footsteps and maintain the family's religious and hierarchical traditions.

Daughters: Daughters are often assigned traditional roles, focusing on homemaking, child-rearing, and supporting the male members of the family. Their choices and activities may be closely monitored to ensure adherence to established gender roles.

Grandparents/Uncles/Aunts: Extended family members may have roles within the hierarchy, with their status determined by age, gender, and the patriarch's discretion. Their influence may vary, but it typically aligns with the overall patriarchal structure.

Children: Children are expected to follow the established family order, adhering to the rules and expectations set by the patriarch. Their upbringing often includes religious indoctrination and strict adherence to hierarchical norms.

WHAT DOES THE GENERAL HIERARCHY LOOK LIKE WITHIN A FAMILY CULT?

It's important to note that the specifics of this hierarchy can vary widely among different Christian cults, and not all Christian groups adhere to such patriarchal structures. In a primarily patriarchal family cult structure, power dynamics are typically hierarchical, with a strong emphasis on male authority. Key features include:

Authoritarian Leadership: The cult is often led by a male figure who holds absolute authority. His decisions are unquestionable, and dissent is typically not tolerated.

Male-Centric Hierarchies: Power is concentrated in male members, who hold leadership roles and are responsible for making important decisions. Women and other members are expected to submit to their authority.

Control over Women's Roles: Women within the cult often have prescribed roles, such as homemaking, child-rearing, and supporting the male leaders. Their autonomy is limited, and they may be subjected to strict gender norms.

Limited Agency for Women: Women may have limited decision-making power and autonomy. Their choices, including those related to education, career, and relationships, may be heavily influenced or controlled by male leaders.

Use of Religious or Cultural Justifications: Patriarchal power structures may be justified using religious or cultural beliefs, reinforcing the idea that male authority is divinely ordained and non-negotiable.

Control over Information and Communication: Male leaders may control the flow of information within the cult, deciding what members are allowed to know. Communication channels may be monitored to prevent dissent or independent thinking.

Enforcement of Traditional Gender Roles: Traditional gender roles are often strongly enforced, with little room for deviation. Deviating from these roles may result in punishment or ostracism.

Rigid Social Hierarchies: Social status within the cult is often determined by one's position in the patriarchal hierarchy. Those who challenge or question the male leadership may be marginalized or punished.

In a family cult with a focus on female submission, women are often assigned specific roles and expected to conform to rigid gender norms. Key aspects include:

Assigned Roles: Women within the cult are typically assigned traditional roles such as homemaking, child-rearing, and supporting the male leaders. These roles are often presented as fulfilling a woman's "divine purpose."

Limited Autonomy: Female members may have limited decision-making power, especially in matters beyond their assigned roles. Their choices regarding education, career, and personal relationships may be heavily influenced or restricted.

Submission to Male Authority: Female members are expected to submit to the authority of male leaders, whether familial or cult-related. Obedience is often framed as a virtue, reinforcing a hierarchical structure.

Control over Appearance and Behavior: Strict guidelines regarding dress code, grooming, and behavior may be imposed on women to ensure conformity to established gender norms. Deviations may be met with scrutiny or punishment.

Reinforcement through Religious or Ideological Beliefs: The submission of women may be justified using religious or ideological beliefs, emphasizing the supposed inherent roles and qualities of men and women as defined by the cult's doctrine.

Limited Educational Opportunities: Educational pursuits for women may be restricted, with an emphasis on practical skills related to their assigned roles rather than broader intellectual development.

Isolation from External Influences: Women may be discouraged from interacting with external influences, limiting exposure to alternative perspectives and reducing the likelihood of questioning the established gender roles.

HOW DOES THE PATRIARCHAL SYSTEM WORK WITHIN A FUNDAMENTAL CHRISTIAN FAMILY CULT?

Within a fundamental Christian family cult, the patriarchal system often plays a central role, shaping various aspects of individuals' lives. Understanding the patriarchal system within a fundamental Christian family cult is crucial for comprehending the dynamics that individuals, particularly women, may face. Here are some key features of the patriarchal system within such a cult:

Male Leadership: The patriarchal system typically involves male leadership, where authority and decision-making power are concentrated in the hands of male leaders, often the cult's founder or designated male figures.

Submission of Women: Women are expected to submit to male authority, following a strict hierarchy where their roles and decisions are subordinate to those of men. This submission is often justified using specific interpretations of religious texts.

Rigid Gender Roles: The patriarchal system enforces rigid gender roles, prescribing specific behaviors, responsibilities, and expectations for men and women. Men are often viewed as the primary breadwinners and spiritual leaders, while women are relegated to supportive and domestic roles.

Limited Educational Opportunities for Women: In line with traditional gender roles, women within the cult may have limited access to education, with a focus on domestic skills rather than pursuing academic or professional endeavors.

Control Over Family Planning: Men typically have control over family planning decisions, including the number of children a family should have. This control may be justified by religious teachings promoting procreation and adherence to specific family structures.

Marriage Arrangements: The patriarchal system may involve arranged marriages, with leaders or elders determining suitable matches for individuals. This practice reinforces the authority of male leaders in shaping the personal lives of their followers.

Emphasis on Obedience: Obedience to male authority figures is highly emphasized, instilled through religious teachings and cultural norms. Members, particularly women, may be taught that obedience is a virtue and disobedience is a sin.

Male-Centric Interpretation of Scriptures: Religious scriptures are often interpreted in a male-centric manner, justifying and reinforcing the patriarchal structure. This interpretation supports the idea that men are divinely ordained to lead and women to submit.

Limited Leadership Opportunities for Women: Women are often excluded from leadership positions within the cult. Decision-making roles, especially those related to doctrinal interpretation, are reserved for men, further solidifying the patriarchal hierarchy.

Perpetuation of Patriarchal Norms: The cult actively perpetuates patriarchal norms by indoctrinating members with specific teachings and reinforcing traditional gender roles. This can create a cycle where subsequent generations adhere to the same hierarchical structure.

Guilt and Shame for Non-Conformity: Individuals, particularly women, who question or resist the patriarchal norms may be subjected to guilt and shame. Non-conformity is often framed as a deviation from God's plan, leading to feelings of unworthiness.

Limited Autonomy for Women: Autonomy and personal agency for women are restricted within the patriarchal system. Major life decisions, including those related to education, career, and relationships, are subject to the approval of male leaders.

WHAT DOES INDOCTRINATION AND BRAINWASHING LOOK LIKE WITHIN A FAMILY CULT?

Indoctrination and brainwashing within a family cult can involve the systematic manipulation of beliefs and behaviors, often driven by a charismatic leader. Family members may be subjected to relentless psychological control, isolation from external influences, and the reinforcement of a distorted worldview. This process can create a closed system where critical thinking is suppressed, and loyalty to the cult becomes paramount.

Indoctrination and brainwashing within a family cult typically involve a combination of psychological tactics aimed at shaping individuals' beliefs and behaviors to conform to the cult's ideology. Key elements include:

Isolation: Members may be cut off from external influences, limiting exposure to alternative perspectives and reinforcing dependence on the cult for social interaction.

Control of Information: The cult often controls the narrative, presenting a distorted version of reality. Access to outside information is restricted, and members may be discouraged from questioning the cult's teachings.

Manipulation of Fear and Guilt: Cult leaders may instill fear of consequences for disobedience or leaving the group. Guilt is used as a tool to maintain control, making members reluctant to question or challenge the cult's principles.

Charismatic Leadership: A charismatic leader often plays a central role in the indoctrination process, using their personality and influence to captivate followers and solidify their authority.

Repetition and Conditioning: Constant repetition of the cult's doctrines, rituals, and beliefs reinforces the desired mindset. This repetition can create a sense of familiarity and acceptance over time.

Mind-altering Practices: Some cults employ mind-altering techniques, such as meditation, chanting, or sleep deprivation, to induce altered states of consciousness and enhance suggestibility.

Hierarchy and Obedience: Cults establish a rigid hierarchy, demanding strict obedience from members. Questioning authority is discouraged, and dissent is often met with punishment or isolation.

Exploitation of Vulnerabilities: Cults may target individuals during vulnerable periods in their lives, exploiting personal crises, insecurities, or the search for meaning to draw them into the group.

EXAMPLE

Matthew, a 36 year old gay man, grew up within a family cult that seeped into every aspect of the believers' lives, particularly eroding the autonomy of individuals like Matthew. From early childhood, Matthew's every decision, no matter how trivial, was scrutinized through the lens of the cult's doctrines. Choices in clothing, friendships, and even career aspirations were subject to the rigid guidelines laid out by the cult's leaders.

The doctrine's pervasive influence went beyond external behaviors; it infiltrated the very core of Matthew's thoughts, shaping his beliefs, desires, and ambitions to align with the cult's prescribed path. Autonomy, the essence of personal choice and self-determination, became an illusion as Matthew's mind was systematically molded to conform, leaving him entangled in a web of obedience that stifled any semblance of independent thought or action.

Matthew found himself ensnared in a delicate dance of conformity within the confines of his family cult. Despite recognizing his authentic identity as a gay man, the stringent doctrines of the cult dictated that any deviation from heterosexual norms was not only sinful but outright forbidden.

Fearful of the consequences—ranging from ostracism to losing his family and community support—Matthew chose to suppress his true self and adhered to the prescribed life path.

He entered into a heterosexual marriage, concealing the intricate web of emotions that bound him. Behind the facade of marital bliss and fatherhood, Matthew grappled with the weight of his secret, navigating the delicate balance between the expectations of the cult and the authenticity he yearned for. The internal conflict left him torn between loyalty to the cult's doctrines and the desire to live a life true to his own identity.

Breaking free from such a coercive environment can be challenging, as individuals may experience cognitive dissonance, emotional manipulation, and a profound sense of loss if they consider leaving the cult.

WHAT DOES GROOMING AND COERCION OF MINORS LOOK LIKE WITHIN A FAMILY CULT?

The grooming and coercion of minors within a family cult involve manipulative tactics employed by leaders or influential members to exploit and control young individuals. These practices are deeply unethical and often result in severe psychological, emotional, and physical harm to the victims. Here are some aspects of grooming and coercion within such contexts:

Trust Building: Perpetrators in family cults may establish trust with minors through seemingly caring and supportive behaviors. This trust-building phase aims to create a sense of dependence and reliance on the perpetrator.

Isolation: Cult leaders may isolate minors from external influences, including friends, extended family, and other support systems. This isolation prevents the victims from receiving alternative perspectives or help, reinforcing the cult's control.

Emotional Manipulation: Groomers use emotional manipulation to control minors, often exploiting their vulnerabilities, insecurities, or emotional needs. This manipulation can involve guilt-tripping, gaslighting, or creating a sense of obligation.

Introduction of Sexual Content: Groomers gradually introduce sexual content, discussions, or activities, desensitizing the minors to boundaries. This process is often calculated to make the victims more susceptible to further exploitation.

Conditional Affection: Perpetrators may provide affection, attention, or approval to minors but make it contingent upon compliance with their wishes. This conditions the victims to seek validation through compliance with the cult's expectations.

Threats and Intimidation: Coercion often involves the use of threats or intimidation to ensure compliance. Victims may fear negative consequences, both within the cult and from the outside world, if they resist or disclose the abuse.

Spiritual or Moral Justifications: Groomers within family cults may use spiritual or moral justifications to rationalize their actions. They may frame the exploitation as part of a divine plan or claim that it is necessary for the minor's spiritual growth.

Control of Information: Groomers control the narrative by limiting access to information and controlling communication. Minors may be discouraged from sharing their experiences or seeking help from external sources.

Normalization of Abuse: Groomers may attempt to normalize inappropriate behaviors, making minors believe that the abuse is acceptable, deserved, or even beneficial for their spiritual development.

Secrecy: Groomers enforce a code of secrecy, warning minors not to disclose the abuse to anyone. This secrecy further isolates victims and allows the abuse to continue without intervention.

Addressing grooming and coercion within family cults requires a multidimensional approach, including legal intervention, counseling for victims, and efforts to dismantle the structures that allow such abuse to persist. Creating awareness and providing support for those who have experienced grooming and coercion is crucial for breaking the cycle of exploitation within these environments.

NATIONAL ABUSE HOTLINES AND CONTACT INFORMATION

If you are in the United States and you or someone you know is experiencing abuse or in immediate danger, please contact the National Domestic Violence Hotline at 1-800-799-SAFE (7233) or visit their website at www.thehotline.org.

For child abuse concerns, you can contact the Childhelp National Child Abuse Hotline at 1-800-4-A-CHILD (1-800-422-4453) or visit www.childhelp.org.

It's essential to reach out to local authorities, law enforcement, or relevant support organizations based on your specific situation and location. If you are in a different country, please let me know, and I can provide information based on your region.

HOMESCHOOLING

In a family cult, the culture of homeschooling is often a tool used by parents to exert control over their children's education and shape their worldview in alignment with the group's beliefs. The decision to homeschool within a cult is driven by a desire to isolate children from external influences, ensuring that their education is tightly controlled to reinforce the ideologies propagated by the cult. Parents in a family cult may choose homeschooling for various reasons, including:

Control of Information: Homeschooling allows parents to carefully curate the information their children are exposed to, ensuring that it aligns with the specific doctrines and beliefs of the cult. This control extends to limiting exposure to alternative perspectives or critical thinking.

Cult Indoctrination: Homeschooling provides a platform for systematic indoctrination. The curriculum often revolves around reinforcing the cult's ideology, shaping the children's worldview to conform to the group's beliefs, and fostering a sense of loyalty to the cult.

Isolation from Outside Influences: By keeping children away from traditional school environments, parents in a cult can minimize the risk of exposure to ideas that may challenge or contradict the group's teachings. This isolation serves to strengthen the cult's influence over the family unit.

Maintaining Power Dynamics: Homeschooling allows parents within a family cult to maintain a high level of control over their children's lives. The lack of exposure to diverse perspectives and external support systems can make it more challenging for children to question or resist the authority of the cult.

It's essential to recognize that these practices can have detrimental effects on a child's social, emotional, and educational development, limiting their ability to think critically and make informed decisions independently.

Breaking free from such an environment often involves overcoming the educational gaps and psychological conditioning imposed by the cult's homeschooling approach.

FREQUENTLY ASKED QUESTIONS AND ANSWERS

WHAT ARE SOME LONG-TERM CONSEQUENCES OF HOMESCHOOLING WITHIN A FAMILY CULT?

Homeschooling a child within a family cult can have profound and lasting effects on various aspects of their life. Some long-term consequences may include but are not limited to:

Limited Exposure to Diverse Perspectives: Homeschooled children within a family cult may face challenges in understanding and appreciating diverse perspectives, leading to difficulties in navigating a pluralistic society.

Stunted Social Development: Isolation from peers and limited social interactions can hinder the development of social skills. This may result in challenges forming relationships and adapting to social dynamics outside the family cult.

Delayed Educational Development: The homeschooling curriculum within a family cult often prioritizes indoctrination over a well-rounded education. As a result, children may experience educational gaps, hindering their academic progress and potentially limiting future opportunities.

Psychological Impact: Growing up in an environment where critical thinking is discouraged and conformity is enforced can lead to long-term psychological effects. Individuals may struggle with autonomy, self-esteem, and the ability to question authority.

Cultural Shock upon Leaving the Cult: When individuals break free from the family cult and enter mainstream society, they may experience a significant cultural shock. Adapting to new beliefs, values, and social norms can be challenging after years of indoctrination.

Navigating Independence: Homeschooled children within a family cult may find it challenging to navigate life independently. Breaking free from the control of the cult and establishing autonomy can be a complex and ongoing process.

WHAT IS TYPICALLY LACKING IN THE CURRICULUM?

Curricula within fundamental Christian education systems often emphasize religious teachings and values. While these curricula may be comprehensive in certain areas, they may lack diversity and inclusivity, and there might be gaps in coverage across various subjects. Here are some subjects that are often underrepresented or lacking in fundamental Christian curricula:

Comprehensive Sex Education: Fundamental Christian curricula might lack comprehensive sex education, focusing primarily on abstinence and moral teachings. This may leave students without essential information about reproductive health, safe practices, and relationships.

Evolutionary Biology: Due to adherence to literal interpretations of creationist beliefs, fundamental Christian curricula may downplay or omit the teaching of evolutionary biology. This omission can hinder students' understanding of mainstream scientific concepts.

Diverse World Religions: A focus on Christianity within these curricula may result in limited exposure to other world religions. Students may lack an understanding of the beliefs, practices, and cultural significance of religions outside their own.

LGBTQ+ Education: Topics related to sexual orientation, gender identity, and LGBTQ+ issues are often either ignored or presented within a framework that aligns with traditional Christian teachings. This can contribute to a lack of understanding and empathy toward LGBTQ+ individuals.

Critical Thinking and Philosophy: Fundamental Christian curricula may not adequately emphasize critical thinking skills or the study of philosophy. Encouraging students to question, analyze, and engage in philosophical discussions is essential for a well-rounded education.

Comprehensive History: Historical events and figures may be presented from a narrow perspective, emphasizing aspects that align with the Christian worldview. This can result in a limited understanding of global history and cultural diversity.

Environmental Science: Environmental science, particularly discussions related to climate change and ecological sustainability, may be downplayed in favor of human-centric views that prioritize biblical teachings about human dominion over the Earth.

Cultural Competency: Curricula may lack a focus on cultural competency and global awareness. Understanding and appreciating cultural diversity is important for fostering open-mindedness and preparing students for an interconnected world.

Mental Health Education: Mental health education may be insufficient or approached from a strictly spiritual perspective. Comprehensive mental health education, covering various conditions, coping strategies, and support systems, is crucial for student well-being.

Technology and Computer Science: As technology becomes increasingly integral to various fields, fundamental Christian curricula may lack emphasis on technology education and computer science. This can leave students unprepared for the demands of a technology-driven society.

Economics and Financial Literacy: Education about economics and financial literacy may be limited. Understanding economic systems, personal finance, and global economic issues is vital for students entering the workforce.

It's important to note that the content of Christian fundamental curricula can vary, and some educational institutions within this framework may incorporate elements from these subjects.

WHY MAY IT BE NECESSARY TO RE-EDUCATE YOURSELF AFTER LEAVING A FAMILY CULT WHERE YOU WERE HOMESCHOOLED?

Re-educating oneself after leaving a family cult where homeschooling was the norm is often a crucial step in overcoming the limitations imposed by the cult's educational practices. In many family cults, homeschooling is tightly controlled, focusing primarily on indoctrination and restricting exposure to diverse perspectives.

After leaving such an environment, individuals may find gaps in their knowledge, critical thinking skills, and exposure to a well-rounded education. Re-education becomes necessary to broaden one's understanding of various subjects, foster critical thinking, and develop the skills needed to navigate the broader world. It allows individuals to break free from the narrow confines of the cult's teachings, enabling them to pursue independent thought, academic exploration, and personal growth outside the constraints of the family cult's educational framework.

WHAT ARE SOME STEPS YOU CAN TAKE TO RE-EDUCATE YOURSELF AFTER LEAVING A FAMILY CULT WHERE YOU WERE HOMESCHOOLED?

Adult children who were homeschooled within a family may need to take several steps to re-educate themselves after breaking free from the cult's influence, such as:

Formal Education: Pursuing formal education, whether through enrolling in a traditional school, community college, or university that offers a structured and comprehensive approach to learning. Adult education programs or online courses can also provide flexible options.

Independent Learning: Embracing self-directed learning is essential. Utilizing online resources, libraries, and educational platforms allows individuals to explore diverse subjects at their own pace. This promotes curiosity and critical thinking outside the constraints of the cult's ideology.

Seeking Professional Guidance: Working with educational counselors or mentors can provide personalized guidance. They can help identify educational goals, recommend suitable courses, and offer support during the reeducation process.

Joining Supportive Communities: Connecting with support groups, online forums, or local communities for individuals who have left cults can be invaluable. These networks provide emotional support and insights into navigating the challenges of reeducation.

Attending Workshops and Seminars: Participating in workshops, seminars, and conferences on various subjects broadens perspectives and facilitates networking. These events offer opportunities to learn from experts and engage with people from diverse backgrounds.

Counseling and Therapy: Addressing psychological and emotional aspects is crucial. Seeking counseling or therapy can help individuals process their experiences within the cult, build self-esteem, and develop coping mechanisms for the challenges of reeducation.

Building a Social Network: Actively engaging with a diverse range of people helps in developing social skills and understanding different perspectives. Volunteering, joining clubs, or participating in community activities fosters connections beyond the confines of the family cult.

Continuous Curiosity and Exploration: Cultivating a mindset of continuous learning and exploration is essential. Reading books, articles, and engaging in conversations on a wide range of topics contributes to ongoing personal development.

PURITY CULTURE

Purity culture is a set of beliefs and practices, often rooted in conservative religious ideologies, that emphasize sexual abstinence, modesty, and the preservation of "purity" until marriage. This cultural phenomenon, prevalent in certain fundamentalist Christian circles, places a strong emphasis on controlling and regulating individuals' sexuality. It often includes teachings on avoiding premarital sex, discouraging certain forms of physical affection, and promoting traditional gender roles.

Purity culture can have both positive and negative impacts, with supporters arguing for moral values and critics pointing out potential harmful effects such as shame, guilt, and unrealistic expectations surrounding sexuality.

Purity culture within a family cult refers to a set of beliefs and practices that place a strong emphasis on sexual purity, often imposing strict standards and expectations, particularly on women.

In such environments, slut-shaming may be prevalent, perpetuating harmful judgments and stigmatization based on perceived violations of these purity standards.

Some examples of purity culture can include but are not limited to the following:

Emphasis on Sexual Purity: Purity culture typically idealizes abstinence until marriage and promotes traditional gender roles. The focus is on maintaining a perceived moral purity, and deviations from this standard may be met with condemnation.

Shaming of Sexual Expression: Individuals within a family cult influenced by purity culture may experience shame and guilt regarding any form of sexual expression outside the prescribed boundaries. This includes dressing modestly, avoiding physical contact, and refraining from any sexual activity.

Double Standards: Purity culture often imposes stricter standards on women, holding them responsible for maintaining the family's moral standing. This can lead to double standards, where women are disproportionately shamed and blamed for any perceived breaches of purity.

Fear-Based Messaging: Messages within purity culture are often fear-based, emphasizing the potential consequences of sexual impurity, such as loss of familial approval, tarnished reputation, or eternal damnation. This fear is used as a mechanism of control.

Control of Female Autonomy: Purity culture in family cults can be a tool for controlling female autonomy. Women may face restrictions on their clothing choices, relationships, and overall life decisions based on the expectation of preserving their sexual purity.

Cultural and Religious Justifications: Purity culture within family cults is often justified through cultural or religious beliefs, framing adherence to these standards as a divine mandate. This makes it challenging for individuals to question or challenge the imposed norms.

Slut-Shaming: When individuals, particularly women, are perceived to have violated purity standards, they may experience slut-shaming. This involves judgment, ostracization, or verbal abuse based on perceived sexual behavior, real or imagined.

Repression of Healthy Sexuality: Purity culture may contribute to the repression of healthy sexual attitudes and behaviors. Individuals may struggle with guilt and shame around their natural sexual development, hindering their ability to form healthy relationships.

Addressing the impact of purity culture and slut-shaming within a family cult requires a nuanced understanding of the psychological and emotional toll it can take on individuals.

In the insular realm of a fundamental Christian family cult, purity culture weaves an intricate tapestry that dictates the very fabric of individuals' lives. Rooted in conservative religious ideologies, this cultural phenomenon becomes a pervasive force, shaping beliefs and behaviors surrounding sexuality within the confines of the cult.

Purity culture, with its emphasis on sexual abstinence, modesty, and the preservation of "purity" until marriage, becomes a cornerstone of the indoctrination process. The boundaries set by purity culture extend beyond personal choices, permeating relationships, societal roles, and even self-worth. Within the family cult, adherents find themselves navigating a complex landscape where adherence to these stringent principles is not just encouraged but mandated, intertwining with the broader web of doctrines that dictate every facet of their existence.

EXAMPLE

Amanda a 17 year old girl, was brought up in a family cult immersed in the tenets of purity culture. From a young age, she absorbed the teachings that linked her virtue to her sexual purity, fostering a sense of shame around any romantic inclinations. However, Amanda's life took a dark turn when, tragically, she became a victim of sexual assault before marriage.

A traumatic incident shattered the carefully constructed narrative of purity culture that had been woven into Amanda's identity. Conflicted by the cult's teachings and the violation she endured, Amanda faced an agonizing internal struggle. The pervasive shame instilled by purity culture intensified, leaving her grappling with a profound sense of guilt, as if the assault had tarnished her perceived purity.

Amanda's tragic experience underscored the damaging consequences of rigid purity culture within the family cult, where victims like her not only contend with the trauma of assault but also bear the additional burden of a culture that often blames survivors for perceived breaches of purity. The incident would mark a turning point in Amanda's perception of the world, forcing her to confront the stark realities of the toxic blend between purity culture and the insular confines of the family cult.

NATIONAL SEXUAL ASSAULT HOTLINE AND CONTACT INFORMATION

If you or someone you know has been a victim of Sexual Assault, it's important to reach out to the appropriate professionals and organizations directly. In the United States, you can contact the National Sexual Assault Hotline at 1-800-656-HOPE (4673). If you're located in a different country, local hotlines and resources may be available. Remember that support is available, and you don't have to face difficult situations alone.

DATING AND COURTING

In a fundamental Christian family cult, the courting process is often highly controlled and influenced by the cult's leaders or central authority figures. It reflects the group's specific interpretation of religious doctrines and tends to prioritize adherence to the cult's principles. Here are elements that might be typical in such a courting process:

Leadership Approval: The courting process usually begins with seeking approval from the cult's leaders or elders. Individuals may be required to obtain permission before pursuing a romantic relationship.

Doctrinal Compatibility: Doctrinal alignment is a primary consideration. Prospective partners are expected to share the cult's specific interpretation of Christian teachings and adhere to its unique set of beliefs.

Limited External Interaction: Interaction with potential partners from outside the cult is often discouraged. Cult members may be expected to find a romantic partner within the cult to maintain doctrinal purity and reinforce group cohesion.

Chaperoned Dates: Dating within the cult is typically chaperoned. This means that couples are accompanied by a trusted member of the cult during their dates to ensure that interactions align with the cult's standards of modesty and purity.

Emphasis on Purity: The courting process places a strong emphasis on maintaining sexual purity. Cult members are expected to abstain from physical intimacy until marriage, and any violations may result in severe consequences.

Counseling and Guidance: Couples in the courting process may be required to undergo counseling or guidance sessions led by the cult's leaders. These sessions aim to ensure that the relationship aligns with the cult's values and expectations.

Swift Progression to Marriage: The courting period tends to be relatively short, with a swift progression toward marriage being encouraged. Delaying marriage is often discouraged, as the cult may associate it with potential moral and or sexual compromise.

Arranged Marriages or Leader Recommendations: In some instances, cult leaders may actively arrange marriages or provide recommendations for potential partners based on their perceived compatibility and adherence to the cult's beliefs.

Isolation from Non-Conforming Individuals: Those who express dissent or do not conform to the cult's teachings may face isolation from the courting process. This exclusion serves as a mechanism to maintain doctrinal purity and control.

Pressure to Conform: There is often external pressure on individuals to conform to the cult's expectations regarding courtship. Deviating from the established process may lead to social ostracism, and in some cases, expulsion from the cult.

Punitive Measures: Individuals who resist the cult's marriage selection process may face punitive measures, including social isolation, expulsion, or other forms of punishment. Fear of these consequences reinforces compliance.

FREQUENTLY ASKED QUESTIONS AND ANSWERS

WHY ARE SO MANY ADULT CHILDREN WITHIN FAMILY CULTS FORCED INTO MARRIAGE?

Adult children within family cults are often forced into marriage for several reasons tied to the cult's dynamics and the leader's control:

Control and Authority: Cult leaders seek to maintain control over every aspect of their followers' lives. Arranging marriages allows leaders to assert authority over individuals' personal relationships, ensuring they dictate even intimate aspects of their followers' lives.

Population Growth: Many cults emphasize the importance of large families and high birth rates to strengthen the cult community. By arranging marriages, cult leaders aim to facilitate rapid population growth among their followers.

Lineage and Legacy: Cult leaders may emphasize the importance of preserving the cult's lineage and legacy. Arranging marriages within the cult ensures that children born from these unions are considered part of the cult's exclusive community.

Isolation from Outsiders: Cults often promote the idea that outsiders are a threat to the community. By arranging marriages within the cult, leaders reduce the likelihood of members forming connections with individuals outside the group, reinforcing isolation.

Control over Members' Lives: Dictating whom members marry allows cult leaders to control their followers' personal lives, influencing their choice of life partner, family structure, and overall happiness.

Preventing Outside Influence: Cult leaders fear the influence of outsiders, especially if a member marries someone not affiliated with the cult. Arranging marriages internally minimizes the risk of external influences challenging the cult's doctrines.

Maintaining Gender Roles: Cults often have rigid gender roles, and arranged marriages may serve to enforce these roles. Leaders may pair individuals based on perceived compatibility with these roles rather than allowing personal choice.

Enforcing Obedience: Arranging marriages reinforces a culture of obedience within the cult. Members are expected to comply with the leaders' directives, including whom they marry, as a demonstration of their unwavering commitment.

Cult Identity and Unity: Cults emphasize a unique identity and unity among their members. Arranged marriages contribute to this sense of identity by ensuring that individuals share common beliefs, practices, and values within the confines of the cult.

Controlled Social Structure: By arranging marriages, cult leaders maintain control over the social structure within the community. This control extends to family relationships, influencing how members interact and reinforcing the hierarchical structure of the cult.

The forced marriages within family cults are a manifestation of the leader's desire to control every aspect of their followers' lives, perpetuate the cult's existence, and solidify a sense of exclusive identity within the community. Breaking away from such marriages can be particularly challenging due to the psychological and emotional manipulation inherent in cult dynamics.

WHAT DOES THE TYPICAL MARRIAGE SELECTION LOOK LIKE WITHIN A FUNDAMENTAL CHRISTIAN FAMILY CULT?

In a fundamental Christian family cult, the marriage selection process is often tightly controlled and guided by the cult's leaders or central authority figures. This process typically reflects the cult's specific interpretation of religious doctrines and may involve several distinct features:

Leadership Influence: Cult leaders often play a significant role in the marriage selection process. They may claim divine guidance or authority, positioning themselves as intermediaries responsible for making decisions on behalf of the individuals seeking marriage.

Doctrinal Compatibility: The cult emphasizes doctrinal compatibility as a primary criterion for potential spouses. Individuals are encouraged to marry within the cult to ensure shared beliefs and adherence to the specific interpretation of Christian principles promoted by the cult.

Arranged Marriages or Approval Process: In some cases, the marriage process may involve arranged marriages, where leaders or elders actively pair individuals based on perceived compatibility. Alternatively, there might be an approval process where leaders must endorse or authorize potential unions.

Limited External Interaction: Individuals within the cult may have restricted interactions with outsiders, making it challenging to form relationships beyond the cult's boundaries. This limitation reinforces the insularity of the community and ensures that marriage candidates are primarily drawn from within the cult.

Emphasis on Obedience: Obedience to the cult's leaders is crucial throughout the marriage selection process. Individuals are expected to submit to the authority of the leaders, trusting their decisions regarding suitable partners.

Gender Roles and Expectations: The cult likely reinforces traditional gender roles and expectations within marriage. These roles are often based on a conservative interpretation of biblical teachings, prescribing specific duties and responsibilities for husbands and wives.

Counseling and Guidance: Before marriage, couples may be required to undergo counseling or guidance sessions led by cult leaders or approved individuals. This ensures that the union aligns with the cult's values and expectations.

Exclusion of Non-Conforming Individuals: Those who express dissent or do not conform to the cult's teachings may face exclusion from the marriage selection process. This exclusion serves as a mechanism to maintain doctrinal purity and control.

Pressure to Marry Early: Cults may encourage individuals to marry early, often associating marital unions with spiritual maturity and fulfillment. This pressure can limit individuals' ability to explore relationships outside the cult or delay marriage until they are more independent.

FAMILY CULT INTERNAL DYNAMICS AND FAMILY SIZE

Within a fundamentalist Christian family cult, you might observe authoritarian parenting styles, where children are expected to unquestioningly obey parental authority and adhere strictly to religious teachings. There could be and typically is limited exposure to the outside world, with education and social interactions tightly controlled to align with the group's beliefs. Emotional manipulation, guilt, and fear tactics may be used to maintain loyalty and conformity within the family unit. Additionally, there might be a strong emphasis on gender roles, with strict expectations for how males and females should behave within the family and society.

Often times within family cults, a focus on large families and reproduction often serves multiple strategic purposes that contribute to the cult's sustainability and control over its members. Here are several reasons why family cults might emphasize these aspects:

Cult Continuity: Encouraging large families ensures the perpetuation of the cult's beliefs and practices across generations. Cult leaders aim to establish a legacy that endures through the family lineage, maintaining the cult's existence over time.

Control and Influence: The larger the family within the cult, the more control and influence the leaders can exert. With a considerable number of offspring, cult leaders can shape the beliefs, behaviors, and loyalty of a substantial group of individuals, extending the reach of their influence.

Dependency and Obedience: Large families within the cult create a network of dependencies. Children raised within the cult are often indoctrinated from a young age, fostering a sense of loyalty and obedience to the family unit and, by extension, to the cult's leaders.

Internal Social Structure: A focus on large families contributes to the internal social structure of the cult. Hierarchies may be established within these families, reinforcing authority and control dynamics that align with the cult's overarching leadership.

Isolation and Insularity: Large families can function as self-contained units, contributing to the isolation of members from external influences. This insularity helps prevent dissent or questioning of the cult's beliefs and practices by limiting exposure to alternative perspectives.

Numbers as a Power Display: A sizable following, symbolized by large families, can serve as a visible display of the cult's power and influence. Leaders may use the number of adherents as a testament to the supposed validity and strength of the cult's teachings.

Economic Contribution: Larger families may contribute economically to the cult, either through direct financial support or through labor and resources. This financial support enhances the cult's sustainability and allows leaders to maintain control over resources.

Propagation of Ideology: Large families provide a platform for the continuous propagation of the cult's ideology. Children raised within the cult are more likely to accept and perpetuate the beliefs and practices instilled by their parents and cult leaders.

Social Identity: The cult may encourage a sense of unique social identity and cohesion within these large family units, fostering an "us versus them" mentality. This strengthens the bonds among family members and reinforces commitment to the cult.

Loyalty and Intergenerational Bonds: Emphasizing large families fosters strong intergenerational bonds within the cult. Loyalty to the family becomes synonymous with loyalty to the cult, creating a multi-generational support system.

It is crucial to recognize that these dynamics in family cults are manipulative and exploitative, often resulting in the limited autonomy and well-being of individuals within the cult. Understanding the motivations behind the emphasis on large families is essential for efforts aimed at supporting those seeking to break free from such environments.

FREQUENTLY ASKED QUESTIONS AND ANSWERS

WHY IS IT COMMON FOR FAMILY CULT LEADERS TO BECOME JEALOUS OF THEIR CHILDREN'S ROMANTIC RELATIONSHIPS?

Family cult leaders may become jealous of their children's romantic relationships for several reasons:

Loss of Control: Romantic relationships often involve a degree of emotional intimacy and autonomy. For a cult leader accustomed to maintaining tight control over their followers, the prospect of losing control over a family member's personal life can trigger jealousy.

Fear of Losing Influence: A romantic partner can introduce alternative perspectives and values, potentially weakening the cult leader's influence. Jealousy may arise from the fear that a romantic relationship could lead the family member to question or challenge the cult's teachings.

Threat to Authority: Cult leaders often thrive on a sense of authority and dominance. A romantic partner can be perceived as a threat to this authority, as the family member may start prioritizing the relationship over the leader's directives.

Competing for Affection: Jealousy may stem from the perceived competition for the family member's affection. A romantic partner can become a significant source of emotional support, potentially challenging the leader's position as the primary influencer in the individual's life.

Desire for Total Loyalty: Cult leaders often seek unwavering loyalty from their followers. The entrance of a romantic partner introduces an external bond that may compete with the leader's expectation of total allegiance.

Risk of Exposure: Romantic partners may encourage the family member to question the cult's practices or beliefs. The leader may fear that the romantic relationship could lead to revelations about the cult's manipulative tactics, potentially exposing them.

Isolation Disruption: Cult leaders thrive on isolating their followers from external influences. A romantic relationship may introduce an intimate connection that challenges the leader's efforts to maintain isolation and control.

Threat to Cult Dynamics: A healthy romantic relationship can foster emotional resilience and support, making it more challenging for the cult leader to manipulate the family member. Jealousy may arise from the perceived threat to the leader's ability to manipulate and exploit their follower.

It's important to note that these dynamics are deeply rooted in the manipulative and controlling nature of cults. Healthy relationships, support networks, and autonomy are essential aspects of personal growth, but cult leaders aim to suppress these elements to maintain dominance over their followers. Understanding these dynamics is crucial for individuals seeking to break free from such environments and establish healthy relationships outside the confines of the family cult.

WHAT IS THE BOND BETWEEN FAMILY CULT LEADER/PARENT, AND THEIR CHILDREN?

The bond between a family cult leader or parent and their children within a cult is complex and often characterized by a mix of loyalty, fear, and dependency. This bond is influenced by the dynamics established within the cult and the tactics employed by the leader to maintain control. Here are key aspects of this bond:

Authoritarian Control: Family cult leaders typically exert authoritarian control over their children. They dictate every aspect of their lives, including beliefs, behaviors, and relationships. This control is often reinforced through strict rules, manipulation, and isolation.

Emotional Manipulation: Cult leaders may use emotional manipulation to create a strong emotional dependence on them. This can involve instilling fear, guilt, and a sense of obligation, making it challenging for children to break away.

Sense of Belonging: Children within a family cult may feel a strong sense of belonging within the group. The cult leader often positions the family as a unique and chosen community, reinforcing the idea that leaving would result in isolation and loss of identity.

Conditional Love: Love within the cult family is often conditional upon adherence to the leader's rules and doctrines. Children may believe that their worthiness and acceptance are tied to their compliance with the cult's ideology.

Identity Formation: The cult leader plays a significant role in shaping the identity of their children. Individuality may be suppressed, and the children's sense of self may be closely tied to their roles within the cult structure.

Fear of Consequences: Children may fear severe consequences if they question or resist the cult leader's authority. This fear can be both physical and psychological, making it challenging for them to contemplate leaving or challenging the established order.

Isolation from External Influences: Cult leaders often isolate their followers, including children, from external influences. Limited exposure to alternative perspectives or support networks reinforces dependence on the cult and its leader.

Cognitive Dissonance: Children may experience cognitive dissonance, where they hold conflicting beliefs about the cult and its leader. They may struggle with the tension between their loyalty to the family and a growing awareness that something is not right.

Dependency on Approval: Children may develop a strong dependency on the leader's approval. This approval becomes a crucial factor in their self-worth, and the fear of disappointing the leader can be a powerful motivator.

WHAT ARE SOME OF THE TACTICS USED BY A CULT LEADER ON THEIR VICTIMS TO ISOLATE THEM WITHIN A FAMILY CULT?

Cult leaders employ various tactics to isolate their victims within a family cult. Here are some common strategies:

Controlled Information Flow: Cult leaders often control the information members receive. They may restrict access to external news, media, or any information critical of the cult, creating a controlled narrative.

Isolation from Outsiders: Cult leaders encourage or enforce isolation from friends, family, or anyone outside the cult. This minimizes external influences and reinforces dependence on the cult for social connection.

Cult Language and Symbols: The use of specific language and symbols creates an exclusive identity within the cult. This linguistic isolation reinforces a sense of belonging and alienates members from those who don't share the same terminology.

Us vs. Them Mentality: Cult leaders foster an "us vs. them" mentality, portraying the outside world as a threat. This psychological isolation strengthens group cohesion and discourages members from seeking support outside the cult.

Guilt and Fear Tactics: Cult leaders use guilt and fear to discourage members from leaving or questioning the cult's beliefs. Fear of punishment, ostracism, or divine retribution reinforces emotional and psychological isolation.

Limited Access to Information: Controlling members' access to information ensures they only receive information approved by the cult. This includes limiting exposure to books, the internet, or any source that contradicts the cult's teachings.

Monitoring and Surveillance: Cult leaders may implement surveillance systems to monitor members' activities, conversations, or relationships. This constant monitoring creates an atmosphere of distrust and hinders free communication.

Emotional Blackmail: Emotional blackmail involves manipulating individuals through guilt, shame, or threats of abandonment. Cult leaders use these tactics to keep members emotionally dependent and less likely to seek outside support.

Financial Dependence: Creating financial dependence on the cult is a powerful isolation tactic. This could involve members surrendering their assets, working for the cult without pay, or being discouraged from pursuing external employment.

Exclusive Social Structure: Cults often establish an exclusive social structure, with members encouraged to associate primarily with fellow cult members. This limits exposure to diverse perspectives and fosters a sense of isolation from the wider community.

Alienation from Family: Cult leaders may encourage or enforce estrangement from family members who are not part of the cult. This further isolates individuals and weakens external support networks.

Phobia Induction: Cult leaders instill irrational fears, convincing members that leaving the cult or associating with outsiders will lead to dire consequences. This phobia induction reinforces psychological isolation.

WHY IS IT DIFFICULT FOR FAMILY CULT PARENTS TO SEE THE TRAUMA THEY INFLICT UPON THEIR CHILDREN?

Family cult leaders may find it difficult to recognize the trauma they inflict upon their children due to various psychological and behavioral factors:

Narcissistic Traits: Cult leaders often exhibit narcissistic traits, including a grandiose sense of self-importance and a lack of empathy. This narcissism can blind them to the emotional needs and suffering of others, especially their own children.

Justification and Rationalization: Cult leaders may justify their actions and rationalize the harm they cause by convincing themselves that their behavior serves a higher purpose or is for the supposed benefit of their children. This cognitive distortion helps them maintain a self-image of righteousness.

Manipulative Tactics: Cult leaders are skilled manipulators who use various tactics to control their followers, including their children. They may intentionally create an environment where dissent is discouraged, making it difficult for anyone, including the children, to express their true feelings or point out the harm being done.

Authoritarian Mindset: Family cult leaders often adopt an authoritarian mindset, asserting absolute control over their followers. This authoritarianism can blind them to the individual needs, emotions, and autonomy of their children, as they prioritize maintaining their own perceived authority.

Delusions of Superiority: Cult leaders may harbor delusions of superiority, believing that they possess unique knowledge, insight, or a divine mandate that justifies their actions. This superiority complex may lead them to dismiss any criticism or evidence of harm as irrelevant or misguided.

Fear of Losing Control: Family cult leaders often fear losing control over their followers, including their children. Acknowledging the trauma they inflict may force them to confront the possibility of rebellion or abandonment, prompting a defensive response to maintain control.

Cognitive Dissonance: Acknowledging the trauma they inflict would create cognitive dissonance for cult leaders— a conflict between their actions and the belief that they are acting for a noble cause. To alleviate this discomfort, they may choose denial or further manipulation to maintain their self-image.

Isolation from External Perspectives: Cult leaders often isolate their followers, including their children, from external influences and differing perspectives. This isolation reinforces the leader's control and shields them from alternative viewpoints that might challenge their behavior.

Lack of Empathy: Empathy is often lacking in cult leaders, making it difficult for them to truly understand or connect with the emotional experiences of their children. This absence of empathy contributes to their inability to recognize the trauma they cause.

Entitlement: Cult leaders may feel entitled to complete obedience and loyalty from their followers, including their children. This entitlement blinds them to the impact of their actions on individual well-being and creates a distorted perspective on what is deemed acceptable behavior.

THE CULT LEADER(S)

Family cult leaders may believe they are vessels of God due to a combination of psychological factors and manipulative tactics that reinforce their self-perceived divine role. Here are several reasons why family cult leaders might feel they are vessels of God:

Narcissism and Grandiosity: Some cult leaders exhibit narcissistic traits, which can lead to an inflated sense of self-importance. They may genuinely believe that they have a special connection with the divine and see themselves as chosen vessels to carry out God's will.

Manipulation and Control: Cult leaders often use their perceived divine connection to manipulate and control followers. By positioning themselves as intermediaries between their followers and God, they gain unquestioning loyalty and obedience.

Justification for Authority: Claiming to be a vessel of God provides a seemingly irrefutable justification for the leader's authority. Followers may be less likely to question or challenge decisions made by someone who presents themselves as carrying out divine mandates.

Psychological Comfort: Believing they are vessels of God may provide cult leaders with a sense of psychological comfort and purpose. It offers an explanation for their leadership role and actions, even if those actions might be harmful or manipulative.

Legitimizing Unconventional Beliefs: Cult leaders often propagate unconventional or extremist beliefs. By positioning themselves as vessels of God, they legitimize these beliefs within the framework of divine revelation, making followers more likely to accept and adopt them.

Fear and Intimidation: Leaders may use the belief in their divine connection to instill fear in followers. The fear of divine retribution or consequences for disobeying the leader's commands can be a powerful tool for maintaining control.

Self-Deception: Some cult leaders may genuinely convince themselves of their divine status. The reinforcement from followers, the isolation from dissenting voices, and a distorted worldview can contribute to a leader's self-deceptive beliefs.

FREQUENTLY ASKED QUESTIONS AND ANSWERS

WHAT BEHAVIORS DO FAMILY CULT LEADS TYPICALLY EXHIBIT?

Family cult leaders often exhibit a combination of charismatic, manipulative, and authoritarian traits that allow them to establish and maintain control over their followers. Here are some common characteristics of family cult leaders:

Charismatic Personality: Cult leaders often possess a charismatic and magnetic charm that draws people to them. They may be eloquent speakers, persuasive communicators, and able to captivate followers with their presence.

Narcissistic Tendencies: Many cult leaders display narcissistic traits, including an exaggerated sense of self-importance, a preoccupation with fantasies of unlimited success, and a belief in their own unique significance.

Authoritarianism: Cult leaders tend to establish strict hierarchies within the family cult, demanding unquestioning obedience from followers. They make decisions with little or no input from others and expect compliance.

Manipulative Tactics: Leaders use psychological manipulation to control and influence their followers. This can include gaslighting, isolation, guilt-tripping, and creating a dependency on the leader for validation and purpose.

Claimed Divine Connection: Family cult leaders often assert that they have a special connection to the divine, presenting themselves as messengers or vessels of God. This claim is used to legitimize their authority and control over followers.

Isolation Strategies: Leaders may isolate followers from external influences, discouraging contact with family and friends who don't belong to the cult. Isolation reinforces the leader's control and limits dissenting voices.

Exploitation of Vulnerabilities: Cult leaders often exploit the vulnerabilities of their followers, such as emotional needs, past traumas, or a search for meaning. They offer solutions to these vulnerabilities, creating a sense of dependency.

Unrealistic Promises: Leaders make grandiose promises, often tied to spiritual salvation or a utopian vision, to keep followers committed. These promises may be unattainable and serve to maintain followers' hope and dedication.

Secrecy and Control of Information: Leaders tightly control information within the cult, limiting access to external sources and manipulating the narrative to suit their agenda. This control prevents followers from questioning the leader's authority.

Fear and Intimidation: Cult leaders use fear tactics to maintain control, instilling a sense of dread regarding potential consequences for disobedience or leaving the cult. This fear can be both psychological and, in some cases, physical.

WHAT IS THE DIFFERENCES BETWEEN A FUNDAMENTAL CHRISTIAN FAMILY CULT LEADER AND A ORGANIZED CULT LEADER?

While there are similarities between leaders of fundamental Christian family cults and leaders of organized cults, there are also distinct differences in their nature, methods, and objectives. Here are some key differences:

Scope and Size:

Organized Cult Leader: Often leads a larger group or organization with a broader scope, involving numerous followers and possibly multiple locations.

Fundamental Christian Family Cult Leader: Primarily operates within the confines of a family unit, exerting control over family members.

Organizational Structure:

Organized Cult Leader: Establishes a hierarchical organizational structure with defined roles and responsibilities for followers. May have a complex system of ranks and divisions.

Fundamental Christian Family Cult Leader: Typically operates within a less formal structure, focusing on direct influence within the family unit. Leadership roles may not be as clearly defined.

Recruitment Methods:

Organized Cult Leader: Utilizes various recruitment strategies, including public events, social media, and targeted outreach to attract new members to the organization.

Fundamental Christian Family Cult Leader: Primarily recruits within the family unit, often through birth and indoctrination rather than active recruitment efforts.

Isolation Tactics:

Organized Cult Leader: May use physical isolation by establishing communal living arrangements or encouraging followers to distance themselves from mainstream society.

Fundamental Christian Family Cult Leader: May isolate family members emotionally and socially, limiting their exposure to external influences while emphasizing the importance of loyalty within the family.

Belief System:

Organized Cult Leader: Develops a comprehensive belief system that may include unique doctrines, rituals, and practices often distinct from mainstream religions.

Fundamental Christian Family Cult Leader: Typically aligns with a fundamentalist interpretation of Christianity, emphasizing strict adherence to specific religious doctrines.

Control Over Finances:

Organized Cult Leader: Often exerts significant control over the financial resources of the entire organization, with followers contributing financially to support the cult's activities.

Fundamental Christian Family Cult Leader: May control the finances within the family unit, making financial decisions that align with the cult leader's directives.

Long-Term Goals:

Organized Cult Leader: May have grandiose and long-term objectives, such as amassing wealth, political influence, or creating a separate society.

Fundamental Christian Family Cult Leader: Often focuses on maintaining control and influence within the family, with less emphasis on broader societal impact.

Exit Challenges:

Organized Cult Leader: Exiting an organized cult can be challenging due to the extensive influence and control the leader has over followers, potentially involving legal or psychological barriers.

Fundamental Christian Family Cult Leader: Leaving a family cult may involve complex emotional and familial dynamics, but the legal and social repercussions may be less extensive than leaving a large organized cult.

It's important to note that these distinctions are generalizations, and specific cults or family groups may exhibit a combination of characteristics. Both types of cult leaders utilize manipulation, control tactics, and psychological coercion to maintain influence over their followers.

WHAT NARCISSISTIC TENDENCIES DO CULT LEADERS TYPICALLY HAVE?

Family cult leaders who exhibit narcissistic traits often display a range of characteristics associated with narcissistic personality disorder (NPD). It's important to note that diagnosing individuals, especially without direct clinical assessment, is not within my capacity. However, common narcissistic traits that may be observed in family cult leaders include:

Grandiosity: Cult leaders often have an exaggerated sense of their own importance and may believe they possess special qualities or a divine mission.

Need for Admiration: Cult leaders seek excessive admiration from their followers. They crave constant affirmation and may react negatively to any perceived criticism or lack of adoration.

Lack of Empathy: A notable trait of narcissism is a lack of empathy. Cult leaders may be indifferent to the needs, feelings, and suffering of their followers, focusing primarily on their own desires and objectives.

Exploitative Behavior: Narcissistic leaders may exploit others for personal gain. In the context of a family cult, this exploitation can manifest in financial, emotional, or physical forms of manipulation and control.

Authoritarianism: Cult leaders often exhibit a need for control and authority. They may establish rigid rules and demand unquestioning obedience from their followers.

Sense of Entitlement: Narcissistic individuals feel entitled to special treatment and may expect unquestioning loyalty from their followers. This entitlement can lead to manipulative behavior and the justification of harmful actions.

Manipulative Tactics: Cult leaders frequently use manipulation to maintain control. This may involve gaslighting, distortion of reality, and coercive tactics to keep followers in a state of dependence.

Intolerance of Criticism: Narcissistic leaders are typically intolerant of any form of criticism or disagreement. They may react defensively, attacking or discrediting anyone who challenges their authority.

Boundary Violations: Narcissistic leaders often disregard the personal boundaries of their followers. In a family cult setting, this can extend to controlling various aspects of individuals' lives, including relationships, education, and personal choices.

Preoccupation with Image: Maintaining a positive public image is crucial for narcissistic leaders. They may go to great lengths to present an idealized version of themselves or the cult, even if it diverges from reality.

It's important to approach these observations with caution, as individuals can exhibit a range of behaviors for various reasons. A comprehensive understanding of narcissistic traits should involve a professional evaluation by mental health experts.

ARE FAMILY CULT LEADERS CAPABLE OF CHANGE AND CORRECTING THEIR BEHAVIOR?

While change is theoretically possible for individuals, including family cult leaders, it is crucial to approach the question of their capability for change with caution. Family cult leaders, particularly those with entrenched narcissistic or authoritarian traits, may face significant barriers to recognizing and correcting their behavior. Several factors contribute to the challenges associated with the potential for change:

Lack of Insight: Family cult leaders may lack insight into the impact of their actions on others, especially if they exhibit narcissistic traits. This lack of self-awareness can impede the recognition of the harm they cause.

Resistance to Criticism: Cult leaders often resist external criticism and maintain a defensive posture against any challenges to their authority. This resistance can make it difficult for them to acknowledge the need for change.

Maintaining Control: Change may be resisted if the cult leader perceives it as a threat to their control and authority. Fear of losing followers or the collapse of the cult structure can be powerful deterrents to change.

Entrenched Belief System: Family cult leaders typically have deeply entrenched belief systems that justify their actions. Challenging these beliefs may be met with resistance, as they may perceive any deviation as a betrayal of their principles.

Lack of Empathy: Empathy is a key factor in recognizing the impact of one's actions on others. If a cult leader lacks empathy, they may struggle to understand or care about the suffering they cause.

Manipulative Tactics: Cult leaders often employ manipulative tactics to control their followers. This manipulation can extend to any attempts at change, with leaders feigning transformation without genuine intention.

Psychological Disorders: In some cases, family cult leaders may exhibit psychological disorders, such as personality disorders, that significantly hinder their ability to change. Treating these disorders is complex and often requires professional intervention.

Legal Ramifications: Family cult leaders may be resistant to change due to legal consequences associated with their actions. Fear of legal repercussions can be a powerful deterrent to acknowledging wrongdoing and initiating change.

While the potential for change exists in theory, it often requires external pressures, such as legal actions, intervention by mental health professionals, or a breakdown of the cult structure. Even then, genuine change is rare, and leaders may be more inclined to adapt superficially or rebrand their beliefs rather than fundamentally altering their behavior. Individuals who have left family cults should prioritize their own well-being, seeking support and professional guidance to navigate the challenges associated with recovery and healing.

WHY DO CULT LEADERS BELIEVE THEY ARE A VESSEL OF GOD?

Cult leaders often believe they are vessels of God or have a special connection to the divine for several reasons:

Control and Authority: Claiming a divine connection allows cult leaders to assert unparalleled authority over their followers. If they present themselves as messengers or vessels of God, followers may be more likely to unquestioningly obey their directives.

Manipulation and Coercion: Cult leaders use the perception of divine authority to manipulate and coerce followers. By positioning themselves as conduits of God's will, they can justify extreme actions, control behavior, and stifle dissent within the group.

Legitimizing Doctrine: Portraying themselves as connected to God lends legitimacy to the cult's doctrines and teachings. Followers may be more inclined to accept and adopt beliefs that are presented as divine revelations.

Charismatic Appeal: The belief that the leader has a direct connection to God enhances their charismatic appeal. This charisma is often a crucial factor in attracting and retaining followers within the cult.

Justification for Unconventional Practices: Cult leaders may use their perceived divine connection to justify unconventional or extreme practices within the group. Followers, trusting in the leader's divine insight, may be more likely to accept practices that seem inconsistent with societal norms.

Creation of Dependency: Cult leaders foster dependency by positioning themselves as the exclusive conduit to divine guidance. Followers may believe that their spiritual well-being depends on adherence to the leader's teachings.

Elevation of Self-Importance: Claiming to be a vessel of God elevates the leader's self-importance. This can appeal to narcissistic tendencies, providing a sense of grandiosity and superiority.

Fear and Control: The belief in a leader's divine connection instills fear among followers. The fear of divine retribution or separation from God can be a powerful tool for maintaining control over the group.

Exploitation of Spiritual Needs: Cult leaders exploit the spiritual needs of individuals by presenting themselves as the ultimate source of spiritual guidance. This can be particularly appealing to those seeking purpose, meaning, or a deeper connection to the divine

It's important to note that not all cult leaders claim to be vessels of God, but many use some form of charismatic authority to establish control. The belief in divine connection is a powerful tool that serves the leader's interests in manipulating and dominating their followers. Understanding these dynamics is crucial for recognizing and addressing the tactics employed by cult leaders.

EXAMPLE

Miren, a 19 year old girl, was raised within a deeply fundamental Christian family cult home. Her mother, Mary, assumed the role of the divinely anointed messenger. Convinced that she was the voice of God, Mary claimed to receive direct revelations and divine instructions guiding the family's every move.

One day, Mary declared to Miren that she had received a sacred vision, unveiling God's plan for her daughter's life. According to Mary's divine revelation, Miren was destined for a particular path that involved strict adherence to the cult's principles, including a predetermined direct role within the cult and a life dedicated to serving the cult's mission.

Caught between the expectations dictated by her mother's divine proclamations and her own desires, Miren, faced the formidable challenge of reconciling personal autonomy with the perceived divine will.

AUTHORITARIANISM WITHIN A FAMILY CULT

Authoritarian rule within a fundamental Christian family cult reflects a system of governance within a religious context where a family structure is organized around rigid adherence to specific religious doctrines. In such a setting:

Patriarchal Leadership: Authoritarian rule often involves a patriarchal structure where the male head of the family assumes a dominant role, wielding authority over family members based on interpretations of religious teachings.

Biblical Literalism: The cult may strictly adhere to a literal interpretation of religious texts, using them as the ultimate authority for all aspects of life. The leader, often the father or male figure, interprets scripture, and family members are expected to follow without question.

Absolute Obedience: Family members are expected to show absolute obedience to the patriarchal leader's interpretation of religious teachings. Disobedience or questioning of these interpretations may be viewed as a challenge to divine authority.

Control of Information: The leader controls the flow of information within the family, dictating what religious texts, teachings, or external influences are permissible. This control limits exposure to alternative viewpoints and maintains a closed ideological system.

Gender Roles and Submission: There may be strict gender roles, emphasizing the submission of women to male authority. Wives and daughters may be expected to submit to the patriarch's decisions without question, reflecting traditional and patriarchal interpretations of religious teachings.

Discouragement of Independent Thought: Critical thinking and independent interpretation of religious texts may be discouraged. Family members are expected to accept the patriarch's interpretations without questioning or challenging the established beliefs.

Fear of Divine Consequences: Authoritarian rule often instills fear of divine consequences for disobedience or deviation from prescribed religious practices. The threat of spiritual punishment is used to maintain control and compliance.

Exclusivity and Isolation: The family may isolate itself from external influences, viewing the broader society as morally corrupt. This isolation reinforces the patriarch's authority and limits exposure to ideas that might challenge the established religious framework.

Religious Rituals and Practices: Authoritarian rule within a Christian family cult may involve strict adherence to religious rituals, practices, and ceremonies. Deviation from these practices may be met with disciplinary measures.

Cultural Conservatism: The family may adopt culturally conservative values, shunning societal changes or progressive views that contradict their interpretation of religious teachings.It's important to recognize that the term "cult" is subjective and may have pejorative connotations. Differentiating between religious groups and cults involves examining the level of control, manipulation, and harm within the particular context. Not all fundamental Christian family structures exhibit authoritarian or cult-like characteristics.

FREQUENTLY ASKED QUESTIONS AND ANSWERS

WHY ARE AUTHORITARIAN POWER DYNAMICS USED WITHIN A FAMILY CULT?

Authoritarian power dynamics within a family cult create a hierarchical structure characterized by strict control, limited individual autonomy, and unwavering obedience to a central authority figure. Here are key aspects of such dynamics:

Centralized Leadership: A single individual, often the patriarch or a charismatic leader, holds absolute authority. Their decisions are final, and dissent is typically not tolerated.

Unquestioning Obedience: Followers are expected to unquestioningly obey the leader's commands and adhere to the established rules and doctrines. Independent thinking and dissent are viewed as disobedience.

Limited Decision-Making Power: Individual members, especially women and those lower in the hierarchy, have minimal decision-making power. Most decisions, whether personal or communal, are made by the authoritarian leader.

Enforcement through Fear and Intimidation: Fear of consequences for disobedience is used to maintain control. Threats of punishment, both psychological and, in extreme cases, physical, reinforce compliance among followers.

Cult of Personality: The leader is often elevated to a near-divine status. Their image is carefully crafted to embody authority, wisdom, and, in some cases, a sense of spiritual or moral superiority.

Rigid Hierarchy: The family cult follows a strict hierarchy, with the leader at the top, followed by family members and perhaps other close associates. The hierarchy serves to maintain order and control.

Control over Information: The leader controls the narrative and selectively disseminates information to maintain a specific worldview. Access to external information is often restricted to prevent followers from questioning the leader's authority.

Isolation from External Influences: Followers may be discouraged or outright prohibited from interacting with outsiders, especially those critical of the cult. Isolation prevents exposure to alternative perspectives and reduces the likelihood of dissent.

Censorship of Expression: Freedom of expression is often curtailed, with followers hesitant to voice opinions that deviate from the leader's teachings. This censorship reinforces the authoritarian control over individual thoughts and beliefs.

Punishment for Deviation: Any form of deviation from established norms can result in punishment. This could range from verbal reprimands to more severe consequences, creating a climate of fear and compliance.

HOW TO RECOGNIZE YOU OR A LOVED ONE MIGHT BE IN A FUNDAMENTAL CHRISTIAN FAMILY CULT?

Recognizing that you or a loved one might be in a fundamental Christian family cult can be challenging, as cult dynamics often involve manipulation and control. Here are some signs that may indicate involvement in a cult:

Authoritarian Leadership: The presence of an authoritarian leader who controls all aspects of family life, including religious beliefs, finances, and personal decisions.

Isolation from Outsiders: A tendency to isolate from friends, family, or anyone outside the religious community, limiting exposure to diverse perspectives and alternative belief systems.

Rigid Doctrine: Strict adherence to a singular, rigid doctrine with little room for questioning or interpretation. Dissent or questioning of beliefs may be discouraged or punished.

Exclusivity and Superiority: A belief in the exclusive truth of their religious doctrine, often leading to feelings of superiority over those who don't share their beliefs.

Control Over Information: Control over access to information, with leaders dictating what members can read, watch, or listen to. Limiting exposure to external influences helps maintain control over belief systems.

Guilt and Fear Tactics: Use of guilt, fear, or shame as tools for control. Members may be made to feel sinful or unworthy if they question the teachings or consider leaving the group.

Financial Exploitation: Financial exploitation, where members are pressured to contribute significant amounts of money to the group, often beyond their means.

Arranged Marriages: Involvement in arranging marriages within the group, with limited autonomy for individuals to choose their partners based on personal preferences.

Strict Gender Roles: Enforcing rigid gender roles, often with women being subservient to men and limited in their roles within the family and community.

Conditional Love and Acceptance: Love and acceptance being conditioned on adherence to the group's rules and doctrines. This can create an environment where members fear rejection if they express doubts or dissent.

Censorship of Communication: Monitoring and censoring communication, especially with those outside the group. Restrictions on talking to family members who have left or discouraging contact with outsiders are common.

Punishment for Dissent: Punishment or shunning for those who express doubt, question leadership, or consider leaving the group. This can include emotional, psychological, or even physical repercussions.

Emphasis on End-Times or Apocalyptic Beliefs: Strong emphasis on end-times or apocalyptic beliefs, fostering a sense of urgency and dependence on the group for salvation.

Lack of Personal Autonomy: Limited personal autonomy, with decisions about education, career, and personal relationships dictated by the group's leaders.

High Demands on Time: High demands on members' time, often involving extensive meetings, rituals, or activities that limit opportunities for outside engagement.

CHAPTER 2

ABUSE AND SEXUAL ASSAULT

Trigger Warning: Sensitive Content

This content may contain information or discussions that could be distressing or triggering for some individuals. Topics may include but are not limited to trauma, abuse, violence, or other potentially upsetting subject matter. Reader discretion is advised. If you find that you are emotionally impacted by such content, it is recommended to seek support or refrain from reading further. Your well-being is important.Abuse refers to the intentional pattern of behavior aimed at gaining power and control over another person. It can manifest in various forms, including physical, emotional, verbal, sexual, financial, or psychological abuse. Abuse often involves manipulation, coercion, intimidation, and exploitation, causing harm to the victim's well-being. Recognizing and addressing abuse is crucial for the safety and support of those affected.

Abuse within a family cult is a sobering reality that extends beyond the confines of typical familial dynamics. In these insular and controlling environments, the consequences of abuse can be particularly profound, affecting individuals on emotional, psychological, and even physical levels. This form of abuse is intricately woven into the fabric of the cult's power structures, creating a toxic and manipulative atmosphere where authority figures exploit their roles to perpetuate harm.

In exploring the dynamics of abuse within family cults, it becomes evident that the consequences extend far beyond the immediate victims, impacting their ability to form healthy relationships, question authority, and navigate the challenges of life outside the cult's influence. Unraveling the complexities of this issue is crucial for understanding the long-lasting repercussions and, ultimately, supporting survivors in their journey toward recovery and reclaiming autonomy. Sexual assault refers to any unwanted or non-consensual sexual activity or behavior inflicted upon a person. It encompasses a wide range of actions, including but not limited to:

Physical Sexual Assault: This involves any form of physical contact of a sexual nature without consent, such as rape, attempted rape, forced penetration, groping, or touching intimate body parts.

Verbal Sexual Assault: This involves using language of a sexual nature to intimidate, coerce, or degrade someone, such as making sexual comments, threats, or demands without consent.

Non-Physical Sexual Assault: This includes actions that do not involve physical contact but are still sexually invasive or coercive, such as voyeurism, exhibitionism, or distributing sexually explicit material without consent.

Sexual assault is a traumatic experience that can have profound and long-lasting effects on the victim, including physical injuries, emotional trauma, psychological distress, and damage to relationships and self-esteem. It is a violation of an individual's bodily autonomy and right to safety and can occur in various contexts, including within relationships, by acquaintances, strangers, or even within family or religious settings.

It is never the fault of the victim and is always a criminal act. It's important to provide support, validation, and resources to survivors of sexual assault and to hold perpetrators accountable for their actions.

OTHER SEXUAL ABUSE

Inappropriate touch:

Inappropriate touch refers to any physical contact that is unwelcome, unwanted, or non-consensual. It can encompass a wide range of behaviors, including touching someone's body without their permission, touching intimate areas without consent, or engaging in any form of physical contact that makes the other person uncomfortable or violates their boundaries.

Inappropriate touch can occur in various contexts, such as in relationships, social interactions, or professional settings, and it is considered a form of sexual harassment or abuse. It's important to respect other people's boundaries and obtain explicit consent before engaging in any physical contact to ensure that interactions are safe, respectful, and consensual.

Molestation:

Molestation refers to the act of engaging in sexual contact or behavior with someone, especially a child, without their consent. It can involve a range of inappropriate behaviors, including touching, fondling, kissing, or other forms of sexual activity.

Molestation is a form of sexual abuse and is illegal and deeply harmful. It can have severe and long-lasting psychological and emotional effects on the victim, including trauma, shame, guilt, and difficulty forming healthy relationships in the future.
It's important to report any suspicions or instances of molestation to the appropriate authorities and to provide support and resources to victims to help them heal from the trauma.

Virginity checks:

Virginity checks within a fundamentalist Christian family cult refer to the practice of inspecting and assessing a person's hymen or other physical indicators to determine whether they have engaged in sexual activity, particularly before marriage. These checks are often performed on young women and girls as a means of enforcing strict sexual purity standards and preserving the concept of virginity until marriage. The practice is based on the belief that a person's worth and virtue are tied to their sexual purity.

Virginity checks can take various forms, ranging from invasive physical examinations to questioning and monitoring a person's behavior and relationships.

In some cases, these checks may be conducted by family members, religious leaders, or community members who uphold strict adherence to traditional gender roles and sexual norms.

It's important to note that virginity checks are not medically or scientifically valid and can be both physically and psychologically harmful. They violate a person's right to bodily autonomy and privacy and can contribute to feelings of shame, guilt, and anxiety surrounding sexuality.

Additionally, they perpetuate harmful myths and misconceptions about virginity and sexual purity, reinforcing patriarchal and oppressive attitudes toward women and sexuality.

Marital rape:

Marital rape refers to sexual intercourse that occurs without the consent of one spouse within a marriage. It involves any sexual act that is forced, coerced, or non-consensual, regardless of the relationship between the individuals involved. Marital rape is a form of sexual violence and is considered a serious violation of human rights and bodily autonomy.

In many fundamental Christian families, marital rape is historically not recognized as a crime, as marriage was often seen as implying permanent consent to sexual activity.

However, attitudes and laws regarding marital rape have evolved over time, with many jurisdictions now recognizing it as a criminal offense, however many fundamental Christian families refuse to acknowledge it as a crime.

Marital rape can have severe physical, emotional, and psychological effects on the victim, including trauma, shame, guilt, and relationship problems.
It's important to understand that marriage does not exempt individuals from the requirement of obtaining consent for sexual activity, and everyone has the right to autonomy over their own body, regardless of their marital status.

FREQUENTLY ASKED QUESTIONS AND ANSWERS

WHAT ARE SOME ABUSE TACTICS A FAMILY CULT MIGHT USE ON THEIR VICTIMS? (THIS CAN AND TYPICALLY DOES INCLUDE ADULT CHILDREN)

It's important to approach this topic with sensitivity, but recognizing the gravity of the issue is crucial. In some instances, parents in a family cult may employ abusive techniques to exert control over their children. Some of these techniques include:

Emotional Manipulation: Cult parents may use guilt, shame, or fear to manipulate their children emotionally. This can involve instilling a sense of unworthiness or constant anxiety about displeasing the cult's doctrines.

Isolation: Parents within a family cult may isolate their children from the outside world, restricting contact with friends, extended family, or any influence that contradicts the cult's beliefs. Isolation can intensify dependence on the cult for emotional and social support.

Physical Abuse: In extreme cases, physical abuse may occur as a means of discipline or control. This can include corporal punishment or more severe forms of violence.

Thought Control: Parents in a family cult often attempt to control their children's thoughts by discouraging independent thinking, critical analysis, or questioning of the cult's ideology. This can lead to a stifling of intellectual and emotional development.

Forced Labor or Exploitation: Children may be subjected to excessive labor or responsibilities within the cult, contributing to physical and emotional exhaustion. This exploitation reinforces dependency and discourages rebellion.

Sexual Abuse: In some distressing cases, sexual abuse may occur within family cults, exploiting the vulnerability of children and adolescents. This heinous form of abuse serves to maintain dominance and instill fear.

Conditional Love: Parents in a family cult may express love conditionally, based on the child's adherence to the cult's beliefs or rules. This conditional affection can create a constant need for approval and validation.

WHAT ARE SOME COERCIVE ABUSE TECHNIQUES FAMILY CULT LEADERS USE TO ENFORCE SUBMISSION? (THIS CAN AND TYPICALLY DOES INCLUDE ADULT CHILDREN)

In family cults, coercive techniques to enforce submission among children and can take various forms. Here are some techniques that may be used:

Isolation: Children may be isolated from external influences, including friends, extended family, or anyone who does not adhere to the cult's beliefs. This prevents exposure to alternative perspectives and reinforces dependence on the cult.

Indoctrination from a Young Age: Children are often subjected to intense indoctrination, with the cult's beliefs and doctrines presented as absolute truths. This continuous exposure shapes their worldview from an early age.

Fear Tactics: Cult leaders may instill fear in children by emphasizing severe consequences, either in this life or the afterlife, for disobedience or questioning the cult's teachings. Fear becomes a powerful tool to control behavior.

Emotional Manipulation: Children may be subjected to emotional manipulation, including guilt-tripping, shaming, or withdrawal of affection, to ensure compliance with the cult's expectations.

Strict Behavioral Controls: The cult may impose strict rules on children's behavior, dress, and activities. Violating these rules could result in punishment, reinforcing the idea that conformity is essential for acceptance and love.

Conditional Love: Love and approval within the cult are often conditional on adherence to its doctrines. Children learn that deviating from the prescribed beliefs or practices puts their familial relationships at risk.

Role Assignments: Children may be assigned specific roles and responsibilities within the cult, reinforcing their commitment and contribution to the group's objectives. Failure to fulfill these roles could lead to negative consequences.

Information Control: Access to external information is restricted, limiting children's exposure to diverse perspectives. This helps in maintaining a closed system where the cult's teachings remain unchallenged.

Peer Pressure and Conformity: Children are encouraged to conform to the beliefs and behaviors of their peers within the cult. This creates a sense of unity and shared purpose, making it more challenging for an individual to deviate.

Physical Punishment or Threats: In extreme cases, physical punishment or the threat of it may be used to enforce compliance. This can include corporal punishment, deprivation of basic needs, or confinement.

EXAMPLE

Sarah, a 13-year-old girl born into a fundamental Christian family cult, finds herself facing an emotionally and physically abusive situation within her home. The cult's leader, her father, strongly enforces patriarchal values, dictating strict gender roles and demanding unquestioning obedience. One day, Sarah innocently questions some of the established norms during a family gathering, expressing curiosity about life outside the cult. This act of inquiry is perceived as defiance against the cult's doctrines, and her father reacts harshly. In response to her questioning, he subjects her to both emotional and physical abuse.

Emotionally, he employs tactics of manipulation and guilt, telling Sarah that her questions demonstrate a lack of faith and loyalty to the family and the cult's teachings. He instills fear in her by describing the dire consequences of disobedience, emphasizing that she risks eternal damnation.

Physically, her father resorts to corporal punishment, using a belt to administer disciplinary action. Sarah is left with physical marks as a painful reminder of her attempt to challenge the established order. This physical abuse is justified within the cult as a means of correcting her behavior in line with their interpretation of religious principles.

In this example, the child experiences abuse through the stifling of curiosity, emotional manipulation, and physical punishment. The cycle of control perpetuates within the family cult, making it challenging for Sarah to envision a life outside the abusive environment and hindering her ability to express individuality or question the cult's authority.

WHY IS PHYSICAL ABUSE AND CORPORAL PUNISHMENT USED WITHIN A FAMILY CULT? (THIS CAN AND TYPICALLY DOES INCLUDE ADULT CHILDREN)

Physical abuse and corporal punishment within a family cult involve the use of force to control and discipline members, often under the guise of enforcing the cult's rules or ideologies. These practices can have severe and lasting effects on the individuals subjected to them:

Disciplinary Measures: Family cults may employ corporal punishment as a means of discipline, enforcing compliance with the cult's strict rules. This can involve physical violence, such as hitting or beating, as a punitive measure.

Fear and Control: The use of physical abuse instills fear in members, creating a sense of helplessness and dependence on the cult for security. The fear of punishment can deter individuals from questioning or resisting the cult's authority.

Isolation: Physical abuse within a family cult may contribute to isolating members. The fear of repercussions may discourage individuals from seeking help or confiding in outsiders, furthering their dependency on the cult for support.

Suppression of Individuality: Physical abuse can suppress individual expression and autonomy. Members may become conditioned to prioritize conformity over personal growth, inhibiting their ability to think independently.

Psychological Impact: Physical abuse leaves deep emotional scars, leading to anxiety, depression, and low self-esteem. The trauma associated with repeated acts of violence can have a lasting impact on an individual's mental health.

Normalization of Violence: In a family cult, physical abuse may become normalized as an acceptable means of maintaining order. This normalization makes it challenging for individuals to recognize the abusive nature of their experiences.

EXAMPLE

Rachel, a 30-year-old adult child living in the confines of a fundamental Christian family cult. Her father, who also happens to be the cult leader, exercises a brutal form of physical abuse to maintain control and discipline within the group.

Rachel, having silently harbored doubts about the cult's teachings, attempts to express her desire for personal freedom and autonomy. In response, her father uses physical violence as a means of asserting authority and quashing any form of dissent.

During a family gathering, Rachel questions certain doctrinal beliefs, challenging the established norms. Her father perceives this act as a direct challenge to his leadership and the cult's principles. In a fit of anger, he physically assaults Rachel, leaving visible marks on her body.

This physical abuse is justified within the cult as a form of correction in line with their interpretation of religious discipline. Rachel is made to believe that enduring this pain is not only a test of her faith but also a necessary purification process to cleanse her of perceived disobedience.

The cycle of physical abuse intensifies as Rachel attempts to resist the cult's authority. Fearful of the consequences, including social isolation and spiritual condemnation, she becomes trapped in a cycle of violence, manipulation, and control. Rachel struggles to envision a life beyond the abuse, torn between loyalty to her family and the desire for individual freedom.

This example highlights the grim reality faced by adult children in fundamental Christian family cults who endure physical abuse from their parent leaders. The manipulation of religious doctrines to justify violence perpetuates a culture of fear, making it extremely challenging for individuals like Rachel to break free from the cycle of abuse. Addressing physical abuse within a family cult requires a comprehensive approach, including intervention by authorities, counseling, and support networks for survivors. Breaking away from the cycle of violence often involves recognizing the harmful nature of the abuse, seeking professional help, and establishing a network of understanding individuals who can provide assistance in the recovery process.

NATIONAL ABUSE HOTLINES AND CONTACT INFORMATION

If you are in the United States and you or someone you know is experiencing abuse or in immediate danger, please contact the National Domestic Violence Hotline at 1-800-799-SAFE (7233) or visit their website at www.thehotline.org.

For child abuse concerns, you can contact the Childhelp National Child Abuse Hotline at 1-800-4-A-CHILD (1-800-422-4453) or visit www.childhelp.org.

It's essential to reach out to local authorities, law enforcement, or relevant support organizations based on your specific situation and location. If you are in a different country, please let me know, and I can provide information based on your region.

WHAT ARE SOME NARCISSISTIC CHARACTERISTIC ABUSE TACTICS USED BY CULT LEADERS?

Gaslighting: This involves manipulating someone's perception of reality, making them doubt their own experiences and sanity.

Gaslighting within a family cult is a manipulative tactic used to distort the reality and perceptions of individuals, making them doubt their own thoughts, feelings, and memories. This psychological abuse is employed by cult leaders or parents to maintain control and reinforce the cult's influence. Gaslighting in a family cult may manifest in various ways:

Denial of Reality: Cult leaders may outright deny events or experiences, creating a false narrative that contradicts an individual's actual memories. This causes confusion and self-doubt.

Minimization of Concerns: Gaslighting often involves downplaying or trivializing concerns raised by individuals, dismissing them as unimportant or exaggerated. This makes it challenging for members to trust their own instincts.

Shifting Blame: Responsibility for negative outcomes or consequences is shifted onto the individual, making them feel at fault even when the issues are a result of the cult's influence.

Invalidation of Emotions: Gaslighters may invalidate or dismiss the emotions of individuals, making them feel that their feelings are unwarranted or irrational. This undermines the person's emotional well-being.

Confusing Narratives: Cult leaders might present conflicting information or alter their stance on certain issues, leaving individuals unsure of what is true. This intentional confusion reinforces dependency on the cult for a perceived sense of stability.

Dividing Loyalties: Gaslighting may involve creating divisions within family members or followers, causing them to question each other's intentions and loyalty. This prevents unity and solidarity against the cult's influence.

Invalidating: Dismissing or minimizing someone's feelings, thoughts, or experiences, making them feel like their opinions don't matter. Invalidation abuse within a family cult involves systematically dismissing, belittling, or rejecting the thoughts, feelings, and experiences of an individual to maintain control and dominance. Here's how it might work:

Undermining Individual Identity: Cult leaders may invalidate individual identities by enforcing strict conformity to a group ideology. Any deviation from prescribed beliefs or behaviors is dismissed as wrong or unworthy.

Suppressing Dissent: Expression of differing opinions or doubts about the cult's doctrines may be met with ridicule or punishment. Cult leaders invalidate dissenting views to maintain a unified and unquestioning following.

Emotional Manipulation: Emotional experiences and reactions are often invalidated by cult leaders who may dismiss genuine emotions as signs of weakness, lack of faith, or moral failure. This manipulation undermines individuals' confidence in their own emotional responses.

Intellectual Suppression: Cult leaders might discourage critical thinking or independent analysis, dismissing alternative viewpoints as misguided or sinful. This invalidation prevents followers from developing their own perspectives.

Criticizing Self-Expression: The cult may discourage self-expression, creativity, or personal interests that deviate from the prescribed norms. Any attempts to express individuality or pursue personal goals may be met with invalidation.

Isolating Dissenters: Individuals who challenge the cult's teachings may face social isolation or shunning, reinforcing the idea that their perspectives are invalid. This social pressure discourages dissent and reinforces groupthink.

Manipulating Self-Worth: Cult leaders may use invalidation to manipulate followers' self-worth, making them believe that their value is contingent on complete adherence to the cult's doctrines. Any deviation is framed as a personal failing.

Controlling Information: Access to information outside the cult's narrative may be restricted, limiting individuals' exposure to alternative perspectives. This control over information reinforces the invalidation of external viewpoints.

Using Religious or Moral Authority: Cult leaders may invoke religious or moral authority to invalidate differing beliefs, framing dissent as a betrayal of faith or moral principles. This manipulation reinforces the power dynamic within the cult.

Invalidation abuse: Leaders within a family cult creates an environment where individual thoughts and feelings are suppressed, fostering dependency on the cult leader and preventing followers from questioning or challenging the established order. Recognizing these manipulative tactics is crucial for individuals seeking to break free from the cycle of abuse within such contexts.

Projection: Blaming others for their own flaws, mistakes, or negative behaviors. Projection abuse within a family cult involves the cult leader attributing their own undesirable thoughts, feelings, or behaviors onto others, often manipulating and gaslighting individuals within the group. Here's how projection abuse might work:

Blaming Others for the Leader's Misdeeds: The cult leader may project their own negative actions or intentions onto followers, blaming them for behaviors that actually originate from the leader. This deflects attention away from the leader's actions.

Creating a Scapegoat: The leader might single out an individual or subgroup within the cult, attributing imagined flaws or sins to them. This scapegoating serves to distract followers from the leader's own shortcomings and consolidates control.

Masking Personal Insecurities: Cult leaders may project their own insecurities, fears, or shortcomings onto followers, presenting themselves as faultless and projecting personal weaknesses onto those who dare to question or resist.

Maintaining Control: Projection abuse serves as a mechanism for the cult leader to maintain control by keeping followers on the defensive.
Individuals within the cult become preoccupied with disproving false accusations rather than questioning the leader's actions.

Justifying Abusive Behaviors: Leaders may project their abusive tendencies onto followers, justifying their mistreatment by falsely claiming that it is a necessary response to the perceived faults of the individual or group.

Shifting Responsibility: Instead of taking responsibility for their actions, the leader shifts blame onto others. This allows them to avoid accountability for any harm caused and maintains a façade of moral superiority.

Creating Division: Projection can create division and mistrust among followers. Those who are accused may become isolated or targeted by other members, fostering an environment where loyalty to the leader is prioritized over critical thinking.

Fostering Dependence: Projection abuse contributes to a culture of dependency, as followers may believe they must adhere unquestioningly to the leader's directives to avoid being targeted by false accusations.

Distorting Reality: The leader's projections distort the reality of the cult, making it difficult for followers to discern the true source of dysfunction and manipulation within the group.

Manipulation: Using tactics like guilt-tripping, stonewalling, or withholding affection to control and influence others. Manipulation abuse within a family cult involves the systematic use of deceptive and coercive tactics by the cult leader to control and exploit followers. Here's how manipulation abuse might work within such a context:

Deceptive Ideology: The cult leader establishes a distorted or extreme ideology that serves as the basis for manipulation. This ideology often involves absolute loyalty to the leader and may include unique beliefs or interpretations of religious or spiritual doctrines.

Exploiting Vulnerabilities: Leaders identify and exploit the vulnerabilities of individuals within the family, such as emotional needs, fears, or personal insecurities. They use this information to gain leverage and control over followers.

Isolation Techniques: Cult leaders employ various methods to isolate followers from external influences, including family members, friends, or mainstream society. Isolation makes it more challenging for individuals to question the leader's authority.

Emotional Manipulation: Leaders use emotional manipulation to control followers' feelings and behaviors. This can include guilt-tripping, love-bombing, or creating a dependency on the leader for emotional support.

Fear Tactics: Cult leaders instill fear in followers by emphasizing the consequences of disobedience or questioning the cult's doctrines. Fear tactics may involve threats of divine punishment, social ostracism, or harm to family members.

Mind Control Techniques: Techniques such as thought-stopping, repetitive rituals, and the control of information are used to manipulate and control the thought processes of followers. This reinforces the cult leader's narrative and discourages independent thinking.

Conditional Love and Approval: Cult leaders make their love and approval contingent upon followers' compliance with the established rules and ideologies. This conditional affection creates a constant need for validation, reinforcing dependence on the leader.

Financial Exploitation: Leaders may exploit followers financially, encouraging substantial contributions or even demanding the surrender of assets. Financial control serves as a method of reinforcing commitment and dependence.

Sexual Exploitation: In some cases, leaders may engage in sexual exploitation, using their position of authority to coerce followers into inappropriate or non-consensual relationships. This creates a further sense of vulnerability and control.

Cognitive Dissonance: Manipulation abuse induces cognitive dissonance by creating a conflict between followers' existing beliefs and the behaviors demanded by the cult. This psychological tension makes it difficult for individuals to break free from the manipulation.

False Promises: Leaders make grand promises or predictions to motivate followers and keep them invested in the cult. False assurances of salvation, enlightenment, or special privileges serve to maintain allegiance.

Devaluation: Frequently criticizing, belittling, or devaluing someone's worth or achievements, leading to them feeling insignificant or worthless. Devaluation abuse within a family cult involves systematically diminishing the worth and value of individuals, eroding their self-esteem, and fostering dependency on the cult leader. Here's how devaluation abuse might work:

Constant Criticism: Cult leaders subject followers to relentless criticism, attacking their abilities, decisions, and personal qualities. This continuous negativity undermines individuals' confidence and self-worth.

Withholding Affection and Approval: Leaders use affection, approval, or positive reinforcement as a tool for control. By withholding love or approval, they create an environment where followers feel they must constantly strive to earn the leader's acceptance.

Public Shaming: Followers may be subjected to public humiliation or shaming as a means of control. This can take the form of public confessions, exposing personal details, or assigning blame in front of the group.

Comparisons and Competition: Leaders may foster an environment of competition among followers, constantly comparing them to one another. This creates a sense of rivalry and inadequacy, reinforcing dependency on the leader for validation.

Attributing Faults and Failures: Cult leaders attribute any faults, failures, or setbacks experienced by followers to inherent personal flaws rather than external circumstances. This reinforces a narrative of inadequacy and justifies the need for the leader's guidance.

Emotional Withholding: Leaders selectively withhold emotional support, compassion, or empathy, creating a dynamic where followers must conform to the leader's expectations to receive emotional nourishment.

Control Over Personal Choices: Leaders dictate and control various aspects of followers' lives, from major life decisions to daily routines. This control reinforces the message that followers are incapable of making choices independently.

Instilling Guilt and Shame: Leaders manipulate followers by instilling deep feelings of guilt or shame. This emotional manipulation keeps individuals in a perpetual state of penance, seeking redemption from the leader.

Dismissal of Achievements: Any personal achievements or successes by followers are downplayed or dismissed by the cult leader. This prevents individuals from feeling a sense of accomplishment and reinforces a narrative of inadequacy.

Shifting Blame: Leaders consistently shift blame onto followers for any perceived shortcomings within the cult. This deflects responsibility and reinforces the notion that the leader is faultless.

Triangulation: Creating conflicts or tension between individuals by involving a third party, usually to gain control or validation. Triangulation abuse within a family cult involves manipulating interpersonal relationships to create tension, division, and control among members. Here's how triangulation abuse might work:

Creating Alliances: The cult leader establishes alliances or favored relationships with certain members, creating a sense of competition and hierarchy within the group. This fosters a climate of favoritism and exclusion.

Selective Communication: The leader controls communication channels, selectively sharing information with different members or groups. This selective communication can breed mistrust and create confusion among followers.

Pitting Members Against Each Other: Cult leaders may deliberately pit members against each other, either by spreading false information, encouraging competition, or creating situations where individuals vie for the leader's favor.

Encouraging Spying or Reporting: The leader may encourage members to spy on one another, report perceived infractions, or disclose private information. This creates an environment of constant vigilance and mistrust.

Using Confessions Against Members: If members share personal confessions or struggles with the leader, the information may be later used against them to manipulate or control behavior. This vulnerability discourages open communication.

Rewarding Loyalty: The leader rewards loyalty and compliance by offering special privileges, attention, or affirmation. This reinforces a system where members vie for the leader's approval and are reluctant to question the established order.

Isolating Dissenters: Individuals who express dissent or question the leader's authority may be isolated or excluded from certain activities. This isolation reinforces conformity and discourages independent thinking.

Creating Rivalries: Triangulation fosters rivalries and divisions among members, diverting attention from the leader's actions. This internal strife prevents solidarity among followers and makes it difficult for dissenting voices to unite.

Using Relationships as Leverage: The leader may exploit personal relationships within the group, using them as leverage to control behavior. Threatening to sever relationships or expose private information creates dependence on the leader.

Manipulating Group Dynamics: By manipulating group dynamics, the leader can shift alliances and loyalties strategically. This keeps members on edge, unsure of who to trust, and perpetuates a culture of uncertainty and fear.

<u>**Isolation:**</u> Cutting off someone's social connections, either by directly limiting their contact or by subtly undermining their relationships. Isolation abuse within a family cult involves systematically restricting an individual's access to external influences, information, and support systems. Here's how isolation abuse might work:

Cutting Ties with Outsiders: Cult leaders often discourage or prohibit contact with family members, friends, or anyone outside the cult. This isolation prevents individuals from seeking alternative perspectives or support.

Limiting External Information: Leaders control the information available to followers, often restricting access to outside news, media, or educational materials. This limits exposure to different ideas and reinforces the leader's narrative.

Creating a Cult-Centric Reality: Members are immersed in a closed environment where the cult's beliefs and ideology are the sole focus. This insular reality reinforces groupthink and makes it challenging for individuals to question or critically evaluate their situation.

Discouraging Independent Thought: Leaders discourage independent thought by stigmatizing critical thinking and dissent. Fear of consequences for questioning the leader or the group's beliefs further reinforces conformity.

Controlling Communication: Leaders often control and monitor communication channels within the cult. This may involve censoring written or verbal communication, restricting internet access, or monitoring phone calls to prevent information exchange.

Limiting Mobility: Members may be discouraged or prohibited from leaving the cult's physical premises, further restricting their interactions with the outside world. This confinement reinforces dependence on the cult environment.

Casting Outsiders as Threats: Cult leaders portray outsiders as threats, emphasizing the dangers of interacting with those who don't share the group's beliefs. This fosters an "us versus them" mentality and reinforces the need for internal cohesion.

Creating Fear of Rejection: Members fear rejection or punishment for interacting with outsiders, even family members. This fear serves as a powerful deterrent, reinforcing compliance and discouraging any inclination to seek external support.

Encouraging Dependence on the Cult Community: Isolation fosters a sense of dependency on the cult community for emotional support, validation, and belonging. Members become reluctant to question the group or leave, fearing the loss of this perceived safety net.

Eradicating Personal Boundaries: Leaders may erode personal boundaries, creating an environment where individual thoughts, emotions, and experiences are shared collectively. This blurring of boundaries reinforces the idea that personal identity is inseparable from the cult community.

Breaking free from isolation abuse within a family cult often involves recognizing the manipulative tactics at play, seeking support from external sources, and gradually reintegrating into a broader social context. Reconnecting with friends, family, or supportive communities can be crucial for recovering from the effects of isolation.

Intimidation: Using threats, aggression, or imposing a sense of fear to control or manipulate others. Intimidation abuse within a family cult involves using fear, threats, and coercive tactics to control and manipulate individuals. Here's how intimidation abuse might work:

Threats of Punishment: Cult leaders may use explicit threats of physical harm, psychological punishment, or divine consequences to instill fear in followers. The fear of retribution reinforces compliance.

Fear of Excommunication: Leaders may threaten to excommunicate or shun individuals who question the cult's beliefs or authority. The fear of social isolation can be a powerful tool for maintaining control.

Character Assassination: Cult leaders might engage in character assassination, spreading false rumors or tarnishing the reputation of those who resist or question the leader's authority. This creates a climate of fear and deters dissent.

Isolation and Alienation: Individuals who challenge the leader may be isolated or alienated from the group, fostering a sense of loneliness and vulnerability. This isolation reinforces the fear of being cast out.

Physical Intimidation: In extreme cases, leaders may resort to physical intimidation or violence to exert control. This can include physical punishment, threats of harm, or creating an atmosphere of aggression within the group.

Psychological Manipulation: Leaders may employ gaslighting and other forms of psychological manipulation to make individuals doubt their own perceptions, creating a constant state of anxiety and fear.

Exploiting Personal Secrets: Cult leaders may exploit individuals' vulnerabilities by revealing personal secrets or information shared in confidence. This creates a sense of exposure and vulnerability, discouraging resistance.

Financial Threats: Leaders may control members by threatening financial repercussions, such as confiscating assets or causing economic harm. This economic leverage reinforces dependence on the cult.

Instilling Fear of Divine Consequences: Leaders often use the fear of divine punishment or spiritual consequences to manipulate followers. This can include threats of damnation, eternal suffering, or spiritual isolation.

Cult of Personality: Leaders may create a cult of personality around themselves, presenting themselves as all-knowing or divinely chosen. This exaggerated authority instills fear and submission among followers.

Love-bombing: Initially showering someone with excessive attention, affection, and gifts to gain their trust and admiration, before gradually exploiting or withdrawing these displays of love. Love bombing abuse within a family cult involves the excessive use of affection, attention, and positive reinforcement to manipulate and control individuals. Here's how love bombing abuse might work:

Overwhelming Affection: Cult leaders or members shower newcomers or those who show vulnerability with excessive expressions of love, attention, and affection. This creates a sense of being valued and accepted.

Instant Inclusion: Individuals are quickly and warmly welcomed into the cult, often bypassing normal social boundaries. This rapid inclusion fosters a feeling of belonging and attachment.

Constant Compliments: Love bombers use frequent and exaggerated compliments to boost individuals' self-esteem and create emotional dependence. This positive reinforcement becomes a powerful tool for manipulation.

Gifts and Favors: Cult members may offer gifts, favors, or special privileges to newcomers, reinforcing a sense of indebtedness. This reciprocity creates a dynamic where individuals feel obligated to reciprocate or comply with the group's expectations.

Excessive Communication: Love bombers maintain constant communication, bombarding individuals with messages, calls, or expressions of care. This overwhelming attention serves to create dependency and discourage questioning the group's intentions.

Idealization of the Leader: The cult leader is often idealized as a perfect, infallible figure, worthy of adoration and loyalty. Followers are encouraged to see the leader as a source of unconditional love and wisdom.

Isolation from External Relationships: Love bombers may discourage or actively interfere with individuals' relationships outside the cult, fostering dependence on the group for emotional support and connection.

Conditional Love: The love and acceptance offered are conditional upon individuals conforming to the cult's beliefs and expectations. Non-compliance may result in withdrawal of affection and attention.

Manipulative Charisma: Cult leaders often possess charismatic qualities that make them appear charming and trustworthy. This charisma is used to captivate individuals and manipulate their emotions.

Rapid Escalation and Devaluation: Love bombing is often followed by a rapid escalation of demands or expectations. Once individuals are emotionally invested, the cult may shift to controlling behaviors, and the love bombers may become more critical or demanding.

Recognizing these forms of abuse is crucial for individuals within a family cult to maintain a clear perspective and resist manipulation. Seeking support from trusted friends, family, or professionals can aid in breaking free from the emotional dependency created by these tactics.

EXAMPLE

Alex, a 25-year-old raised in a strict Christian family cult, has started to question the teachings and authority imposed by the cult leader, who is also their parent. Alex has quietly begun exploring alternative perspectives and questioning some of the oppressive practices within the cult. As Alex expresses these doubts, the cult leader parents respond with emotionally manipulative tactics. They use guilt, fear, and tactics of spiritual condemnation, emphasizing that questioning the cult's doctrines is a betrayal of family, faith, and God. The parents claim that Alex is jeopardizing not only their own salvation but the eternal well-being of the entire family.

In addition to emotional abuse, the cult leader parents exert control over Alex's life choices. They dictate whom Alex should marry, expecting compliance with their choice rather than allowing Alex to make personal decisions about relationships. The cult leader parents threaten to cut off emotional and financial support if Alex continues to resist their authority, reinforcing a sense of dependency.

The cult's influence extends into every aspect of Alex's life, from career choices to social interactions. Any attempt to assert independence is met with psychological manipulation, creating a constant atmosphere of fear and guilt. The fear of social isolation, eternal damnation, and the loss of family ties serves as a powerful tool to maintain control over Alex.

HEALTH NEGLECT AND ABUSE

Health neglect and abuse refer to situations where an individual's health is compromised due to intentional harm, lack of care, or negligence. Neglect involves the failure to provide necessary care, leading to harm or risk of harm. Abuse, on the other hand, involves intentional actions causing harm, whether physical, emotional, or psychological, to an individual's health. Both are serious concerns that may require intervention and support.

FREQUENTLY ASKED QUESTIONS AND ANSWERS

WHAT DOES HEALTH ABUSE AND OR NEGLECT LOOK LIKE WITHIN A FUNDAMENTAL CHRISTIAN FAMILY CULT?

Health abuse or neglect within a fundamental Christian family cult can manifest in various ways. It might involve restricting access to medical care based on religious beliefs, imposing extreme dietary restrictions, or using religious doctrines to justify harmful practices. Emotional and psychological abuse may also occur, with manipulation and control tactics under the guise of religious principles.

WHY DO SO MANY FUNDAMENTAL CHRISTIAN FAMILY CULTS BASE HEALTH CARE ON FAITH HEALTH VERSUS MEDICAL CARE?

Some fundamental Christian family cults may base health care on faith rather than conventional medical care due to strong religious beliefs and a literal interpretation of biblical teachings. These groups might believe in the power of prayer and divine intervention for healing, viewing medical interventions as a lack of faith or a compromise of their spiritual principles. This approach can stem from a combination of religious doctrines, mistrust of secular institutions, and a desire to maintain strict adherence to their interpretation of scripture. However, it's essential to recognize that views on health care vary widely within the Christian faith, and not all Christians adopt such practices.

WHAT ARE SOME CHRISTIAN RELIGIOUS PRACTICES CENTERED AROUND HEALING?

Christian religious practices centered around healing often involve prayer, laying on of hands, anointing with oil, and seeking divine intervention for physical, emotional, or spiritual well-being. Many Christian denominations believe in the power of prayer for healing and have rituals or ceremonies dedicated to this purpose.

The practice of anointing with oil is derived from biblical passages, symbolizing the Holy Spirit's presence and healing. Additionally, some Christian communities have specific healing services or ministries where members gather to pray for the sick and seek God's healing grace. It's important to note that practices may vary among denominations and individual beliefs within the Christian faith.

WHAT ARE SOME OF THE PRACTICES THAT MIGHT BE USED WITHIN A FUNDAMENTAL CHRISTIAN FAMILY CULT?

Faith Healing: Faith healing within a fundamental Christian family cult is a practice where individuals believe in seeking healing through unwavering faith in God's power. Members of such cults may attribute physical, emotional, or spiritual healing to their strong belief and trust in divine intervention. This form of healing often involves prayer, laying on of hands, anointing with oil, and other faith-based rituals.

It's important to recognize that faith healing in this context is rooted in religious convictions, and adherents may prioritize it over conventional medical care, relying solely on their faith for healing. This approach can pose risks, and it's crucial to consider the well-being of individuals involved.

Prayer Healing: Prayer healing within a fundamental Christian family cult involves seeking healing through fervent prayers and reliance on divine intervention. Members of the cult may believe that through prayer, they can connect with God's healing power to address physical, emotional, or spiritual ailments. This practice is rooted in the belief that God has the ability to bring about restoration and well-being in response to faithful prayers.

It's important to note that prayer healing is specific to the religious context of the cult, and its effectiveness is understood through the lens of faith rather than scientific validation.

Hands-On Healing: In a fundamental Christian family cult, hands-on healing typically involves the practice of laying on of hands as a form of prayer for healing. Members of the cult may believe that by physically touching an individual and praying fervently, they can channel divine or spiritual energy to promote healing—whether it be physical, emotional, or spiritual. This practice is often grounded in a literal interpretation of biblical passages that mention the laying on of hands for healing purposes.

It's important to recognize that such practices can vary widely among Christian groups, and the efficacy is viewed through the lens of religious faith rather than conventional medical standards.

Claimed Healing: Claimed healing within a fundamental Christian family cult refers to instances where individuals or leaders within the cult assert that healing has taken place through their faith-based practices. This could involve attributing improvements in health, relief from ailments, or recovery to the power of prayer, laying on of hands, anointing with oil, or other religious rituals. The term "claimed" emphasizes that these assertions are made within the context of the cult's beliefs and practices, and the effectiveness of such healing may not be scientifically validated.

Healing by Exorcism: Healing by exorcism within a fundamental family cult involves the belief that certain physical or mental ailments are caused by demonic possession, and the process of exorcism is deemed necessary for healing. Members of the cult may perform rituals, prayers, or other practices to expel what they believe to be malevolent spirits or demons from the afflicted individual. This practice is rooted in a literal interpretation of biblical passages describing exorcism.
It's important to note that within mainstream Christianity, exorcism is a less common and more controversial practice, and it is typically approached cautiously.

In the context of a fundamental family cult, the beliefs and practices surrounding healing by exorcism can vary widely and may not align with mainstream Christian traditions. This approach to healing can have significant emotional, psychological, and physical consequences for individuals involved, and it may lack scientific validity.

WHAT ARE THE LONG TERM EFFECTS ON CHILDREN DENIED MEDICAL CARE BASED ON FAITH WITHIN A FUNDAMENTAL CHRISTIAN FAMILY CULT?

Children denied medical care based on faith, especially within a fundamentalist context, can face severe and potentially life-altering consequences. The long-term effects may include:

Worsening Health Conditions: Without proper medical intervention, treatable health conditions may worsen, leading to chronic illnesses, disabilities, or even fatalities.

Emotional and Psychological Impact: Children may experience emotional and psychological distress due to untreated illnesses, prolonged pain, or witnessing the suffering of others. This can lead to long-lasting trauma.

Stunted Growth and Development: Lack of necessary medical care can impede a child's physical and cognitive development, affecting their overall well-being and potential.

Legal Consequences: In some jurisdictions, denying essential medical care to children based on faith may result in legal consequences, including charges of child neglect or endangerment.

Strained Relationships: Children may face challenges in their relationships, both within and outside the family, as a result of their unique health experiences and the impact of their caregivers' decisions.

It's important to prioritize the best interests and well-being of children by balancing faith with responsible and evidence-based medical care. In situations where children are at risk due to the denial of medical care, intervention from authorities or child protective services may be necessary to ensure their safety and health.

WHY IS PHYSICAL HEALTH CARE FOR CHILDREN OF CULT LEADERS/ MEMBERS TYPICALLY DENIED?

Physical health care for children of cult leaders or members may be denied or limited due to various factors within the cult environment:

Control and Isolation: Cults often exert strict control over their members, including their children. This control extends to medical decisions, and cult leaders may limit access to healthcare to maintain authority and isolation.

Distrust of External Authorities: Cults frequently foster a distrust of external authorities, including healthcare professionals. Members, including children, may be conditioned to avoid seeking medical care outside the cult community.

Fear of Judgment: Cult members may fear judgment or negative consequences if they seek medical care independently. This fear can be particularly heightened for children who may be more vulnerable to the influence of the cult.

Alternative Healing Practices: Some cults promote alternative or unconventional healing practices, often guided by the cult leader's beliefs. Members may be discouraged from seeking traditional medical care in favor of these alternative methods.

Financial Dependence: Children within cults may be financially dependent on the cult community. The fear of losing this financial support can discourage them from seeking medical care independently, especially if the cult discourages such actions.

Lack of Autonomy: Children in cults typically have limited autonomy and decision-making power. Their ability to independently seek medical care may be restricted by the cult's rigid structure.

Cult Leader as Authority Figure: The cult leader often assumes the role of the ultimate authority figure, and members may believe that the leader possesses unique insights or healing abilities. This perception may deter them from seeking medical care outside the cult.

Psychological Manipulation: Cult leaders may use psychological manipulation to convince members that physical ailments are a result of spiritual issues or lack of faith. This can create a false belief that seeking medical care is unnecessary or counterproductive.

Isolation from Outsiders: Cults frequently isolate their members from the outside world. This isolation can extend to healthcare, with members discouraged from interacting with healthcare professionals who might challenge the cult's teachings.

It's important to note that the denial of healthcare within a cult environment is a form of control and manipulation. Recognizing the importance of physical health care and gaining access to independent medical assistance are crucial steps for individuals, including children, seeking to break away from the harmful influences of cults.

WHY IS MENTAL HEALTH CARE FOR CHILDREN OF CULT LEADERS/ MEMBERS TYPICALLY DENIED? (THIS CAN AND TYPICALLY DOES INCLUDE ADULT CHILDREN)

Mental health care for children of cult leaders or members may be denied or overlooked for several reasons:

Cult Control and Isolation: Cults often exert extreme control over their members, including their children. This control extends to various aspects of life, including medical decisions. Cult leaders may discourage or outright forbid seeking mental health care, viewing it as a threat to their authority.

Stigmatization of Mental Health: Some cults stigmatize mental health care, portraying it as a sign of weakness or lack of faith. Members, including children, may fear judgment or punishment for seeking help for mental health issues.

Manipulation and Gaslighting: Cult leaders may use manipulation and gaslighting techniques to convince followers that their mental health concerns are imagined or exaggerated. This can create a sense of self-doubt and reluctance to seek professional help.

Fear of Outsiders: Cults often foster a fear of outsiders, including mental health professionals. Members may be conditioned to believe that seeking help from external sources, especially in the realm of mental health, is dangerous and may lead to negative consequences.

Limited Access to Information: Children in cults may have restricted access to information about mental health and available resources. They might be unaware of the potential benefits of seeking professional help or may be actively prevented from accessing such information.

Lack of Autonomy: Children within cults typically have limited autonomy and decision-making power. Even if they recognize the need for mental health care, their ability to act on it may be restricted by the cult's rigid structure.

Dependency on the Cult Community: Children of cult members may be emotionally and financially dependent on the cult community. The fear of losing this support system can discourage them from seeking mental health care independently.

Cult Leaders as Pseudo-Therapists: Cult leaders may position themselves as pseudo-therapists, claiming to have the ability to address members' mental health concerns. This false sense of support can dissuade individuals, including children, from seeking professional help outside the cult.

EXAMPLE

Sarah, is a 16-year-old girl living in a fundamental Christian family cult led by her father, who is the cult leader. Sarah experiences a medical issue, and the denial of care is influenced by the cult leader's control and adherence to religious doctrines:

Onset of a Medical Issue: Sarah develops a persistent cough and breathing difficulties, symptoms that suggest a potential respiratory problem. Concerned about her well-being, she approaches her father, who is not only her parent but also the authoritative cult leader.

Cult's Teachings on Divine Healing: The cult strongly advocates for divine healing through prayer and faith. Cult members are taught that seeking medical care demonstrates a lack of trust in God's ability to heal and solve problems. The leader, Sarah's father, adheres strictly to this doctrine.

Fear of External Influence: The cult instills a deep fear of external influences, especially secular medical professionals and government agencies. Members are discouraged from seeking help outside the cult, as it may lead to unwanted scrutiny and interference with the cult's practices.

Control and Authority: Sarah's father, as both her parent and the cult leader, holds significant control over her life. Seeking medical care without his approval is seen as an act of disobedience not only to a parent but to the cult's authority structure.

Religious Manipulation: The cult leader manipulates religious teachings to dissuade Sarah from seeking medical attention. He convinces her that enduring suffering is a form of spiritual purification and that seeking worldly solutions contradicts their faith.

In this example, Sarah's access to medical care is denied due to the cult leader's strict adherence to religious doctrines, fear of external influence, and the exertion of control over the member's life. The combination of religious manipulation and authority dynamics within the family cult creates a situation where Sarah's health needs are neglected for the sake of the cult's teachings.

WHY DO SO MANY CHILDREN STRUGGLE TO FEEL SAFE IN AN ABUSIVE FUNDAMENTAL CHRISTIAN FAMILY CULT?

Children in abusive fundamental Christian family cults often struggle to feel safe due to a combination of psychological, emotional, and physical factors:

Authoritarian Control: Cult leaders, often the parents or authority figures, exercise strict and authoritarian control over every aspect of a child's life. This lack of autonomy can lead to feelings of helplessness and insecurity.

Fear of Punishment: Children in such environments are often raised with a fear of divine consequences or harsh punishment for perceived disobedience or sins. This constant fear creates an atmosphere of anxiety and insecurity.

Conditional Love: Love within the cult is often conditional, based on adherence to strict rules and conformity to the leader's expectations. Children may fear losing the love and approval of their parents or the group if they deviate from the established norms.

Isolation: Cults often isolate their members from external influences, including friends, family, or outside support networks. This isolation prevents children from seeking help or finding alternative perspectives, exacerbating their feelings of vulnerability.

Guilt and Shame: Children may be burdened with a sense of guilt and shame, often instilled through teachings emphasizing inherent sinfulness. This constant self-blame can erode their sense of self-worth and safety.

Emotional Manipulation: Children may experience emotional manipulation, including gaslighting and other tactics that distort their reality. This can lead to confusion, self-doubt, and a constant sense of instability.

Cult of Personality: Cult leaders often create a cult of personality, portraying themselves as infallible and divinely guided. Children may fear challenging the authority of the leader or questioning their teachings, contributing to a lack of safety in expressing their true feelings.

Inconsistent Parental Care: In some cases, children in cults may experience inconsistent or unpredictable parental care. The whims of the cult leader or the rigid adherence to cult practices may disrupt normal caregiving routines, leaving children without a stable source of comfort.

Exposure to Abuse: Children may witness or experience various forms of abuse within the cult, whether it's physical, emotional, or sexual. Such exposure further undermines their sense of safety and well-being.

Lack of Boundaries: Cults often blur or eliminate healthy boundaries, making it challenging for children to develop a sense of personal space and safety. Their autonomy is frequently disregarded, contributing to feelings of vulnerability.

It is important for children in such environments to find avenues for support, whether through trusted adults, friends, or external organizations. Breaking free from an abusive family cult often involves recognizing the harmful dynamics at play and seeking help to establish a safe and nurturing environment.

WHY DO CULT/FAMILY LEADERS ISOLATE THEIR VICTIMS?

Isolation within a fundamental Christian family cult serves as a powerful tool, intricately woven into the fabric of control and manipulation. In this insular environment, the concept of isolation extends beyond physical separation, encompassing emotional, social, and intellectual realms. Cult leaders, often wielding religious doctrines as their weapon, intentionally curate an environment where members find themselves secluded from external influences, dissenting opinions, and diverse perspectives.

This isolation is not merely geographical but extends to the very core of individual identity, restricting personal autonomy and critical thinking.

As we delve into the dynamics of isolation within these family cults, we unearth the profound impact it has on the psychological well-being of members, shaping their beliefs, behaviors, and relationships in ways both subtle and profound. It is a journey into the shadowed corridors of control, where isolation becomes a formidable force, molding the contours of individuals' lives within the stringent parameters set by the cult's leaders.

Control of Information: Isolation helps control what information followers have access to. By restricting external influences, cult leaders can shape and manipulate the narrative to align with their doctrines, preventing contradictory viewpoints.

Prevention of Dissent: Isolating followers minimizes the chances of dissent or critical thinking. Exposure to alternative perspectives could lead followers to question the leader's authority, so isolation serves to maintain a closed system where the leader's teachings go unchallenged.

Dependency on the Leader: Isolation fosters a sense of dependency on the cult leader for emotional, social, and sometimes even practical needs. This dependence makes it more difficult for followers to contemplate leaving the group or questioning the leader's directives.

Cult of Personality: Cult leaders often promote a charismatic and authoritarian image. Isolation ensures that the leader remains the primary and, in some cases, the only source of guidance, creating an environment where followers are heavily influenced by the leader's persona.

Fear and Intimidation: By cutting off external connections, cult leaders can instill fear in followers. The threat of consequences for contacting outsiders or leaving the group may be used as a means of control.

Psychological Manipulation: Isolation is a powerful tool for psychological manipulation. It can lead to feelings of loneliness, anxiety, and a distorted sense of reality, making followers more susceptible to the leader's influence.

Us-versus-Them Mentality: Isolation reinforces an "us-versus-them" mentality. Followers may come to view the outside world as a threat, further binding them to the group and discouraging any inclination to seek help or information from external sources.

Social Pressure and Conformity: Cult leaders often emphasize conformity. Isolation from dissenting opinions creates an echo chamber where social pressure to conform to the group's beliefs is intensified, making it difficult for followers to express doubt or disagreement.

Secrecy and Exclusive Knowledge: Cults often claim to possess exclusive knowledge or insights. Isolation adds an element of secrecy, making followers feel privileged to be part of an elite group with access to hidden truths, reinforcing their commitment.

Erosion of Personal Identity: Isolation contributes to the erosion of personal identity. Without external perspectives, followers may gradually lose touch with their individuality, adopting the beliefs and behaviors dictated by the cult leader.

EXAMPLE

Grace, a 39-year-old woman whose life began within a fundamental Christian family cult led by her domineering parents, the revered cult leaders. Grace's existence has been a symphony of isolation, an entwined melody of obedience and seclusion within the walls of the cult's stronghold.

Born into this insular community, Grace's isolation is profound, reaching beyond physical boundaries into the very fabric of her thoughts and beliefs. The teachings of her parents, hailed as divine revelations, have shaped every aspect of her worldview. Her education is confined to the doctrines approved by the cult, shielding her from the diverse perspectives of the outside world.

Grace's social interactions are meticulously controlled within the cult's cloistered environment. Friendships are scrutinized, and any deviation from the prescribed norms is met with suspicion. The fear of isolation from the only community she has ever known acts as an invisible shackle, binding her to the cult's rigid ideology.

As Grace contemplates breaking free, she faces a myriad of obstacles. The psychological toll of isolation weighs heavily on her, and the outside world seems both alluring and intimidating. The very concept of autonomy is an uncharted territory, and the fear of isolation, this time from her family and the only reality she has ever known, is a formidable barrier to her quest for freedom.

Grace's story epitomizes the struggles of those born into the clutches of a fundamentalist Christian family cult. Breaking away from the pervasive isolation is not merely a physical escape; it is an intricate dance with the deeply ingrained psychological and emotional bonds that tether her to the only life she has ever known.

Grace, embarking on her journey to break free from the clutches of the fundamental Christian family cult, encounters a stark landscape of scarce resources. The very isolation that defined her life within the cult becomes a formidable barrier as she steps into the unfamiliar terrain outside its walls.

One of the immediate challenges Grace faces is the lack of practical skills and knowledge essential for survival beyond the confines of the cult. Her education, tailored to fit the cult's narrative, leaves significant gaps in practical life skills, hindering her ability to navigate the complexities of the outside world. Basic tasks like managing finances, securing employment, and even accessing public services proves daunting in the absence of a comprehensive education. Financial independence becomes a distant goal for Grace as she grapples with the scarcity of resources.

The cult's control over its members often extends to economic aspects, leaving those who leave without the necessary means to support themselves. Grace's lack of exposure to alternative worldviews further limits her employment prospects, exacerbating the financial challenges she faces post-cult.

Social isolation compounds Grace's struggle for resources. The cult has been her entire social ecosystem, and breaking away means severing ties with the only community she has ever known. This leaves her without the essential support networks that often play a pivotal role in overcoming challenges during times of transition.

Limited access to mental health resources further exacerbates Grace's predicament. The deep emotional scars left by a lifetime of isolation and indoctrination require specialized support, but such services are often scarce or inaccessible, adding an additional layer of complexity to her journey of recovery.

As Grace confronts these resource-related challenges, her story sheds light on the harsh realities faced by individuals leaving family cults. The lack of education, financial resources, and a robust support system makes the journey to independence a daunting and arduous path.

Grace's story forces us to look at the face of these very real challenges and underscores the urgent need for broader societal awareness and support structures to aid those seeking to rebuild their lives after leaving a family cult.

WHY IS ISOLATION DETRIMENTAL, ESPECIALLY WITHIN A FAMILY CULT?

It is crucial to clarify that isolating a child or victim within a family context, particularly for harmful purposes, is deeply unethical and can have severe negative consequences. While some perpetrators may attempt to isolate individuals within family cults or abusive situations, this behavior is not justified, and it's essential to emphasize the importance of protecting vulnerable members.

Isolating a child or victim within a family culture can be detrimental for several reasons:

Psychological Manipulation: Isolation creates an environment where the perpetrator can exert greater control over the child or victim. Limited exposure to external influences makes it easier for the perpetrator to manipulate thoughts, beliefs, and emotions.

Prevention of External Support: Isolation hinders the child or victim's ability to seek help from external sources, such as friends, teachers, or extended family. Lack of support makes it more challenging for individuals to recognize and escape abusive situations.

Distorted Worldview: Isolation often involves restricting access to diverse perspectives and information. This can result in a distorted worldview, where the child or victim is only exposed to the beliefs and narratives promoted by the perpetrator or the family cult.

Dependence on the Perpetrator: Isolation fosters dependence on the perpetrator for emotional, psychological, and even physical needs. The victim may develop a reliance on the abuser, leading to increased vulnerability and difficulty breaking free from the abusive situation.

Impaired Social Development: Children require social interactions for healthy development. Isolation can impede social skills, emotional intelligence, and the ability to form meaningful connections outside the abusive environment.

Fear and Intimidation: Perpetrators may use the fear of consequences for seeking help or disclosing abuse to maintain control. Isolation amplifies this fear, making it more challenging for victims to break their silence.

Normalization of Abuse: Isolation may contribute to a normalization of abusive behaviors within the confined environment. Lack of external feedback or contrasting viewpoints can make victims believe that the abusive conduct is acceptable or normal.

NATIONAL ABUSE HOTLINES AND CONTACT INFORMATION

If you are in the United States and you or someone you know is experiencing abuse or in immediate danger, please contact the National Domestic Violence Hotline at 1-800-799-SAFE (7233) or visit their website at www.thehotline.org.

For child abuse concerns, you can contact the Childhelp National Child Abuse Hotline at 1-800-4-A-CHILD (1-800-422-4453) or visit www.childhelp.org.

It's essential to reach out to local authorities, law enforcement, or relevant support organizations based on your specific situation and location. If you are in a different country, please let me know, and I can provide information based on your region.

NATIONAL SEXUAL ASSAULT HOTLINE AND CONTACT INFORMATION

If you or someone you know has been a victim of Sexual Assault, it's important to reach out to the appropriate professionals and organizations directly. In the United States, you can contact the National Sexual Assault Hotline at 1-800-656-HOPE (4673). If you're located in a different country, local hotlines and resources may be available. Remember that support is available, and you don't have to face difficult situations alone.

CHAPTER 3

VICTIM EXPERIENCE

Trigger Warning: Sensitive Content

This content may contain information or discussions that could be distressing or triggering for some individuals. Topics may include but are not limited to trauma, abuse, violence, or other potentially upsetting subject matter. Reader discretion is advised. If you find that you are emotionally impacted by such content, it is recommended to seek support or refrain from reading further. Your well-being is important.

Within the intricate tapestry of the victim experience after leaving a fundamental Christian family cult, the threads of mental and emotional challenges are woven with profound significance. Liberation from the cult's oppressive environment doesn't necessarily mark an immediate end to the psychological toll endured during indoctrination. Survivors often grapple with profound mental and emotional scars.

The intense conditioning, manipulation, and emotional abuse experienced within the family cult can lead to a range of mental health challenges. Anxiety, depression, and post-traumatic stress disorder (PTSD) are common companions on the journey to recovery. The very mechanisms that sustained individuals within the cult – control, fear, and guilt – leave enduring imprints on the psyche, demanding careful unraveling in the aftermath.

Emotionally, survivors may confront a turbulent sea of conflicting feelings. The ruptured connections with family members and the rupture of the only social structure they've known can evoke a profound sense of loss. Guilt, shame, and self-doubt may persist as remnants of the indoctrination, making the process of self-discovery and healing a delicate dance.

The victim experience encapsulates the courageous struggle to reclaim mental and emotional well-being. Establishing new patterns of thought, overcoming ingrained fears, and learning to trust oneself again become integral parts of the journey. Access to mental health resources is often a vital component in this process, offering survivors the support needed to navigate the complexities of their emotional landscape.

In the unfolding chapters of post-cult life, the mental and emotional challenges serve as poignant reminders of the resilience required to break free. Through therapy, community support, and a commitment to self-discovery, survivors embark on a transformative journey to reclaim their mental and emotional well-being, forging a path towards a future liberated from the haunting echoes of the family cult.

FREQUENTLY ASKED QUESTIONS AND ANSWERS

WHAT DOES SOMEONE EXPERIENCE LIVING INSIDE THE INVISIBLE PRISON THAT IS A FAMILY CULT?

Living in an invisible prison within a family cult can be an emotionally and psychologically challenging experience. Here are some aspects of that experience:

Control and Manipulation: Family cults often thrive on control, manipulation, and strict adherence to the cult leader's ideologies. Members may feel compelled to conform to rigid rules and expectations, limiting their autonomy.

Isolation: Cults often isolate their members from the outside world, creating a sense of exclusivity. This isolation can lead to a distorted worldview, as individuals are cut off from diverse perspectives and alternative ways of thinking.

Fear and Intimidation: Cult leaders may instill fear through tactics such as emotional manipulation, threats of punishment, or the promise of dire consequences for disobedience. This atmosphere of fear can keep members compliant and hesitant to question authority.

Guilt and Shame: Cults frequently use guilt and shame as tools for control. Members may be made to feel guilty for questioning the cult's teachings or expressing dissenting opinions, fostering a sense of self-blame and inadequacy.

Limited Information Access: In a family cult, information is often tightly controlled. Members may have restricted access to external sources of information, preventing them from critically evaluating the cult's teachings or seeking alternative viewpoints.

Dependency on the Cult: Family cults may create an environment where members become emotionally, financially, or socially dependent on the cult structure. This dependency can make it challenging for individuals to envision a life outside the cult.

Cognitive Dissonance: Members may experience cognitive dissonance, where their beliefs clash with observable reality. This internal conflict can lead to confusion, anxiety, and a sense of being trapped between conflicting thought patterns.

Loss of Individual Identity: Cults often demand conformity, and individual identity may be suppressed or subsumed by the collective identity of the cult. Members may lose a sense of self as their thoughts, feelings, and actions become aligned with the cult's agenda.

Conditional Love and Acceptance: Love and acceptance within the family cult may be conditional on adherence to the cult's doctrine. Members might fear rejection or ostracism if they deviate from the prescribed beliefs or behaviors.

Psychological Manipulation: Cult leaders may employ mind-control techniques, exploiting psychological vulnerabilities to maintain control over their followers. This manipulation can erode critical thinking skills and impair decision-making.

Limited Freedom: Members may find their freedom curtailed, with restrictions on personal choices, relationships, and life decisions. This limited freedom reinforces the sense of living within an invisible prison.

Breaking free from the invisible prison of a family cult often requires immense courage, support, and a gradual awakening to the realization that life beyond the cult is possible. Seeking professional help and connecting with supportive communities can be crucial steps in the process of reclaiming one's autonomy and rebuilding a life outside the confines of the cult.

WHAT ARE SOME OF THE DIAGNOSES YOU MIGHT GO THROUGH AFTER LEAVING YOUR FAMILY CULT?

Leaving a family cult and transitioning to life outside can be a complex process that may involve various emotional and psychological challenges. It's important to note that clinical diagnoses are determined by mental health professionals based on a comprehensive assessment of an individual's symptoms, experiences, and functioning. The following are some mental health conditions that individuals who have left a family cult may commonly encounter, but it's crucial to consult with a qualified mental health professional for accurate diagnosis and appropriate treatment:

Post-Traumatic Stress Disorder (PTSD): Individuals who have experienced trauma within the family cult may develop symptoms of PTSD, such as intrusive memories, flashbacks, hyper-vigilance, and emotional numbness.

Complex Post-Traumatic Stress Disorder (C-PTSD): C-PTSD is associated with prolonged exposure to trauma, often involving interpersonal relationships. Leaving a family cult may lead to symptoms such as difficulties with emotional regulation, identity, and relationships.

Anxiety Disorders: Generalized Anxiety Disorder (GAD), social anxiety, panic disorder, and other anxiety disorders may manifest due to the stressors and uncertainties associated with leaving a family cult.

Depressive Disorders: Major Depressive Disorder (MDD) or persistent depressive symptoms may arise as individuals grapple with the aftermath of their experiences, loss of community, and challenges in adapting to a new life.

Dissociative Disorders: Dissociation may occur as a coping mechanism during or after traumatic experiences. Dissociative Identity Disorder (DID) and other dissociative disorders may be relevant in some cases.

Adjustment Disorders: Difficulties adjusting to the new environment, establishing new relationships, or coping with the aftermath of cult experiences can lead to adjustment disorders.

Personality Disorders: Individuals leaving family cults may exhibit traits associated with personality disorders, such as borderline personality disorder (BPD), which can involve challenges in identity, self-image, and interpersonal relationships.

Substance Use Disorders: Coping with the aftermath of cult experiences may lead some individuals to turn to substance use as a way of managing emotional distress.

Eating Disorders: Trauma and control mechanisms within the cult may contribute to the development of eating disorders, such as anorexia nervosa, bulimia nervosa, or binge-eating disorder.

Note: The information provided above is a generalization and may not apply to everyone who has left a family cult. Individual experiences and mental health conditions can vary widely. It is essential for individuals seeking support to consult with qualified mental health professionals for personalized assessments, accurate diagnoses, and appropriate treatment plans based on their unique circumstances.

PTSD

It's important to emphasize that each individual's experience is unique, and the manifestation of mental health challenges can vary widely. Seeking professional mental health support is crucial for accurate assessment, diagnosis, and the development of an appropriate treatment plan tailored to the individual's needs. A mental health professional can provide guidance, support, and therapeutic interventions to aid in the recovery process.

Post-Traumatic Stress Disorder (PTSD) is a mental health condition that can develop in individuals who have experienced or witnessed a traumatic event. Traumatic events that can lead to PTSD include:

Childhood trauma: Individuals who experienced abuse, neglect, or other traumatic events during childhood.

Physical or sexual assault: Survivors of rape, abuse, or other violent crimes.

Accidents: Survivors of physical accidents, or other serious accidents.

Medical trauma: Individuals who have undergone life-threatening medical procedures or experienced severe illnesses.

PTSD is characterized by a range of symptoms that can persist long after the traumatic event has occurred. These symptoms are generally grouped into four categories:

Intrusive Thoughts: Individuals may experience recurrent, distressing memories, nightmares, or flashbacks related to the traumatic event.

Avoidance: People with PTSD often go to great lengths to avoid reminders of the traumatic event. This can include avoiding certain places, people, or activities associated with the trauma.

Negative Changes in Thinking and Mood: PTSD can lead to persistent negative thoughts about oneself or others, feelings of guilt or shame, and a reduced ability to experience positive emotions.

Changes in Reactivity and Arousal: Individuals with PTSD may become easily startled, experience heightened irritability or anger, have difficulty sleeping, or have difficulty concentrating.

The symptoms of PTSD can vary in intensity and may interfere with an individual's daily life and functioning. It's important to note that not everyone who experiences a traumatic event will develop PTSD, and the disorder can affect individuals of all ages. Treatment for PTSD often involves psychotherapy, particularly approaches such as Cognitive Behavioral Therapy (CBT) and Eye Movement Desensitization and Reprocessing (EMDR).

Medications may also be prescribed in some cases to alleviate specific symptoms. If you or someone you know is experiencing symptoms of PTSD, seeking help from mental health professionals is crucial for appropriate diagnosis and support.

FREQUENTLY ASKED QUESTIONS AND ANSWERS

WHY IS IT COMMON FOR SOMEONE RECOVERING FROM A FAMILY CULT TO HAVE PTSD?

Individuals recovering from a family cult may commonly experience Post-Traumatic Stress Disorder (PTSD) due to the pervasive and severe nature of trauma within these environments. Several factors contribute to the likelihood of developing PTSD:

Systematic Abuse: Family cults often involve systematic abuse, including emotional, physical, and sometimes sexual abuse.
The chronic and repetitive nature of this abuse can contribute to the development of PTSD symptoms.

Mind Control and Manipulation: Cult leaders employ tactics of mind control and manipulation, creating an environment that induces fear, dependency, and submission. The psychological impact of such control can lead to long-lasting trauma.

Ritualistic Practices: Some family cults engage in ritualistic practices that involve traumatic experiences, further intensifying the impact on individuals. These rituals can create lasting psychological scars.

Loss of Autonomy: Individuals in family cults often experience a loss of autonomy and personal agency. The lack of control over one's life and choices contributes to a sense of helplessness, a common aspect of trauma.

Isolation and Control of Information: Cults often isolate members from the outside world and tightly control information. This isolation can create a distorted worldview and contribute to difficulties in adjusting to non-cult society.

Fear of Retribution: Exiting a family cult can be accompanied by a genuine fear of retribution from the cult or its members. This fear can persist even after leaving, contributing to hyper-vigilance and anxiety.

Betrayal and Exploitation: Individuals in family cults may experience profound betrayal by those they trusted, including family members and leaders. Exploitation of trust can lead to deep emotional wounds.

Cognitive Distortions: Cult environments foster distorted beliefs about the world, self, and others. These cognitive distortions can contribute to symptoms of PTSD, such as negative changes in thinking and mood.

Traumatic Exits: Leaving a family cult is often a traumatic experience itself. The challenges of rebuilding life outside the cult, combined with the fear of retaliation, contribute to the overall trauma experienced by survivors.

Complex Trauma: The cumulative impact of ongoing, multiple traumas over an extended period can result in Complex PTSD. This form of PTSD is characterized by additional symptoms such as difficulties with emotional regulation, interpersonal relationships, and a distorted self-concept.

It's important for individuals recovering from family cults to seek professional support and engage in trauma-focused therapy. Therapeutic interventions can help survivors process their traumatic experiences, develop coping strategies, and work toward healing and recovery. Additionally, building a supportive network and connecting with others who have experienced similar situations can be valuable in the recovery journey.

WHY IS IT IMPORTANT FOR SOMEONE THAT IS SUPPORTING A VICTIM OF FAMILY CULT ABUSE TO UNDERSTAND PTSD?

Understanding Post-Traumatic Stress Disorder (PTSD) is crucial for someone supporting a victim of family cult abuse for several significant reasons:

Validation of Experiences: Knowledge of PTSD allows support providers to recognize and validate the survivor's experiences. Understanding the impact of trauma helps avoid minimizing or dismissing the severity of what the survivor has endured.

Recognizing Triggers: Individuals with PTSD may have specific triggers that elicit intense emotional responses or flashbacks. Support providers who understand these triggers can help create environments that minimize potential distress and promote a sense of safety.

Compassionate Communication: Understanding PTSD enables support providers to communicate with empathy and sensitivity. They can approach conversations with awareness of potential triggers, use non-triggering language, and provide support without inadvertently causing additional distress.

Promoting Safety and Trust: Trauma survivors often struggle with feelings of vulnerability and fear. Knowledge of PTSD helps support providers create a safe and trusting environment, essential for survivors to feel comfortable seeking help and sharing their experiences.

Encouraging Professional Help: Support providers, armed with knowledge about PTSD, can encourage survivors to seek professional help from therapists or mental health professionals specializing in trauma. This guidance is crucial for comprehensive and effective treatment.

Avoiding Re-traumatization: Uninformed interactions can unintentionally trigger trauma responses in survivors. Understanding PTSD helps support providers avoid behaviors or statements that could re-traumatize the survivor.

Facilitating Coping Strategies: Knowledge of PTSD allows support providers to assist survivors in developing and utilizing coping strategies. This may involve encouraging healthy self-care practices, mindfulness techniques, or other methods to manage symptoms.

Trauma-Informed Support: Adopting a trauma-informed approach is essential. This involves recognizing the impact of trauma on an individual's life and behaviors. Support providers can align their approach with trauma-informed principles to create a supportive and understanding atmosphere.

Understanding Hyper-arousal and Hyper-vigilance: PTSD often involves symptoms of hyper-arousal and hyper-vigilance, where individuals may be overly alert to potential threats. Support providers who understand these aspects can offer assistance in managing heightened states of arousal.

Long-Term Support and Patience: PTSD recovery is often a long-term process. Understanding this helps support providers offer sustained, patient assistance, recognizing that healing takes time and may involve setbacks.

CPTSD

Complex Post-Traumatic Stress Disorder (CPTSD) is a mental health condition that can develop in response to prolonged exposure to traumatic events or situations, particularly those involving interpersonal trauma and a lack of escape or support. CPTSD is considered a more complex and severe form of post-traumatic stress disorder (PTSD). Key features of CPTSD include:

Exposure to Prolonged Trauma: CPTSD often arises from exposure to long-term, chronic trauma rather than a single, isolated event. This can include experiences such as ongoing abuse, captivity, or severe neglect.

Interpersonal Trauma: The trauma typically involves interpersonal relationships, where the individual feels trapped, helpless, or unable to escape. This can occur in abusive relationships, cults, human trafficking situations, or other contexts with persistent threats to physical or psychological well-being.

Dysregulation of Emotions: Individuals with CPTSD may struggle with the regulation of emotions. This can manifest as intense and unpredictable emotional responses, difficulty managing stress, and a heightened state of arousal.

Negative Self-Concept: CPTSD can lead to a negative self-concept, including feelings of shame, guilt, and a distorted perception of oneself as damaged or fundamentally flawed.

Distorted Relationships: The impact of chronic trauma can extend to interpersonal relationships, resulting in difficulties forming and maintaining healthy connections. Trust issues, fear of abandonment, and challenges with boundaries may arise.

Loss of Meaning and Identity: Prolonged exposure to trauma can lead to a loss of a coherent sense of self and a diminished sense of purpose or meaning in life.

Somatic Symptoms: CPTSD can manifest in physical symptoms, such as chronic pain, gastrointestinal issues, or other somatic complaints, often with no clear medical explanation.

Cognitive Distortions: Individuals with CPTSD may develop distorted beliefs about themselves, others, and the world. These cognitive distortions can contribute to negative thought patterns and hinder the ability to trust.

It's important to note that while CPTSD shares some similarities with PTSD, it also includes additional symptoms related to disturbances in self-organization. The concept of CPTSD is not universally recognized in all diagnostic systems, but it has gained recognition and is included in the International Classification of Diseases (ICD-11) as a distinct diagnosis. Treatment for CPTSD often involves a combination of psychotherapy, support groups, and holistic approaches to address the various symptoms and challenges associated with prolonged trauma. Seeking professional help is essential for individuals experiencing CPTSD to navigate their healing journey effectively.

FREQUENTLY ASKED QUESTIONS AND ANSWERS

WHAT IS THE DIFFERENCE BETWEEN PTSD AND CPTSD?

Post-Traumatic Stress Disorder (PTSD) and Complex Post-Traumatic Stress Disorder (CPTSD) share similarities, but they differ in the nature of the traumatic experiences and the resulting symptoms. While both disorders involve a response to trauma, CPTSD acknowledges the impact of sustained, interpersonal trauma over an extended period.

It recognizes the cumulative effects of ongoing stressors and acknowledges the broader range of symptoms that may result from complex trauma. It's important to note that these distinctions help in understanding the nuances of trauma-related disorders, but a mental health professional should make an accurate diagnosis based on an individual's specific experiences and symptoms.

PTSD (Post-Traumatic Stress Disorder):

Traumatic Event: PTSD typically results from exposure to a single traumatic event, such as combat, assault, natural disaster, or a serious accident.

Symptoms: Individuals with PTSD may experience symptoms like flashbacks, nightmares, hypervigilance, and avoidance behaviors. These symptoms are often triggered by reminders of the traumatic incident.

CPTSD (Complex Post-Traumatic Stress Disorder):

Prolonged, Repeated Trauma: CPTSD is associated with prolonged, repeated trauma, often involving interpersonal relationships and power dynamics. This can include situations like long-term emotional, physical, or sexual abuse, or being exposed to chronic stressors over an extended period.

Additional Symptoms: In addition to symptoms similar to PTSD, CPTSD may involve difficulties with emotion regulation, distorted self-perception, interpersonal problems, and a pervasive sense of emptiness.

EXAMPLE

For Caleb, a 30-year-old man who has emerged from the shadow of his fundamental Christian family cult close to 2 years ago, life unfolds against the backdrop of a complex tapestry woven with the threads of Post-Traumatic Stress Disorder (PTSD) and Complex Post-Traumatic Stress Disorder (CPTSD). The journey beyond the confines of the cult has led him to a landscape where the echoes of sustained trauma reverberate through his daily existence. Caleb's experience encapsulates the lingering impact of prolonged, interpersonal trauma endured within the family cult.

Diagnosed with PTSD and CPTSD, he grapples with the aftermath of a reality shaped by years of emotional manipulation, control, and the erosion of personal autonomy. The relentless exposure to a distorted belief system and the scars left by sustained abuse color his perceptions of self and the world around him.

Within the realm of PTSD or CPTSD, Caleb navigates the terrain of intrusive memories, hyper-vigilance, and the intricate dance of emotional regulation.

The very fabric of his identity bears the imprints of the cult's influence, and forging connections with others becomes a delicate dance fraught with the ghosts of past traumas. Yet, within the struggle lies resilience. Caleb's journey is one of rediscovery and piecing together the fragments of his true self that were obscured beneath layers of indoctrination.

As he confronts the challenges of managing triggers, rebuilding shattered trust, and finding a sense of safety, he embodies the profound courage required to transcend the shackles of cult-induced trauma.

Caleb's narrative echoes the collective experiences of survivors who, having broken free from the chains of a family cult, embark on a path of healing and self-discovery. Through therapy, community support, and a commitment to reclaiming his autonomy, Caleb confronts the shadows of his past with the hope of forging a future liberated from the haunting echoes of the family cult.

WHY IS IT IMPORTANT FOR SOMEONE THAT IS SUPPORTING A VICTIM OF FAMILY CULT ABUSE TO UNDERSTAND CPTSD?

Understanding Complex Post-Traumatic Stress Disorder (CPTSD) is crucial for individuals supporting victims of family cult abuse for several reasons:

Informed Support: Knowledge of CPTSD equips support providers with a deeper understanding of the unique challenges faced by survivors of family cult abuse.
This awareness enables more informed and empathetic support.

Recognition of Symptoms: CPTSD can manifest in various ways, including flashbacks, emotional dysregulation, dissociation, and difficulties with interpersonal relationships. Understanding these symptoms helps support providers recognize and respond appropriately to the survivor's needs.

Trauma-Informed Approach: A trauma-informed approach involves recognizing the pervasive impact of trauma on an individual's life. Understanding CPTSD allows support providers to adopt a trauma-informed perspective, promoting a safer and more supportive environment for the survivor.

Avoiding Re-traumatization: Uninformed interactions may inadvertently trigger trauma responses in survivors. Knowledge of CPTSD helps support providers avoid potential triggers and behaviors that could re-traumatize the survivor.

Effective Communication: Understanding CPTSD aids in effective communication with survivors. It allows support providers to navigate conversations with sensitivity, validate the survivor's experiences, and create a space for open and respectful dialogue.

Encouraging Professional Help: Familiarity with CPTSD enables support providers to encourage survivors to seek professional help from therapists or mental health professionals who specialize in trauma and its complex effects.

Promoting Self-Care: CPTSD often involves challenges related to self-worth and self-care. Support providers who understand these dynamics can encourage survivors to prioritize self-care practices and advocate for their well-being.

Understanding Triggers: Recognizing potential triggers for individuals with CPTSD is essential. Support providers can help create environments that minimize triggers and work collaboratively with survivors to develop coping strategies.

Validation of Experiences: Understanding CPTSD allows support providers to validate the survivor's experiences. This validation is crucial for building trust, as survivors may have faced gaslighting or denial of their reality within the family cult.

Advocacy and Empowerment: Armed with knowledge about CPTSD, support providers can advocate for the survivor's needs and empower them to take steps toward recovery. This may involve connecting them with appropriate resources or helping them navigate the mental health system.

Long-Term Support: CPTSD often requires long-term support. Understanding the chronic nature of the disorder helps support providers offer sustained, patient assistance throughout the survivor's healing journey.

In summary, familiarity with CPTSD enhances the quality and effectiveness of support provided to survivors of family cult abuse. It allows support providers to approach their role with sensitivity, empathy, and a well-informed perspective, ultimately contributing to the survivor's healing and recovery process.

ANXIETY DISORDERS

WHAT IS ANXIETY DISORDERS AND WHAT ARE THE SYMPTOMS?

Anxiety disorders are a group of mental health conditions characterized by excessive and persistent worry, fear, or apprehension. These feelings can interfere with daily functioning, impact overall well-being, and may be accompanied by physical symptoms. There are various types of anxiety disorders, each with its own specific features. Common anxiety disorders include Generalized Anxiety Disorder (GAD), Social Anxiety Disorder, Panic Disorder, and Specific Phobias.

General Symptoms of Anxiety Disorders:

Excessive Worry: Persistent and uncontrollable worry about various aspects of life, even when there is no apparent reason for concern.

Restlessness: A feeling of restlessness or being on edge, making it difficult to relax or sit still.

Fatigue: Feeling easily fatigued, both physically and mentally, due to heightened anxiety.

Difficulty Concentrating: Trouble focusing or concentrating on tasks because of intrusive thoughts or worry.

Irritability: Increased irritability and a sense of being easily agitated.

Muscle Tension: Physical symptoms such as muscle tension, aches, or soreness, often without a clear physical cause.

Sleep Disturbances: Difficulty falling asleep, staying asleep, or experiencing restful sleep due to racing thoughts or anxiety.

Physical Symptoms: Various physical symptoms, such as headaches, stomachaches, trembling, sweating, dizziness, or shortness of breath, can accompany anxiety.

Specific Anxiety Disorders:

Generalized Anxiety Disorder (GAD): Excessive worry and anxiety about a variety of everyday concerns. Individuals with GAD often anticipate disaster and may have physical symptoms such as muscle tension and restlessness.

Social Anxiety Disorder: Intense fear of social situations and a strong desire to avoid scrutiny or judgment. This fear may lead to avoidance of social activities and interactions.

Panic Disorder: Recurrent and unexpected panic attacks, which are sudden episodes of intense fear or discomfort accompanied by physical symptoms like a racing heart, sweating, trembling, and a feeling of impending doom.

Specific Phobias: Intense and irrational fears of specific objects, situations, or activities. Common phobias include fear of heights, flying, animals, or certain environments.

Obsessive-Compulsive Disorder (OCD) and Post-Traumatic Stress Disorder (PTSD): While OCD and PTSD are not classified as anxiety disorders, they can involve significant anxiety symptoms.

OCD: Intrusive and distressing thoughts (obsessions) followed by repetitive behaviors or mental acts (compulsions) to reduce the anxiety associated with the obsessions.

PTSD: Anxiety and distress following exposure to a traumatic event, with symptoms such as flashbacks, nightmares, and hyper-vigilance.

It's important to note that experiencing occasional anxiety is a normal part of life. However, when anxiety becomes overwhelming, persistent, and interferes with daily functioning, seeking professional help is advisable.

Mental health professionals can provide a thorough assessment, diagnosis, and recommend appropriate interventions, such as therapy, medication, or a combination of both, to manage anxiety effectively.

FREQUENTLY ASKED QUESTIONS AND ANSWERS

WHY IS IT VERY COMMON FOR PEOPLE LEAVING A FAMILY CULT TO EXPERIENCE ANXIETY DISORDERS?

Leaving a family cult is often accompanied by numerous challenges and stressors that can contribute to the development or exacerbation of anxiety disorders. Here are some reasons why individuals leaving a family cult commonly experience anxiety:

Trauma and Abuse: Many family cults involve abusive and manipulative practices. Leaving such an environment can trigger trauma, leading to heightened anxiety as individuals confront and process past experiences.

Loss of Support System: Family cults often create a tightly knit community. Leaving means losing the support of that community, which can result in feelings of isolation and a lack of a social safety net, contributing to anxiety.

Fear of Retribution: Cults may instill fear in members, warning of dire consequences for leaving. The fear of retaliation or punishment can lead to persistent anxiety even after leaving the cult.

Cognitive Dissonance: Leaving a family cult may entail a significant shift in beliefs and values. The cognitive dissonance that arises from reconciling conflicting perspectives can be emotionally distressing, contributing to anxiety.

Identity Crisis: Cults often dictate members' identities. Leaving may result in a loss of self and a struggle to establish a new identity, leading to existential anxiety.

Social Reintegration: Individuals leaving a cult may find it challenging to integrate into mainstream society. The fear of judgment, rejection, or not fitting in can contribute to social anxiety.

Grief and Loss: Leaving a family cult involves leaving behind relationships, belief systems, and a way of life. Grieving these losses can be a prolonged and complex process, contributing to anxiety.

Uncertain Future: Cults often control various aspects of members' lives. The uncertainty of the future, coupled with the lack of guidance and structure, can evoke anxiety about navigating the unknown.

Manipulative Conditioning: Cults use manipulation and mind control techniques that leave lasting psychological effects. Breaking free from this conditioning can result in ongoing anxiety as individuals grapple with distorted thought patterns.

Financial and Practical Challenges: Leaving a family cult may entail practical challenges, such as finding employment, housing, and establishing financial independence. These stressors can contribute to anxiety about the practical aspects of starting anew.

Addressing anxiety after leaving a family cult requires a supportive network, professional mental health intervention, and time for healing. Therapy and counseling can help individuals process their experiences, develop coping mechanisms, and gradually rebuild their lives.

WHAT ARE SOME BEST PRACTICES TO SUPPORT SOMEONE STRUGGLING WITH ANXIETY ISSUES?

Supporting someone struggling with anxiety issues involves a combination of empathy, understanding, and practical assistance. Here are some best practices to offer support:

Educate Yourself: Learn about anxiety disorders to better understand what your loved one is experiencing. Knowledge about the condition can help you provide informed and compassionate support.

Listen Actively: Allow your loved one to express their feelings without judgment. Practice active listening, and validate their emotions. Sometimes, having someone who listens attentively can be immensely comforting.

Be Non-Judgmental: Avoid making assumptions or passing judgment. Understand that anxiety is a complex condition, and individuals may not always have full control over their symptoms.

Offer Reassurance: Reassure your loved one that you are there for them. Remind them that it's okay to seek help and that they are not alone in their struggle.

Encourage Professional Help: Suggest seeking professional support from therapists, counselors, or mental health professionals. Offer assistance in finding appropriate resources and even accompany them to appointments if needed.

Respect Boundaries: Understand that individuals with anxiety may need space at times. Respect their boundaries while also expressing your willingness to support them when they're ready.

Encourage Self-Care: Promote healthy habits, such as regular exercise, sufficient sleep, and a balanced diet. These can positively impact mental well-being.

Help Identify Triggers: Work together to identify triggers that may contribute to anxiety. Understanding specific situations or stressors can be the first step in finding coping strategies.

Explore Coping Mechanisms: Support your loved one in finding healthy coping mechanisms for anxiety. This could include deep breathing exercises, mindfulness, or other relaxation techniques.

Be Patient: Recovery from anxiety is a process that takes time. Be patient, and recognize that progress may be gradual. Celebrate small victories and encourage continued effort.

Stay Calm in Crisis: If your loved one is experiencing a crisis, remain calm and provide reassurance. Encourage them to contact a mental health professional or crisis hotline if necessary.

Include Them Socially: Anxiety can lead to social withdrawal. Encourage social activities, but respect their comfort level. Create supportive environments where they feel safe and understood.

Remember that each person's experience with anxiety is unique, and what works for one individual may not work for another. Open communication, empathy, and ongoing support are key components in helping someone navigate their anxiety challenges. If the anxiety is severe, professional intervention may be necessary, and your encouragement to seek such help can be crucial.

DEPRESSION

Depression is a mental health disorder characterized by persistent feelings of sadness, hopelessness, and a lack of interest or pleasure in activities. It can affect how individuals think, feel, and handle daily activities. Some common symptoms of depression include:

Persistent Sadness: Feeling persistently sad, empty, or having a sense of hopelessness.

Loss of Interest or Pleasure: Losing interest in activities or hobbies that were once enjoyable.

Changes in Sleep Patterns: Experiencing changes in sleep patterns, such as insomnia or oversleeping.

Fatigue or Lack of Energy: Feeling consistently fatigued or having low energy levels.

Changes in Appetite: Significant changes in appetite, leading to weight loss or gain.

Difficulty Concentrating: Experiencing difficulties in concentration, decision-making, or memory.

Feelings of Worthlessness or Guilt: Having feelings of worthlessness or excessive guilt over perceived failures.

Agitation or Restlessness: Feeling restless, irritable, or having trouble sitting still.

Physical Symptoms: Experiencing physical symptoms such as headaches or digestive issues without a clear medical cause.

Suicidal Thoughts: Thoughts of death or suicide, or suicide attempts.

NATIONAL SUICIDE PREVENTION LIFELINE

In the United States, the National Suicide Prevention Lifeline can be reached at 1-800-273-TALK (1-800-273-8255). This hotline provides free and confidential support for individuals in crisis or anyone concerned about someone who may be at risk of suicide. It's available 24/7, and the call is routed to the nearest crisis center in the Lifeline's national network.

FREQUENTLY ASKED QUESTIONS AND ANSWERS

WHY SHOULD DEPRESSION BE TAKEN SERIOUSLY?

Depression should be taken seriously due to its significant impact on individuals' mental, emotional, and physical well-being. Here are several reasons why depression warrants serious attention:

Impact on Quality of Life: Depression can severely affect a person's overall quality of life. It interferes with the ability to experience joy, engage in daily activities, and maintain fulfilling relationships.

Physical Health Consequences: Depression is not only a mental health concern but can also have physical consequences. It has been linked to various health issues, including cardiovascular problems, compromised immune function, and increased susceptibility to other illnesses.

Suicide Risk: Depression is a major risk factor for suicide. Individuals experiencing severe depressive symptoms may have thoughts of self-harm or suicide. Taking depression seriously is crucial to prevent such tragic outcomes.

Interference with Daily Functioning: Depression can significantly interfere with a person's ability to perform everyday tasks, maintain employment, and fulfill responsibilities. This can lead to financial difficulties and strain on relationships.

Negative Impact on Relationships: Depressive symptoms, such as irritability, withdrawal, and a lack of interest, can strain relationships with family, friends, and colleagues. Addressing depression is vital for maintaining healthy connections.

Impaired Cognitive Functioning: Depression can impair cognitive functions, including concentration, memory, and decision-making. This can affect work performance, academic achievements, and overall cognitive abilities.

Chronic Nature: Depression often becomes chronic if left untreated. Addressing it early can prevent long-term suffering and improve the chances of recovery.

Physical Pain: Some individuals with depression may experience physical symptoms such as chronic pain or gastrointestinal issues. Treating depression can alleviate these physical symptoms.

Impact on Sleep Patterns: Depression frequently disrupts sleep patterns, leading to insomnia or excessive sleep. Sleep disturbances can worsen overall well-being and contribute to other health problems.

Financial and Occupational Consequences: Persistent depression can lead to difficulties maintaining employment, resulting in financial instability. Taking depression seriously is crucial for addressing these occupational challenges.

Positive Treatment Outcomes: With appropriate treatment, many individuals with depression can experience significant improvement in their symptoms and overall well-being. Ignoring or dismissing depression may delay access to beneficial treatments.

Taking depression seriously involves recognizing its impact on various aspects of a person's life and seeking professional help when needed. Timely intervention and appropriate support contribute to better outcomes and an improved quality of life for individuals struggling with depression.

If you or someone you know is experiencing depressive symptoms, it's important to reach out to a mental health professional for assessment and support.

WHY IS DEPRESSION COMMON AMONG CHILDREN AND THE ADULT CHILDREN OF FAMILY CULT MEMBERS?

Depression can be common among children and adult children of family cult members for several reasons, given the unique challenges and experiences associated with growing up in such environments:

Trauma and Abuse: Many family cults involve elements of psychological, emotional, or even physical abuse. Children raised in such environments may experience trauma, contributing to the development of depression.

Isolation and Lack of Social Support: Family cults often isolate members from the outside world, limiting social interactions. Children may grow up without a diverse social support network, increasing the risk of depression due to social isolation.

Authoritarian Control: The authoritarian and controlling nature of family cults can lead to a lack of autonomy for children. This lack of individual agency and decision-making can contribute to feelings of helplessness and depression.

Restricted Education and Development: Family cults may limit access to mainstream education, stifling intellectual and emotional development in children. Limited exposure to diverse ideas and experiences can impact mental well-being.

Guilt and Shame: Children raised in family cults may internalize feelings of guilt and shame associated with not conforming to cult rules or expectations. These negative emotions can contribute to depressive symptoms.

Fear of Punishment: Fear of punishment or rejection within the cult can create a constant state of anxiety. Chronic fear and stress are risk factors for the development of depression.

Loss of Identity: Family cults often demand conformity and discourage individual expression. This loss of personal identity and the inability to explore one's true self can lead to a sense of emptiness and contribute to depression.

Cognitive Dissonance: Growing up in a family cult may expose children to conflicting beliefs and practices. This cognitive dissonance can lead to internal conflict and emotional distress, potentially contributing to depression.

Cult Exit Challenges: Adult children who choose to leave the family cult may face significant challenges, including social isolation, loss of family ties, and difficulties adjusting to life outside the cult. These challenges can contribute to depression during the recovery process.

It's important to note that each individual's experience within a family cult is unique, and not everyone raised in such an environment will develop depression. However, the cumulative impact of various stressors, trauma, and restricted life experiences can elevate the risk. Seeking professional support, such as therapy and counseling, is crucial for individuals navigating the challenges of recovering from a family cult and managing depression.

WHAT ARE SOME SIGNS TO RECOGNIZE SOMEONE MIGHT BE SUFFERING FROM DEPRESSION?

Recognizing signs of depression in someone requires paying attention to changes in their behavior, emotions, and overall well-being. While everyone's experience of depression is unique, here are some common signs that someone might be suffering from depression:

Persistent Sadness: A pervasive and prolonged feeling of sadness, hopelessness, or emptiness that persists throughout the day.

Loss of Interest or Pleasure: Diminished interest in activities or hobbies that were once enjoyable. A person may withdraw from social engagements.

Changes in Sleep Patterns: Significant alterations in sleep, including insomnia (difficulty falling or staying asleep) or hypersomnia (excessive sleep).

Fatigue and Low Energy: Consistent feelings of fatigue, lethargy, or a lack of energy, even after adequate rest.

Appetite Changes: Noticeable changes in appetite, leading to significant weight loss or gain. This can include overeating or loss of interest in food.

Difficulty Concentrating: Challenges with focus, concentration, and decision-making. Completing tasks may become more difficult.

Feelings of Guilt or Worthlessness: Experiencing excessive guilt or feelings of worthlessness, even when there is no apparent reason for these emotions.

Irritability or Agitation: Unexplained irritability, restlessness, or feelings of agitation that are out of character.

Social Withdrawal: Withdrawing from friends, family, or social activities. Avoidance of social interactions may become more pronounced.

Physical Symptoms: Experiencing physical symptoms such as headaches, digestive issues, or unexplained aches and pains.

Suicidal Thoughts: Expressing thoughts of death or suicide, even if indirectly. Any mention of suicide should be taken seriously.

Negative Self-Talk: Engaging in negative self-talk and pervasive feelings of self-criticism. A person may excessively focus on perceived failures.

Changes in Appearance: Neglecting personal grooming and hygiene. A decline in self-care may be evident.

Slowed Movement or Speech: Observable changes in physical movement or speech, such as slowed pace or reduced speech.

Seeking Isolation: Preferring to be alone and avoiding social interactions. Isolation may become a coping mechanism.

It's important to note that individuals experiencing depression may not exhibit all these signs, and the severity can vary. If you notice several of these symptoms persisting for an extended period, especially if they significantly impact daily functioning, it's advisable to encourage the person to seek professional help from a mental health provider. Prompt intervention and support can make a positive difference in their recovery journey.

WHAT CAN SOMEONE DO WHEN SUPPORTING A PERSON SUFFERING FROM DEPRESSION AFTER LEAVING THEIR FAMILY CULT?

Supporting someone dealing with depression after leaving a family cult requires a delicate and understanding approach:

Listen Empathetically: Allow the individual to express their feelings without judgment. Validate their experiences and offer a non-judgmental space for them to share.

Encourage Professional Help: Suggest seeking therapy or counseling from mental health professionals experienced in cult recovery. Professional guidance can be crucial in addressing the complex emotional aftermath.

Educate Yourself: Learn about the unique challenges faced by cult survivors and how these experiences can contribute to depression. Understanding the context helps in providing more informed and compassionate support.

Be Patient: Recovery is a gradual process. Be patient and understanding, recognizing that healing from the impact of a family cult takes time. Encourage small steps toward positive changes

Offer Practical Assistance: Help with daily tasks or responsibilities to alleviate some stress. This can include providing resources for therapists, helping with job searches, or offering a supportive environment.

Promote Self-Care: Emphasize the importance of self-care activities. Encourage healthy habits such as regular exercise, proper nutrition, and sufficient sleep. These can positively impact mental well-being.

Stay Connected: Cultivate a sense of community and belonging. Supportive relationships outside of the cult can play a vital role in recovery. Encourage social interactions and participation in supportive groups.

Monitor Suicidal Thoughts: If the person expresses thoughts of self-harm or suicide, take it seriously. Encourage them to contact a mental health professional or a helpline immediately. If necessary, involve emergency services.

Remember that supporting someone with depression is a complex task, and professional assistance is often crucial. Encourage them to reach out to mental health experts who specialize in cult recovery and trauma.

EXAMPLE

For Ellen, stepping into the role of support for Jamie becomes an intricate journey into the complex aftermath of leaving a fundamental Christian family cult. Jamie, having severed ties with the oppressive confines of her familial cult, now grapples with the weight of depression and anxiety, and it is in this pivotal moment that Ellen extends a compassionate hand.

Navigating the emotional journey of Jamie's recovery, Ellen becomes a steadfast ally, witnessing the intricacies of healing and the resilience required to rebuild a fractured sense of self. The shadows of cult-induced beliefs and practices cast a long shadow over Jamie's psyche, contributing to the profound anxiety and melancholy that shape her daily existence.

As Jamie confronts the ghosts of her past, Ellen stands as a pillar of strength, offering empathetic support in the face of Jamie's internal struggles. Together, they navigate the tumultuous waters of therapy, self-discovery, and the gradual unfurling of Jamie's true identity obscured beneath layers of cult-induced conditioning.

In this partnership, Ellen embodies the power of empathy, creating a safe haven for Jamie to share the burdens of her mental health journey.

The duo delves into the intricacies of depression and anxiety, recognizing that these challenges are not isolated, but intertwined with the broader tapestry of Jamie's recovery from the family cult.

Ellen's narrative unfolds as a testament to the transformative potential of support and understanding in the face of post-cult adversities. Through their shared endeavor, Ellen and Jamie embark on a journey of healing, embracing the hope that the scars of the past can gradually give way to a future defined by resilience, self-love, and the triumph over the shadows of the family cult's legacy.

DISSOCIATIVE DISORDERS

Dissociative disorders are a group of mental health conditions characterized by disruptions in a person's consciousness, identity, memory, or perception. These disruptions often involve a sense of detachment or disconnection from one's thoughts, feelings, identity, or surroundings. Dissociation is a coping mechanism that the mind employs to manage overwhelming stress, trauma, or distressing experiences.

There are several types of dissociative disorders, and symptoms can vary based on the specific condition. Common dissociative disorders include Dissociative Identity Disorder (DID), Dissociative Amnesia, and Depersonalization/Derealization Disorder.

Dissociative Identity Disorder (DID):

Symptoms:
- Presence of two or more distinct personality states or identity states, each with its own way of perceiving and interacting with the world.
- Recurrent gaps in memory that go beyond ordinary forgetfulness and cannot be explained by other medical conditions.

Dissociative Amnesia:

Symptoms:
- Inability to recall important personal information, often related to traumatic or stressful events.
- Memory gaps may be selective, affecting specific periods or aspects of the individual's life.

<u>Depersonalization/Derealization Disorder:</u>

Symptoms:
- Depersonalization: Feeling detached from one's own body or self, as if observing oneself from outside.
- Derealization: A sense of unreality or detachment from the external world, including people, objects, and surroundings.

It's important to note that dissociative disorders are often associated with a history of trauma, particularly early childhood trauma or repeated exposure to distressing events.

FREQUENTLY ASKED QUESTIONS AND ANSWERS

WHY IS IT VERY COMMON FOR PEOPLE LEAVING A FAMILY CULT TO EXPERIENCE DISSOCIATIVE DISORDERS?

Leaving a family cult can be a profoundly traumatic experience, and the development of dissociative disorders among individuals who have exited such environments is not uncommon. Several factors contribute to the prevalence of dissociative disorders in this context:

Trauma and Abuse: Many family cults employ coercive tactics, emotional manipulation, and various forms of abuse. The trauma inflicted on individuals within these environments can lead to dissociative responses as a coping mechanism to disconnect from overwhelming and distressing experiences.

Mind Control and Manipulation: Cults often engage in mind control techniques that aim to manipulate and influence the thoughts, emotions, and behaviors of their members. This manipulation can contribute to a dissociative response as individuals grapple with conflicting beliefs and realities.

Cognitive Dissonance: Leaving a family cult may result in cognitive dissonance, where individuals confront a misalignment between their former beliefs and the new reality. Dissociation can serve as a defense mechanism to manage the internal conflict and distress associated with this dissonance.

Identity Crisis: Family cults often dictate members' identities, beliefs, and behaviors. Upon leaving, individuals may experience an identity crisis, and dissociation can be a way of navigating the profound loss of self and restructuring one's identity outside the cult.

Fear and Anxiety: The fear of retribution, abandonment, or punishment for leaving the cult can contribute to heightened anxiety. Dissociation may serve as a means of escaping or numbing the overwhelming emotional distress associated with these fears.

Loss of Community and Support: Leaving a cult means severing ties with a tightly knit community that provided a sense of belonging. The loss of this support system can lead to feelings of isolation, and dissociation may become a way of distancing oneself from the pain of abandonment.

Grief and Loss: Leaving a family cult involves significant losses, including relationships, beliefs, and a familiar way of life. Dissociation can be a way of numbing the emotional pain associated with grieving these losses.

Recovery and Reintegration: The process of recovering from the effects of the cult and reintegrating into mainstream society can be overwhelming. Dissociation may manifest as a way of navigating the challenges and uncertainties of adapting to a new environment.

It's important to note that dissociative disorders exist on a spectrum, and individuals may experience a range of dissociative symptoms. Seeking professional mental health support, such as therapy and counseling, is crucial for those leaving family cults to address dissociative symptoms, process trauma, and work towards healing and integration.

WHAT ARE SOME BEST PRACTICES TO SUPPORT SOMEONE STRUGGLING WITH DISSOCIATIVE DISORDERS?

Supporting someone struggling with dissociative disorders requires a thoughtful and understanding approach. Here are some best practices to provide support:

Educate Yourself: Learn about dissociative disorders to gain a better understanding of the condition. Familiarize yourself with the different types of dissociation and the experiences your loved one may be going through.

Open Communication: Encourage open and non-judgmental communication. Let your loved one know that you are there to listen and that they can share their experiences without fear of criticism.

Respect Their Experience: Acknowledge and respect their subjective experiences, even if you may not fully understand them. Avoid invalidating their feelings or dismissing their dissociative episodes.

Learn Triggers: Work together to identify potential triggers for dissociation. Understanding the situations or stimuli that contribute to dissociation can help both of you manage and navigate challenging circumstances.

Create a Safe Environment: Foster a safe and supportive environment where your loved one feels comfortable expressing themselves. Knowing they have a secure space can be crucial in managing dissociative symptoms.

Encourage Professional Help: Recommend seeking professional support from therapists or mental health specialists experienced in dissociative disorders. Encourage your loved one to explore therapy options such as dialectical behavior therapy (DBT) or Eye Movement Desensitization and Reprocessing (EMDR), which are often used in treating dissociation.

Develop Coping Strategies: Collaborate on developing coping strategies for managing dissociative episodes. This may include grounding techniques, sensory interventions, or other methods recommended by mental health professionals.

Maintain Consistency: Establish routines and maintain consistency in daily life. Predictability and structure can provide a sense of stability, which may be beneficial for someone experiencing dissociative disorders.

Stay Calm During Episodes: If your loved one is experiencing dissociation, remain calm and provide reassurance. Avoid pressuring them to "snap out of it" and instead offer support when they are ready.

Be Patient: Recovery from dissociative disorders is a gradual process. Be patient and understanding, celebrating progress and acknowledging the challenges without judgment.

Respect Boundaries: Understand that your loved one may need space during times of dissociation. Respect their boundaries while expressing your availability when they are ready to reconnect.

Involve Them in Decision-Making: Involve your loved one in decisions regarding their mental health treatment and support. Empower them to be active participants in their recovery journey.

Remember that professional guidance is crucial for managing dissociative disorders. Encouraging your loved one to seek therapy and offering ongoing support can make a positive impact on their journey toward recovery.

PERSONALITY DISORDERS

Personality disorders are a group of mental health conditions characterized by enduring patterns of behavior, cognition, and inner experience that deviate significantly from cultural expectations and cause distress or impairment in functioning. These patterns typically emerge in adolescence or early adulthood and persist over time. There are several types of personality disorders, each with its own specific features.

The Diagnostic and Statistical Manual of Mental Disorders (DSM-5) outlines three clusters of personality disorders: Cluster A (Odd or Eccentric), Cluster B (Dramatic, Emotional, or Erratic), and Cluster C (Anxious or Fearful). Here are examples of personality disorders from each cluster along with their key symptoms:

Cluster A: Odd or Eccentric Disorders

Paranoid Personality Disorder:

Symptoms:
- Distrust and suspicion of others' motives.
- Unwarranted belief that others are trying to harm, deceive, or exploit them.
- Reluctance to confide in others.

Schizoid Personality Disorder:

Symptoms:
- Lack of interest in social relationships.
- Limited range of emotional expression.
- Preference for solitary activities.

Schizotypal Personality Disorder:

Symptoms:
- Social anxiety and discomfort in close relationships.
- Odd or eccentric beliefs or magical thinking.
- Unusual perceptual experiences.

Cluster B: Dramatic, Emotional, or Erratic Disorders:

Antisocial Personality Disorder:
Symptoms:
- Disregard for the rights of others.
- Lack of empathy and remorse.
- Impulsivity and aggression.

Borderline Personality Disorder:

Symptoms:
- Intense fear of abandonment.
- Unstable relationships marked by idealization and devaluation.
- Impulsivity, self-harm, or suicidal behavior.

Histrionic Personality Disorder:

Symptoms:
- Excessive need for attention.
- Inappropriately seductive or provocative behavior.
- Shallow and rapidly shifting emotions.

Narcissistic Personality Disorder:

Symptoms:
- Grandiosity and a sense of self-importance.
- Lack of empathy.
- Need for excessive admiration.

Cluster C: Anxious or Fearful Disorders

Avoidant Personality Disorder:

Symptoms:
- Fear of criticism or rejection.
- Avoidance of social interactions.
- Feelings of inadequacy and inferiority.

Dependent Personality Disorder:

Symptoms:
- Excessive reliance on others to make decisions.
- Difficulty initiating and maintaining relationships.
- Fear of separation and being alone.

Obsessive-Compulsive Personality Disorder:

Symptoms:
- Perfectionism and preoccupation with orderliness.
- Inflexibility and difficulty delegating tasks.
- Excessive devotion to work.

It's important to note that individuals with personality disorders may not always recognize the impact of their behavior on themselves and others. Diagnosis and treatment are typically provided by mental health professionals, and therapeutic approaches, such as psychotherapy, can be beneficial for managing symptoms and improving functioning.
The specific symptoms and severity of personality disorders can vary widely among individuals.

FREQUENTLY ASKED QUESTIONS AND ANSWERS

WHY IS IT VERY COMMON FOR PEOPLE LEAVING A FAMILY CULT TO EXPERIENCE PERSONALITY DISORDERS?

The experience of leaving a family cult can contribute to the development or exacerbation of personality disorders due to the complex and often traumatic nature of the cult environment. Several factors may contribute to the prevalence of personality disorders in individuals who have left family cults:

Abuse and Trauma: Family cults frequently involve abusive practices, emotional manipulation, and coercive control. The trauma resulting from these experiences can contribute to the development of personality disorders as individuals attempt to cope with and adapt to the adverse conditions.

Mind Control and Manipulation: Cults often engage in mind control techniques that aim to shape members' thoughts, beliefs, and behaviors.

The manipulation and conditioning within the cult can lead to distorted self-perceptions and interpersonal difficulties, which are common features of personality disorders.

Identity Disturbance: Family cults often dictate members' identities, beliefs, and roles within the group. Leaving the cult may lead to a profound loss of identity and a struggle to establish a new sense of self, potentially contributing to personality disorders.

Social Isolation: Cults often isolate their members from mainstream society, limiting social interactions and support systems. The lack of healthy socialization may impact interpersonal skills and contribute to the development of personality disorders characterized by difficulties in forming and maintaining relationships.

Controlled Environment: Cults create a highly controlled and authoritarian environment where individual autonomy is restricted. Leaving this environment may result in challenges adapting to a more open and autonomous lifestyle, potentially leading to personality disorders.

Cognitive Dissonance: Leaving a family cult often involves confronting conflicting beliefs and realities, leading to cognitive dissonance. The internal conflict associated with this dissonance may contribute to personality disorders characterized by instability in self-image, relationships, and emotions.

Grief and Loss: Exiting a family cult involves significant losses, including relationships with cult members, a sense of belonging, and the loss of a familiar way of life. The grief and loss associated with leaving may contribute to personality disorders marked by difficulties in managing emotions and coping with stress.

Post-Cult Adjustment: Individuals leaving a cult may struggle with adapting to life outside the cult, dealing with societal norms, and establishing a new identity. The challenges in adjusting to the post-cult environment may contribute to the development of personality disorders.

It's important to note that personality disorders are complex conditions influenced by a combination of genetic, biological, and environmental factors. Seeking professional mental health support, such as therapy and counseling, is essential for individuals leaving family cults to address underlying issues, process trauma, and work towards mental health and well-being.

WHAT ARE SOME BEST PRACTICES TO SUPPORT SOMEONE STRUGGLING WITH PERSONALITY DISORDERS?

Supporting someone struggling with personality disorders involves adopting a compassionate and informed approach. Here are some best practices to provide effective support:

Educate Yourself: Gain knowledge about the specific personality disorder your loved one is dealing with. Understanding the characteristics, triggers, and treatment options can help you offer informed support.

Encourage Professional Help: Recommend seeking professional assistance from mental health experts. Therapists with experience in treating personality disorders can provide specialized guidance and therapy.

Promote Open Communication: Foster open and honest communication. Create a safe space for your loved one to share their thoughts and feelings without judgment. Encourage them to express their needs and concerns.

Set Healthy Boundaries: Establish clear and healthy boundaries to maintain a balanced relationship. Be mindful of your own well-being and communicate your limits while offering support.

Avoid Stigmatizing Language: Use non-judgmental language to discuss the challenges associated with personality disorders. Avoid stigmatizing terms and focus on fostering understanding and empathy.

Practice Active Listening: Be an attentive listener. Allow your loved one to express themselves without interruption, and validate their experiences. Reflective listening can enhance your understanding of their perspective.

Be Patient and Understanding: Recognize that managing personality disorders can be a long-term process. Be patient and understanding as your loved one navigates their challenges, and avoid placing unrealistic expectations on them.

Celebrate Small Achievements: Acknowledge and celebrate any progress, no matter how small. Recognizing achievements, no matter how incremental, can boost your loved one's confidence and motivation.

Offer Consistent Support: Be a consistent and reliable source of support. Consistency helps build trust and reassures your loved one that you are there for them through ups and downs.

Encourage Self-Care: Emphasize the importance of self-care. Support your loved one in adopting healthy habits, including regular exercise, sufficient sleep, and engaging in activities they enjoy.

Collaborate on Coping Strategies: Work together to identify coping strategies for challenging situations. Encourage the development of healthy coping mechanisms that align with therapeutic goals.

Respect Autonomy: Respect your loved one's autonomy and decision-making. While providing support, avoid being overbearing or making decisions on their behalf. Collaborate on choices that empower them.

Remember that supporting someone with a personality disorder can be complex, and professional guidance is often essential.

EXAMPLE

Samantha, a 22-year-old, navigates the intricate challenges of Dissociative Identity Disorder (DID) stemming from her upbringing in a family cult and ultimate escape. DID, formerly known as multiple personality disorder, manifests as the development of distinct identities or personality states to cope with severe trauma. Samantha's journey is marked by the struggle to integrate these fragmented aspects of herself while contending with the complex legacy of her family cult experiences.

Understanding and supporting Samantha requires a nuanced approach, acknowledging the profound impact of her past on her present identity and mental well-being.

Samantha's daily struggles with Dissociative Identity Disorder (DID) are profound and complex. Here are some aspects she navigates:

Identity Shifts: Samantha experiences shifts in her identity, where different personality states emerge, each with its own set of memories, behaviors, and emotions. These transitions can be disorienting and challenging to manage.

Memory Gaps: DID often involves significant memory gaps or amnesic periods. Samantha may find herself unable to recall parts of her daily life or experiences, contributing to a sense of confusion and loss.

Internal Communication: The internal communication among Samantha's distinct identities may vary. Coordinating and communicating between alters can be a constant struggle, impacting her ability to function seamlessly.

Triggers and Flashbacks: Triggers from her past in the family cult may provoke intense emotional responses or flashbacks. Samantha must navigate these triggers daily, seeking ways to ground herself and manage overwhelming emotions.

Coping Mechanisms: Each alter may have its own coping mechanisms developed during the family cult experiences. Samantha works to understand and integrate these coping strategies into her daily life while fostering healthier alternatives.

Therapeutic Engagement: Samantha likely engages in ongoing therapy to explore and integrate her alters, process traumatic memories, and develop coping skills. Consistent therapeutic support is crucial for her overall well-being.

Social Interactions: Managing relationships and social interactions can be challenging as Samantha grapples with the impact of DID on her ability to connect with others consistently.

Self-Integration: Samantha's journey includes the ongoing work of self-integration, aiming to establish a cohesive sense of self that incorporates all aspects of her identity. This process is gradual and requires patience and understanding.

Samantha's daily struggles emphasize the importance of a supportive and compassionate environment, ongoing therapeutic intervention, and a commitment to self-discovery and healing.

CULTURE SHOCK AND ADJUSTMENT DISORDERS

Culture shock or adjustment disorder refers to the psychological and emotional impact individuals may experience when adapting to a new and unfamiliar cultural environment. It's characterized by a range of symptoms that can affect a person's mental well-being as they navigate the challenges of acclimating to a different culture. Symptoms may include:

Anxiety: Feeling uneasy, nervous, or stressed in the new cultural context.

Depression: Experiencing feelings of sadness, hopelessness, or isolation due to cultural differences.

Homesickness: Longing for one's familiar cultural environment, including family, friends, and customs.

Irritability: Being easily frustrated or agitated as a result of cultural misunderstandings or challenges.

Withdrawal: Social withdrawal or avoiding interactions due to difficulties in communication or cultural differences.

Physical Symptoms: Some individuals may experience physical symptoms such as headaches, fatigue, or digestive issues.

Difficulty Concentrating: Struggling to focus or concentrate on tasks due to the stress of adjusting to a new culture.

Loss of Identity: Feeling a loss of one's cultural identity or a sense of disorientation.

Culture shock is a natural response to the unfamiliar, and individuals may go through stages such as the honeymoon phase (initial excitement), followed by the negotiation, adjustment, and mastery phases. Coping strategies often involve seeking support, developing cultural competence, and gradually adapting to the new cultural context.

FREQUENTLY ASKED QUESTIONS AND ANSWERS

WHAT KIND OF CULTURE SHOCK CAN SOMEONE EXPERIENCE AFTER LEAVING A FUNDAMENTAL CHRISTIAN FAMILY CULT?

Leaving a fundamental Christian family cult can result in a profound culture shock as individuals transition from a highly controlled and isolated environment to the broader society. The nature and intensity of the culture shock may vary based on factors such as the specific cult's practices, the individual's background, and the degree of isolation experienced. Here are potential aspects of culture shock someone might encounter:

Diversity of Beliefs: Exposure to a diverse range of beliefs, values, and lifestyles outside the cult may be overwhelming. Individuals may encounter viewpoints that challenge their previously held convictions, leading to a reevaluation of their belief system.

Freedom and Autonomy: The newfound freedom and autonomy can be disorienting. Individuals may struggle with decision-making, personal choices, and the responsibility that comes with independence, as these were often dictated within the cult.

Social Interaction: Cult members are often socially isolated, and leaving may expose individuals to unfamiliar social dynamics. Building relationships, navigating social norms, and understanding non-cult environments can be challenging.

Educational Gaps: Individuals leaving a family cult may have gaps in their education, particularly if the cult restricted access to certain subjects or provided a limited curriculum. Adjusting to mainstream educational standards may pose challenges.

Cultural and Technological Changes: Rapid changes in technology and cultural norms may be overwhelming, especially if the cult discouraged or limited exposure to external influences. Adapting to new technologies, social media, and contemporary cultural trends can be a significant adjustment.

Gender Roles and Equality: Fundamental Christian family cults often adhere to strict gender roles. Adjusting to societies where gender equality is emphasized may challenge preconceived notions about roles and expectations.

Career and Employment: Cult members may lack exposure to the broader job market, career opportunities, and professional development. Entering the workforce and navigating career paths can be a novel and potentially intimidating experience.

Freedom of Expression: Cult environments may suppress individual expression. Experiencing the freedom to express oneself, whether through clothing choices, personal opinions, or artistic pursuits, can be liberating but also initially overwhelming.

Family Relationships: Leaving a family cult may strain relationships with family members who remain in the cult. Rebuilding or establishing relationships with non-cult family members can also be challenging.

Consumer Culture: Exposure to consumer culture and the abundance of choices in mainstream society may be disconcerting for those accustomed to a more restricted lifestyle with limited material options.

Legal and Civic Responsibilities: Understanding and navigating legal and civic responsibilities may be challenging for individuals who were sheltered from broader societal norms within the cult.

Secular Values: Adjusting to a secular society with a wide range of values and ethics can be both enlightening and overwhelming for individuals leaving a family cult with a strong religious focus.

Navigating culture shock after leaving a fundamental Christian family cult is a gradual process. Seeking support from mental health professionals, joining support groups, and connecting with others who have gone through similar experiences can be instrumental in facilitating a smoother transition and promoting long-term well-being.

EXAMPLE

Triston, a 25-year-old navigating the difficult landscape of adjustment disorder and culture shock after breaking free from the chains of a fundamental Christian family cult. Raised within the confines of strict beliefs and isolating doctrines, Triston now finds himself in a world that is both liberating and overwhelming.

The clash between the values ingrained by the cult and the reality of the broader society has thrust him into a state of emotional turbulence. As he grapples with anxiety, confusion, and the challenge of redefining his identity, Triston embarks on a journey to reconstruct his life beyond the confines of the only reality he's ever known.

Triston's life is upside down now because he has recently broken free from the fundamental Christian family cult where he was raised. The abrupt transition from the tightly controlled environment of the cult to the broader, more diverse society has upended his sense of normalcy.

The strict beliefs and isolating doctrines that once defined his reality are now in stark contrast to the new, unfamiliar world he's encountering. Triston is grappling with the challenge of reevaluating his identity, beliefs, and social interactions. This profound shift in perspective, coupled with the cultural differences and the need to navigate a world outside the cult, contributes to the disorientation and upheaval he is currently experiencing and will be for many years to come.

WHAT ARE SOME WAYS SOMEONE CAN HELP THEMSELVES ACCLIMATE TO SOCIETY AFTER LEAVING A FAMILY CULT?

Acclimating to society after leaving a family cult is a significant and sometimes challenging transition. Here are some ways individuals can help themselves during this acclimation process:

Seek Professional Support: Engage with mental health professionals experienced in trauma and cult recovery. Therapists can provide guidance, support, and coping strategies tailored to your specific needs.

Join Support Groups: Connect with support groups or communities for individuals who have left similar cults. Sharing experiences and insights with others who understand can provide validation and a sense of community.

Establish a Support System: Cultivate relationships with non-cult family members, friends, or individuals who can offer emotional and practical support. Building a strong support system is crucial during the acclimation process.

Educate Yourself: Learn about the world outside the cult environment. Stay informed about current events, cultural norms, and societal expectations to enhance your understanding of the broader context.

Gradual Exposure: Gradually expose yourself to different aspects of society. Start with small steps, such as attending local events, exploring new neighborhoods, or participating in community activities.

Cultural Integration: Immerse yourself in the local culture and community. Attend cultural events, visit museums, and engage with activities that reflect the diversity of the society you are acclimating to.

Educational Pursuits: Pursue educational opportunities to fill any gaps in knowledge or skills. This may involve taking classes, attending workshops, or enrolling in courses that align with your interests and goals.

Employment Preparation: Equip yourself for the job market by updating your resume, acquiring new skills, and seeking guidance on employment opportunities. Employment can be a key aspect of acclimating to societal expectations.

Social Skills Development: Cultivate social skills by participating in group activities, clubs, or volunteer work. Practice effective communication, active listening, and building relationships with diverse individuals.

Personal Development: Focus on personal development and self-improvement. Set goals, both short-term and long-term, to help shape your path and foster a sense of purpose.

Mindfulness and Self-Care: Incorporate mindfulness and self-care practices into your routine. This can include activities such as meditation, yoga, or simply taking time for reflection to manage stress and maintain well-being.

Legal Assistance: If there are legal matters associated with leaving the cult, consult with legal professionals for guidance. Resolving any legal issues can provide a sense of security and stability.

Establishing Routine: Create a daily routine that suits your new lifestyle. Consistency can provide a sense of stability and help you gradually adapt to societal expectations.

Celebrate Achievements: Acknowledge and celebrate your achievements, no matter how small. Recognizing progress and milestones in your acclimation process boosts confidence and motivation.

Remember that acclimating to society is a gradual process, and it's okay to take your time. Be patient with yourself, and seek support when needed. The journey of acclimation involves self-discovery, learning, and adapting to a new way of life.

COPING STRUGGLES

People in fundamentalist Christian family cults often struggle with coping because they face intense pressure to conform to strict beliefs and practices that may be oppressive or harmful. This environment can lead to feelings of guilt, shame, and fear for those who question or dissent. Additionally, the isolation from mainstream society can limit access to support networks and resources that might offer alternative perspectives or help in times of need.

The authoritarian control within these cults can also undermine individual autonomy and self-esteem, making it challenging for members to assert their own identities and make independent decisions.

FREQUENTLY ASKED QUESTIONS AND ANSWERS

WHAT IS SELF-MEDICATING (ADDICTION) AND WHY IS IT COMMON AMONG PEOPLE WHO ARE IN RECOVERY FROM A FAMILY CULT?

Self-medicating refers to the use of substances or behaviors to cope with emotional, psychological, or physical distress without the guidance or prescription of a medical professional. It can involve the misuse of alcohol, drugs, or other substances, as well as engaging in certain behaviors like excessive eating, gambling, or risky activities as a means of seeking relief from emotional pain or stress.

Self-medicating is common among individuals within a family cult for several reasons:

Trauma Coping Mechanism: Survivors of family cults often experience deep emotional and psychological trauma. Self-medicating may be a way for individuals to cope with the intense emotions and distress associated with their traumatic experiences.

Escaping Painful Memories: Substance use or addictive behaviors can provide a temporary escape from painful memories or intrusive thoughts related to the cult experience. It serves as a way to numb emotional pain.

Coping with Anxiety and Depression: Family cult survivors may struggle with heightened anxiety, depression, or other mental health challenges. Self-medicating can seem like a quick solution to alleviate these symptoms temporarily.

Lack of Healthy Coping Skills: Individuals exiting family cults may not have developed healthy coping mechanisms. The cult environment often suppresses individual autonomy and the development of essential life skills, leaving survivors without effective tools for handling stress.

Seeking Comfort and Control: Self-medicating behaviors may be an attempt to regain a sense of control or find comfort in a world that previously felt chaotic and oppressive.

Social Isolation: Exiting a family cult can lead to social isolation, as survivors may have severed ties with their cult community. Self-medicating can be an attempt to fill the void of lost social connections and cope with loneliness.

Unresolved Trauma: Family cult survivors may carry unresolved trauma that manifests in various ways. Self-medicating becomes a way to manage ongoing symptoms of trauma that affect daily functioning.

Lack of Access to Mental Health Resources: Some individuals in recovery from family cults may face barriers to accessing mental health resources. Self-medicating can be an easily accessible, albeit harmful, way to cope in the absence of proper support.

It's crucial to recognize that while self-medicating may provide temporary relief, it doesn't address the root causes of trauma and can lead to additional challenges.

HOW TO RECOGNIZE SOMEONE MIGHT BE SELF MEDICATING?

Recognizing signs of self-medication in someone involves observing changes in their behavior, emotions, and lifestyle. While these signs do not necessarily confirm self-medication, they may indicate a need for further assessment. Here are some common signs to look for:

Increased Substance Use: A noticeable increase in alcohol, drug, or medication consumption beyond what is considered typical or socially acceptable.

Changes in Social Behavior: Withdrawal from social activities or a decline in the quality of relationships. A person may isolate themselves to engage in self-medicating behaviors.

Neglect of Responsibilities: Neglecting personal, professional, or academic responsibilities. Self-medicating can lead to a lack of motivation to fulfill daily obligations.

Mood Swings: Unexplained and extreme mood swings. Someone engaged in self-medication may use substances to manage mood fluctuations.

Changes in Sleep Patterns: Disrupted sleep patterns, including insomnia or oversleeping, which may be indicative of attempts to self-medicate for emotional distress.

Physical Changes: Observable physical changes, such as weight loss or gain, changes in personal hygiene, or the appearance of unusual physical symptoms.

Defensiveness About Substance Use: Becoming defensive or evasive when asked about substance use. Someone engaged in self-medication may resist discussing their habits.

Engaging in Risky Behaviors: Engaging in risky behaviors under the influence, such as driving under the influence, taking excessive risks, or participating in dangerous activities.

Loss of Interest: A sudden loss of interest in previously enjoyed activities or hobbies. Self-medication can lead to a decrease in activities that once brought pleasure.

Financial Issues: Financial difficulties or unexplained financial strain. Self-medication often involves the purchase of substances, leading to increased financial burdens.

Changes in Eating Habits: Significant changes in eating habits, including overeating or under-eating. Substance use may impact appetite and eating behaviors.

Inability to Stop or Cut Down: An inability to stop or cut down on substance use despite recognizing its negative impact on health, relationships, or other aspects of life.

It's important to approach these observations with sensitivity and empathy. If you suspect someone is self-medicating, encourage open communication and express your concern. Professional help, such as counseling or addiction treatment, may be necessary to address underlying issues and support the individual in developing healthier coping mechanisms.

WHEN IS IT TIME TO STEP IN IF YOU ARE THE SUPPORT SYSTEM FOR SOMEONE IN FAMILY CULT, THAT YOU SUSPECT IS SELF MEDICATING?

If you suspect that someone in a family cult, whom you are supporting, is self-medicating, it's crucial to approach the situation with care. Here are indicators that it may be time to step in as a support system:

Observable Behavioral Changes: If you notice significant changes in their behavior, mood swings, or a decline in their overall well-being that aligns with patterns of substance misuse.

Communication Breakdown: If there is a breakdown in communication and they become defensive or avoid discussing their behaviors, particularly when it comes to substance use.

Neglect of Responsibilities: If the person neglects important responsibilities at work, in relationships, or in their personal life, suggesting that self-medicating behaviors are impacting their daily functioning.

Physical and Mental Health Decline: If there's evidence of declining physical health, mental health struggles, or the emergence of physical symptoms related to substance use.

Increased Isolation: If the individual withdraws further from social activities, isolates themselves, or exhibits signs of increasing social isolation as a result of self-medicating.

Risky Behaviors: If the person engages in risky behaviors while under the influence, putting themselves or others in danger.

Financial Strain: If there are observable financial difficulties or strain that may be linked to the purchase of substances.

Concerns from Others: If friends, family members, or colleagues express concern about the person's well-being and potential self-medicating behaviors.

If you observe these signs, it's important to approach the individual with empathy and express your concern for their well-being. Encourage open communication, and let them know that you are there to support them. Suggest seeking professional help, such as counseling or addiction treatment, and offer assistance in finding appropriate resources.

Remember that addressing self-medicating behaviors requires sensitivity, as the individual may be facing complex emotional and psychological challenges. Professional guidance can provide them with the necessary tools and support to navigate their recovery journey more effectively.

WHAT ARE SOME TREATMENTS FOR SOMEONE THAT IS SELF MEDICATING?

Treating self-medicating behaviors in the context of family cult recovery involves addressing both the addiction aspects and the unique challenges associated with leaving a cult. Here are some treatments that can be beneficial:

Cult-Informed Therapy: Working with therapists who understand the dynamics of family cults can provide tailored support. Therapists can help individuals process their experiences within the cult and develop strategies to overcome the associated challenges.

Trauma-Informed Care: Trauma-focused therapies, such as EMDR (Eye Movement Desensitization and Reprocessing) or trauma-focused cognitive-behavioral therapy, can be effective in addressing the psychological impact of family cult experiences.

Cult Education and Deconstruction: Providing education about the characteristics of cults and helping individuals deconstruct the belief systems instilled by the family cult can be crucial in the recovery process.

Support Groups for Cult Survivors: Engaging in support groups specifically designed for cult survivors creates a space for shared experiences and understanding. Connecting with others who have faced similar challenges can provide a sense of validation and support.

Rebuilding Autonomy and Identity: Therapeutic interventions focused on rebuilding autonomy, identity, and self-esteem can help individuals rediscover their true selves apart from the influences of the family cult.

Mindfulness and Grounding Techniques: Incorporating mindfulness practices and grounding techniques can assist individuals in staying present and managing the anxiety or distress associated with cult recovery.

Life Skills Training: Learning and enhancing essential life skills, which may have been suppressed or neglected within the family cult, is vital for independent living and self-sufficiency.

Dual Diagnosis Treatment: If there are co-occurring mental health conditions, addressing both the addiction and mental health aspects through dual diagnosis treatment is essential.

Community Integration: Encouraging participation in healthy community activities and building a supportive network outside of the cult environment is crucial for long-term recovery.

Relapse Prevention Planning: Developing a comprehensive relapse prevention plan that addresses triggers specific to cult recovery is important in maintaining progress.

Crisis Intervention: Having access to crisis intervention resources is essential, as leaving a family cult can sometimes lead to crises. Knowing how to navigate these situations with professional support is critical.

It's important to involve mental health professionals who are experienced in cult recovery and trauma-informed care. The treatment plan should be tailored to the individual's unique experiences and needs, recognizing the complexities associated with family cult recovery.

THE SUBSTANCE ABUSE AND MENTAL HEALTH SERVICES ADMINISTRATION (SAMHSA)

National Helpline is a confidential, free, 24/7 hotline that provides assistance for individuals facing substance abuse and mental health issues. You can contact them at **1-800-662-HELP (4357)** for support, information, and resources related to drug and alcohol addiction.

EATING DISORDERS

Eating disorders are serious mental health conditions characterized by persistent disturbances in eating patterns, body image, and emotions related to food and weight. These disorders can have severe physical and emotional consequences and often require professional intervention for diagnosis and treatment. The most common types of eating disorders include Anorexia Nervosa, Bulimia Nervosa, and Binge Eating Disorder.

Anorexia Nervosa:

Symptoms:
- Intense fear of gaining weight or becoming fat, despite being underweight.
- Distorted body image and a preoccupation with body size and shape.
- Restricted food intake leading to significant weight loss.
- Denial of the seriousness of low body weight.

Bulimia Nervosa:

Symptoms:
- Recurrent episodes of binge eating, characterized by eating an excessive amount of food in a discrete period.
- Compensatory behaviors to prevent weight gain, such as vomiting, laxative use, fasting, or excessive exercise.
- A sense of lack of control during binge episodes.

- Preoccupation with body weight and shape.

Binge Eating Disorder:

Symptoms:
- Recurrent episodes of binge eating, similar to bulimia, without compensatory behaviors.
- Eating rapidly, eating large amounts when not physically hungry, and eating until uncomfortably full.
- Feelings of guilt, shame, or distress after binge eating episodes.
- Lack of control during binge episodes.

Avoidant/Restrictive Food Intake Disorder (ARFID):

Symptoms:
- ARFID is characterized by limited food preferences, avoidance of certain foods or textures, and difficulty meeting nutritional needs. Unlike anorexia, ARFID is not driven by a desire for thinness.

Common Features Across Eating Disorders:

Preoccupation with Food, Weight, or Shape: A significant amount of time and mental energy is devoted to thoughts about food, weight, or body image.

Distorted Body Image: Perceiving one's body size or shape inaccurately, often feeling overweight even when underweight.

Impaired Social and Occupational Functioning: Eating disorders can significantly impact relationships, work, and daily functioning.

Physical Consequences: Eating disorders can lead to a range of physical health issues, including malnutrition, electrolyte imbalances, gastrointestinal problems, and more.

Early detection and intervention are crucial for the successful treatment of eating disorders. A multidisciplinary approach involving medical, nutritional, and psychological support is often necessary to address the complex nature of these conditions. Professional guidance, such as therapy and, in some cases, medication, can aid individuals in their recovery journey.

FREQUENTLY ASKED QUESTIONS AND ANSWERS

WHY IS IT VERY COMMON FOR PEOPLE LEAVING A FAMILY CULT TO EXPERIENCE EATING DISORDERS?

Leaving a family cult can contribute to the development of eating disorders due to the complex interplay of psychological, emotional, and environmental factors associated with the cult experience. Here are some reasons why individuals leaving family cults may be at an increased risk of experiencing eating disorders:

Control and Autonomy Issues: Cults often exert strict control over various aspects of members' lives, including their dietary choices. Leaving the cult may lead to a desire for autonomy, but the lack of healthy coping mechanisms could manifest in the form of restrictive eating, bingeing, or purging as a way of regaining control.

Body Image Distortion: Cults may promote distorted ideals of body image and impose specific standards of beauty. Individuals leaving the cult may internalize these ideals, leading to body dissatisfaction and, in some cases, the development of unhealthy eating behaviors.

Guilt and Shame: Cults often use guilt and shame as control mechanisms. Leaving the cult may result in lingering feelings of guilt and shame, which some individuals might attempt to manage through disordered eating patterns as a form of self-punishment or control.

Identity Struggles: Leaving a family cult can lead to a profound identity crisis as individuals navigate the process of redefining themselves outside the cult's influence. Eating disorders may emerge as a way to cope with the uncertainties and anxieties related to establishing a new identity.

Post-Traumatic Stress: Trauma experienced within a family cult can have lasting effects on mental health. Post-traumatic stress and unresolved trauma may contribute to the development of eating disorders as individuals attempt to cope with distressing memories and emotions.

Isolation and Lack of Support: Individuals leaving a cult may face isolation from their former community and a lack of social support. Disordered eating patterns can emerge as a way of coping with loneliness, isolation, and the challenges of reintegrating into mainstream society.

Coping Mechanism: Cult survivors may use disordered eating as a maladaptive coping mechanism to deal with the emotional aftermath of leaving the cult. Food and body-related issues can serve as a distraction from the psychological distress associated with the cult experience.

Perfectionism: Cults often demand perfection from their members. Leaving the cult may lead to a continuation of perfectionistic tendencies, which can contribute to the development of eating disorders characterized by an intense focus on body weight and shape.

It's important to recognize that the relationship between leaving a family cult and eating disorders is complex and multifaceted. Seeking professional help, such as therapy and counseling, is crucial for individuals dealing with the aftermath of cult experiences and struggling with disordered eating behaviors.

WHAT ARE SOME BEST PRACTICES TO SUPPORT SOMEONE STRUGGLING WITH EATING DISORDERS?

Supporting someone struggling with eating disorders requires a sensitive and understanding approach. Here are some best practices:

Educate Yourself: Learn about different types of eating disorders, their symptoms, and the psychological factors involved. Understanding the complexity of these disorders will help you provide more informed support.

Avoid Judgment: Refrain from making judgmental or critical comments about the person's appearance, eating habits, or body size. Judgment can exacerbate feelings of shame and guilt.

Listen Empathetically: Create a non-judgmental and empathetic space for the person to express their feelings and experiences. Active listening without imposing solutions can be beneficial.

Encourage Professional Help: Suggest seeking help from healthcare professionals, such as therapists, nutritionists, or doctors experienced in treating eating disorders. Professional guidance is crucial for comprehensive treatment.

Respect Autonomy: Recognize that recovery is a personal journey, and the individual may need to take ownership of their process. Respect their autonomy and avoid pressuring them to recover at a pace that feels uncomfortable.

Promote a Healthy Relationship with Food: Encourage a balanced and non-restrictive approach to food. Avoid labeling foods as "good" or "bad" and support a positive attitude toward nourishing the body.

Be Patient: Recovery from eating disorders is a gradual process. Be patient and understanding, acknowledging that setbacks may occur. Celebrate small victories and progress.

Foster Body Positivity: Promote body positivity by emphasizing the importance of self-acceptance and self-love. Challenge societal beauty standards and help the individual appreciate their body for its functionality and uniqueness.

Offer Practical Support: Assist in practical ways, such as attending appointments, preparing meals together, or engaging in activities that promote a healthy lifestyle. Practical support reinforces the sense of companionship and care.

Communicate Openly: Foster open communication about feelings, concerns, and the challenges associated with the recovery process. Encourage the person to express themselves and share their thoughts without fear of judgment.

Avoid Triggering Language: Be mindful of language that may be triggering. Avoid discussing weight, dieting, or using language that reinforces harmful stereotypes about body image.

Understand Relapse: Recognize that relapses may occur, and they are part of the recovery journey. Offer support and encouragement during challenging times, emphasizing the importance of resilience.

Remember that supporting someone with an eating disorder can be emotionally challenging, and it's crucial to prioritize your own well-being. Encourage the individual to build a comprehensive support network that includes friends, family, and healthcare professionals. If the situation becomes critical, seek immediate professional assistance.

THE NATIONAL EATING DISORDERS ASSOCIATION (NEDA)

These valuable resources and support for those affected by eating disorders. You can contact their helpline at **1-800-931-2237** for assistance, information, and guidance related to eating disorders. Additionally, their website (https://www.nationaleatingdisorders.org/) offers online resources and tools for individuals and their support systems.

EXAMPLE

Candice, a resilient 32-year-old woman who has faced the relentless grip of eating disorders throughout her life within the confines of her family cult. Since breaking free from the cult, Candice has embarked on a journey of recovery, determined to reclaim her life and heal from the scars of her past. Jack, her steadfast partner, stands by her side as a pillar of support, offering encouragement and understanding in the daily struggle against the shadows of her disorder.

Together, they navigate the challenges of rebuilding a life free from the toxic influence of the family cult, fostering hope and resilience in the face of adversity. Jack, as a supportive partner to Candice in her recovery from eating disorders and the aftermath of leaving a family cult, engages in various actions to provide assistance and encouragement:

Active Listening: Jack actively listens to Candice's thoughts and feelings without judgment, creating a safe space for her to express herself.

Educational Support: Jack seeks to understand the complexities of eating disorders, educating himself about the challenges Candice faces and offering informed support.

Encouragement in Therapy: Jack encourages Candice to attend therapy sessions, respecting her journey toward healing and providing emotional support throughout the therapeutic process.

Promoting Healthy Habits: Jack collaborates with Candice in cultivating positive lifestyle changes, promoting nutritious eating habits, regular exercise, and overall well-being.

Patience and Understanding: Jack practices patience and understanding, recognizing that recovery is a gradual process with ups and downs. He remains supportive during challenging moments.

Celebrating Progress: Jack acknowledges and celebrates Candice's milestones and progress in her recovery, reinforcing positive behaviors and fostering a sense of accomplishment.

Advocacy for Boundaries: Jack respects and advocates for healthy boundaries, understanding the importance of Candice setting limits to maintain her well-being.

Building a Support Network: Jack helps Candice establish a broader support network outside their relationship, connecting her with friends, family, or support groups who can contribute to her recovery.

Participation in Recovery Activities: Jack actively participates in activities that contribute to Candice's recovery, such as attending support group meetings or engaging in mindfulness exercises together.

Unconditional Love: Above all, Jack offers Candice unwavering love and acceptance, reinforcing that he values her for who she is and supporting her in her journey toward a healthier, happier life.

Jack's supportive actions play a crucial role in Candice's recovery by creating an environment that fosters healing, stability, and personal growth. Here's how Jack's efforts are beneficial to Candice:

Emotional Safety: Jack's active listening and understanding provide Candice with emotional safety. Knowing she can express herself without judgment or fear of rejection allows her to process and navigate her emotions more effectively.

Education and Awareness: Jack's commitment to educating himself about eating disorders demonstrates a genuine interest in Candice's struggles. This shared awareness allows them to communicate more effectively and work together toward understanding and overcoming challenges.

Therapeutic Support: Encouraging Candice to attend therapy and offering emotional support during sessions contributes to her therapeutic journey. Having a partner who values and encourages mental health care reinforces the importance of seeking professional help.

Promoting Healthy Habits: Jack's involvement in cultivating healthy habits reinforces positive behaviors. Together, they establish a foundation for physical well-being, which is integral to overcoming eating disorders.

Patience and Understanding: Jack's patience during difficult moments helps Candice feel understood and accepted. This understanding is essential in navigating the complexities of recovery, especially during setbacks.

Celebrating Progress: Acknowledging and celebrating Candice's progress reinforces her sense of achievement. Recognizing milestones provides motivation and reinforces the positive changes she is making in her life.

Advocacy for Boundaries: Respecting healthy boundaries is crucial in creating a supportive environment. Jack's advocacy for boundaries ensures that Candice has the space she needs for self-care and personal growth.

Building a Support Network: Jack's efforts to connect Candice with a broader support network strengthen her overall support system. This network offers diverse perspectives and additional sources of encouragement.

Participation in Recovery Activities: Actively participating in recovery activities together creates shared experiences and strengthens their bond. It also reinforces the idea that they are a team, working collaboratively toward Candice's well-being.

Unconditional Love: Jack's unwavering love and acceptance provide Candice with a stable foundation. Feeling loved and valued for who she is, irrespective of her struggles, contributes significantly to her sense of self-worth and overall recovery.

In essence, Jack's supportive actions contribute to Candice's overall well-being, empowering her to navigate the challenges of recovery with resilience and hope.

CHAPTER 4

OTHER VICTIM EXPERIENCES

Trigger Warning: Sensitive Content

This content may contain information or discussions that could be distressing or triggering for some individuals. Topics may include but are not limited to trauma, abuse, violence, or other potentially upsetting subject matter. Reader discretion is advised. If you find that you are emotionally impacted by such content, it is recommended to seek support or refrain from reading further. Your well-being is important.

COGNITIVE DISSONANCE

When exploring the tapestry of the familial cult, you will often hear the term "cognitive dissonance." It is important to have a complete understanding of its meaning and the impact it has on its victims.

Cognitive dissonance is a psychological concept that refers to the discomfort or tension that arises when an individual holds two or more conflicting beliefs, attitudes, or values simultaneously, or when their behavior conflicts with their beliefs or self-perception. The term was introduced by psychologist Leon Festinger in 1957.

Key aspects of cognitive dissonance include:

Conflict Between Beliefs: Cognitive dissonance occurs when there is a discrepancy between two beliefs or between a belief and a behavior. This conflict creates a sense of psychological discomfort, prompting individuals to seek resolution.

Need for Consistency: Humans have a natural inclination to maintain consistency in their beliefs and behaviors. Cognitive dissonance arises when inconsistencies threaten this need for internal harmony.

Discomfort and Tension: The experience of cognitive dissonance is marked by feelings of discomfort, tension, or anxiety. Individuals are motivated to alleviate this discomfort by resolving the conflicting beliefs or behaviors.

Resolution Strategies: To reduce cognitive dissonance, individuals may employ various strategies. These include changing one's beliefs or attitudes, acquiring new information to support existing beliefs, or altering behaviors to align with beliefs.

Examples: Examples of cognitive dissonance can be found in everyday life. For instance, a person who values health but engages in unhealthy habits might experience discomfort. To resolve this dissonance, they may either change their behavior (adopt healthier habits) or change their belief (convince themselves that the unhealthy behavior is not as harmful).

Impact on Decision-Making: Cognitive dissonance can influence decision-making processes. When faced with choices that challenge existing beliefs, individuals may experience dissonance, leading them to rationalize or justify their decisions to maintain internal consistency.

Role in Change and Growth: While cognitive dissonance can be uncomfortable, it also plays a role in personal growth. Confronting and resolving conflicting beliefs can lead to positive changes in attitudes, behaviors, and perspectives.

Relevance to Cults and Manipulation: Cults often exploit cognitive dissonance to control members. Individuals may experience dissonance between their previous beliefs and the teachings of the cult. To alleviate discomfort, they may adopt the cult's beliefs or engage in behaviors that align with the group's expectations.

Understanding cognitive dissonance is essential in psychology, as it provides insights into how individuals manage conflicting information and maintain a sense of internal coherence. In therapeutic settings, addressing cognitive dissonance can be a crucial aspect of helping individuals navigate personal growth, change, and the resolution of internal conflicts.

FREQUENTLY ASKED QUESTIONS AND ANSWERS

WHY DO RECOVERING FAMILY CULT MEMBERS OFTEN EXPERIENCE COGNITIVE DISSONANCE AFTER LEAVING?

Recovering family cult members often experience cognitive dissonance after leaving due to the profound shift in beliefs, values, and identity. Several factors contribute to this phenomenon:

Contrasting Belief Systems: Leaving a family cult entails a departure from deeply ingrained beliefs and ideologies. The stark contrast between the beliefs promoted within the cult and the emerging understanding outside of it creates cognitive dissonance.

Identity Crisis: Cults often dictate members' identity and self-worth. Leaving the cult results in an identity crisis as individuals grapple with the challenge of defining themselves independently of the cult's influence, leading to conflicting self-perceptions.

Reevaluation of Past Choices: Recovering members may reevaluate their past decisions and actions within the cult. The realization that these choices were made under the influence of manipulative tactics or misinformation can induce cognitive dissonance.

Emotional Attachment and Trauma Bonds: Emotional bonds formed within the cult, often through manipulation and control, can create a strong emotional attachment. Recovering members may feel conflicted emotions, experiencing a sense of loss or attachment that contradicts their newfound understanding.

Fear of Abandonment and Rejection: Cults commonly instill a fear of abandonment or rejection for those who question or leave. Recovering members may grapple with cognitive dissonance as they confront fears of being ostracized or abandoned by the community they once considered family.

Challenging Core Beliefs: Cults often dictate fundamental beliefs about the world, life, and purpose. Exiting the cult requires challenging and revising these core beliefs, triggering cognitive dissonance as individuals confront the inconsistency between old and new perspectives.

Desire for Consistency: Humans naturally seek consistency in their beliefs and behaviors. Leaving a family cult disrupts the consistency that once existed, creating internal conflict that manifests as cognitive dissonance.

Reconstruction of Reality: Recovering members must reconstruct their understanding of reality, acknowledging that the narratives presented within the cult were manipulated or distorted. This process can be mentally challenging and evoke cognitive dissonance.

Social and Emotional Dependency: Cults often foster social and emotional dependency among members. Leaving the cult means severing these ties, and the resulting emotional void can contribute to cognitive dissonance as individuals navigate the loss of their support network.

Fear of Judgment and Stigma: Recovering members may fear judgment or stigma from those outside the cult who may not fully comprehend the dynamics of cult involvement. This fear can intensify cognitive dissonance as individuals strive to reconcile their past with external perceptions.

Addressing cognitive dissonance in the recovery process involves therapeutic support, self-reflection, and a gradual shift in beliefs and behaviors. Professional guidance helps individuals navigate the complexities of reconciling their past with their evolving understanding, promoting personal growth and a more coherent sense of self.

WHAT ARE SOME SIGNS YOU ARE EXPERIENCING COGNITIVE DISSONANCE AFTER LEAVING A FAMILY CULT?

Experiencing cognitive dissonance after leaving a family cult can manifest in various signs and emotional reactions. Some common signs include:

Conflicting Emotions: Feeling simultaneous emotions such as relief and guilt, or freedom and anxiety, reflects the internal conflict and inconsistency associated with cognitive dissonance.

Discomfort or Anxiety: Experiencing discomfort, anxiety, or unease when confronted with information, beliefs, or situations that challenge the teachings of the family cult.

Defensive Behavior: Reacting defensively or becoming agitated when others question or challenge the beliefs held within the cult, as a way to protect one's established beliefs.

Self-Doubt: Struggling with self-doubt and questioning one's decisions, especially when those decisions deviate from the norms established by the family cult.

Rationalizing or Justifying: Engaging in rationalization or justification for past actions or beliefs within the cult, even when presented with evidence or arguments that contradict them.

Avoidance of Conflicting Information: Avoiding exposure to information or perspectives that contradict the beliefs held within the family cult, as a way to maintain internal consistency and avoid discomfort.

Feeling Stuck or Ambivalent: Feeling stuck in a state of ambivalence or uncertainty, especially when attempting to reconcile conflicting beliefs or when making decisions that deviate from the cult's teachings.

Resistance to Change: Resisting changes in belief systems or behaviors that challenge the established norms of the family cult, even when presented with valid reasons for change.

Struggle with Identity: Experiencing a struggle with personal identity, self-worth, or a sense of purpose outside the context of the family cult.

Fear of Consequences: Feeling a lingering fear of potential consequences, punishment, or negative outcomes for leaving the family cult, even when such threats are no longer present.

Isolation or Withdrawal: Withdrawing socially or isolating oneself to avoid potential conflicts or discussions that might challenge the established beliefs, contributing to a sense of separation from others.

Difficulty Trusting Others: Struggling to trust individuals or information outside the cult environment, as a result of the distrust cultivated within the family cult.

Recognizing these signs is an essential step in the process of addressing cognitive dissonance. Seeking support from mental health professionals, engaging in open and honest self-reflection, and gradually exposing oneself to diverse perspectives can contribute to resolving cognitive dissonance and fostering personal growth after leaving a family cult.

WHAT ARE SOME BEST PRACTICES WHEN EXPERIENCING COGNITIVE DISSONANCE?

Experiencing cognitive dissonance can be challenging, but there are several best practices to navigate this internal conflict:

Self-Reflection: Take time for introspection to identify conflicting beliefs or attitudes. Understand the source of the dissonance and reflect on how these conflicts impact your thoughts and emotions.

Open-Mindedness: Cultivate an open mind to consider alternative perspectives. Be willing to explore information that challenges existing beliefs, allowing for a more comprehensive understanding of different viewpoints.

Seek Professional Guidance: Consult with mental health professionals, such as therapists or counselors, who specialize in trauma and cult recovery. They can provide valuable insights, coping strategies, and a supportive space for processing cognitive dissonance.

Gradual Exposure: Introduce conflicting information gradually to avoid overwhelming yourself. Slow exposure allows for a more manageable adjustment and reduces the intensity of cognitive dissonance.

Connect with Supportive Communities: Engage with support groups or communities of individuals who have experienced similar cognitive dissonance after leaving cults. Shared experiences and empathetic understanding can provide valuable support during this challenging process.

Educate Yourself: Educate yourself on critical thinking skills, logical fallacies, and cognitive biases. Understanding these concepts can empower you to critically assess information and navigate cognitive dissonance more effectively.

Mindfulness and Meditation: Practice mindfulness and meditation to cultivate awareness of your thoughts and emotions. Mindfulness can help you observe cognitive dissonance without immediate judgment, providing a clearer perspective.

Journaling: Maintain a journal to document your thoughts, feelings, and the progression of your understanding. Journaling can serve as a tool for self-reflection and tracking the evolution of your beliefs over time.

Connect with Trusted Individuals: Share your thoughts and feelings with trusted friends, family members, or mentors who can provide emotional support and different perspectives. Having a supportive network can ease the process of resolving cognitive dissonance.

Set Realistic Goals: Establish realistic goals for personal growth and change. Break down the process into manageable steps, allowing yourself time to adapt to new beliefs and behaviors.

Focus on Values: Clarify your core values and prioritize them in your decision-making process. Aligning actions with your values can help reduce cognitive dissonance and foster a sense of authenticity.

Celebrate Progress: Acknowledge and celebrate the progress you make in resolving cognitive dissonance. Recognize that personal growth is a gradual process, and each step forward is a significant achievement.

Remember that experiencing cognitive dissonance is a natural part of personal growth and self-discovery.

By implementing these best practices, you can navigate this internal conflict with greater resilience and develop a more coherent and authentic understanding of yourself and the world around you.

EXAMPLE

Don, a 27-year-old, is experiencing cognitive dissonance after bravely breaking free from the confines of a fundamental Christian family cult. Born into a world of strict beliefs and unwavering loyalty, Don recently took the courageous step of going no contact with all family members, leaving him to grapple with the conflicting emotions that come with untangling oneself from deeply ingrained beliefs and familial ties.

The stark contrast between the beliefs and values instilled in him by his fundamental Christian family cult and the newfound independence and different perspectives he's encountered after leaving the group.

The conflict arises as he tries to reconcile the deeply ingrained teachings with his evolving understanding of the world, leading to inner turmoil and dissonance between the old and the new.Don grapples with conflicting emotions and thoughts, such as questioning deeply ingrained beliefs from the cult while simultaneously feeling the weight of guilt or fear instilled by those beliefs.

He may face internal tension as he reevaluates his identity, struggling to align his past worldview with the evolving perspectives he encounters. The dissonance may manifest as emotional distress, confusion, and a sense of unease as Don strives to make sense of his new reality while confronting the echoes of his past.

HYPER-VIGILANCE

Hyper-arousal and hyper-vigilance are common symptoms associated with Post-Traumatic Stress Disorder (PTSD).

Hyper-vigilance refers to a heightened state of alertness and awareness, often characterized by:

Increased Sensitivity: Individuals experiencing hyper-vigilance may have heightened sensitivity to stimuli in their environment. This can include being easily startled by unexpected sounds or movements.

Constant Scanning: A person in a hyper-vigilant state may engage in constant scanning of their surroundings, looking for potential threats. This heightened awareness is a survival mechanism developed in response to past traumatic experiences.

Difficulty Relaxing: Individuals with hyper-vigilance may find it challenging to relax or let their guard down. The persistent sense of imminent danger can make it difficult for them to feel safe even in non-threatening situations.

Physical Symptoms: This state of increased arousal can manifest in physical symptoms such as elevated heart rate, rapid breathing, muscle tension, and a general sense of unease.

Sleep Disturbances: Hyper-vigilance can interfere with sleep, leading to difficulties falling asleep or staying asleep. The individual may remain on high alert even during periods of rest.

Emotional Impact: The constant anticipation of danger can contribute to heightened anxiety and stress levels. Over time, hyper-vigilance can be emotionally exhausting.

Hyper-vigilance is often a learned response to trauma and is one of the ways the body and mind adapt to perceived threats. While it can be a protective mechanism in dangerous situations, it can become maladaptive in non-threatening environments, impacting a person's overall well-being.

EXAMPLE

Misty, a 23-year-old navigating the intricate web of hyper-vigilance within the confines of the family cult she was born into. Raised in an environment where constant surveillance and scrutiny are the norm, Misty finds herself on high alert, with every action and thought scrutinized by the cult's rigid doctrines.

As she grapples with the persistent fear of deviating from the established norms, Misty's journey unfolds against a backdrop of intense vigilance, where each step away from conformity is met with the looming shadows of potential repercussions. Misty is in a constant state of hyper-vigilance due to the intense and controlling environment within the family cult. The cult enforces strict rules, expectations, and constant surveillance, creating an atmosphere where any perceived deviation from the established norms is met with severe consequences.

Misty's vigilance is a coping mechanism developed in response to the constant fear and anticipation of punishment or judgment within the tightly regulated confines of the cult. This heightened state of alertness becomes a way for her to navigate the complexities and potential repercussions of living within such a controlling environment.

Within Misty's family cult, repercussions for deviating from established norms could include social isolation, shunning, or even verbal, physical and emotional abuse.

The hyper-vigilant environment may also lead to a heightened fear of punishment, both within the cult and in the perceived afterlife. Misty may experience anxiety and a constant sense of being watched, making it challenging to express individuality or explore beliefs outside the cult's boundaries without the fear of these severe consequences.

FREQUENTLY ASKED QUESTIONS AND ANSWERS

WHY IS HYPER-VIGILANCE COMMON WITH PEOPLE THAT HAVE LEFT A FAMILY CULT?

Hyper-vigilance is common among individuals who have left a family cult due to the unique and often traumatic experiences associated with cult environments. Several factors contribute to the development of hyper-vigilance in those recovering from family cults:

Cult Mind Control Tactics: Family cults often employ mind control tactics, including manipulation, indoctrination, and fear-based strategies. Survivors may have developed hyper-vigilance as a means of self-protection during their time within the cult.

Fear of Retribution: Exiting a family cult can be accompanied by a genuine fear of retribution from the cult or its members. Survivors may remain hyper-vigilant, anticipating potential threats to their safety or well-being.

Isolation and Control: Family cults thrive on isolating members from external influences and tightly controlling information. Exiting the cult means facing a world that may feel unfamiliar and potentially threatening, contributing to hyper-vigilance.

Traumatic Experiences: Many family cults involve traumatic experiences, including emotional, physical, or sexual abuse. Survivors may carry the impact of these traumas, leading to hyper-vigilance as a response to the ongoing perceived threat.

Loss of Autonomy: Individuals within family cults often experience a profound loss of autonomy and personal agency. Leaving the cult can trigger hyper-vigilance as survivors navigate the challenges of reclaiming control over their lives.

Betrayal and Trust Issues: Survivors may have experienced betrayal by family members or leaders within the cult. This betrayal can lead to deep-seated trust issues and hyper-vigilance in interpersonal relationships.

Rebuilding Life Outside the Cult: Exiting a family cult requires survivors to rebuild their lives in a non-cult environment. The process of establishing a new identity, social connections, and a sense of safety can contribute to hyper-vigilance.

Cognitive Distortions: Cults often instill distorted beliefs about the world, outsiders, and the consequences of leaving the group. These cognitive distortions can fuel hyper-vigilance as survivors grapple with adjusting to a reality that contradicts the cult's teachings.

Uncertainty and Anxiety: Leaving a family cult introduces uncertainty about the future and can lead to heightened anxiety. Hyper-vigilance may be a way for survivors to cope with the unpredictability of their post-cult life.

Recovery Challenges: The recovery journey involves confronting past traumas, rebuilding a sense of self, and establishing new relationships. These challenges can contribute to hyper-vigilance as survivors navigate the complexities of healing.

Understanding the link between hyper-vigilance and the experiences within a family cult is crucial for both survivors and those providing support. Trauma-informed care, professional therapy, and creating environments that foster safety and understanding are essential components of addressing hyper-vigilance in the recovery process.

WHAT ARE SOME SYMPTOMS YOU MIGHT EXPERIENCE WHEN COMING OUT OF HYPER-VIGILANCE?

When coming out of hyper-vigilance, individuals may experience a variety of symptoms as they gradually reduce their heightened state of alertness. These symptoms can vary from person to person, but some common experiences might include:

Increased Sense of Relaxation: As hyper-vigilance diminishes, individuals may notice a heightened sense of relaxation. This can manifest as a general feeling of ease, reduced muscle tension, and a more calm overall demeanor.

Improved Sleep Patterns: Hyper-vigilance often interferes with sleep. Coming out of this state may lead to improved sleep patterns, including an easier time falling asleep, fewer disturbances during the night, and an increased sense of restfulness upon waking.

Decreased Anxiety Levels: One of the primary features of hyper-vigilance is heightened anxiety. As individuals recover, they may notice a decrease in overall anxiety levels, allowing for a more stable and positive emotional state.

Greater Sense of Safety: Overcoming hyper-vigilance contributes to a greater perception of safety. Individuals may start to feel more secure in various environments and may experience a reduced sense of imminent threat.

Improved Concentration and Focus: Hyper-vigilance can impact cognitive functioning. As individuals transition away from this state, they may notice improvements in concentration, focus, and the ability to engage more fully in daily tasks.

Enhanced Emotional Regulation: Hyper-vigilance is often accompanied by emotional dysregulation. As individuals recover, they may find it easier to manage and regulate their emotions, leading to a more stable emotional state.

Decreased Startle Response: Hyper-vigilant individuals often exhibit an exaggerated startle response. Gradually, as they come out of hyper-vigilance, the startle response may decrease, and they may become less reactive to sudden stimuli.

Increased Trust in Others: Building trust can be challenging for those coming out of hyper-vigilance. However, as recovery progresses, individuals may experience a gradual increase in trust in others, fostering healthier relationships.

Enhanced Self-Efficacy: Overcoming hyper-vigilance contributes to a greater sense of control and self-efficacy. Individuals may feel more empowered to navigate challenges and make decisions for themselves.

Exploration of New Activities: As hyper-vigilance lessens, individuals may become more open to exploring new activities, environments, and relationships that were previously perceived as threatening.

It's important to note that the recovery journey is unique to each individual, and the timeline for experiencing these changes can vary. Seeking support from mental health professionals can provide guidance and personalized strategies for managing symptoms during the transition out of hyper-vigilance.

WHAT ARE SOME BEST PRACTICES TO SUPPORT YOURSELF COMING OUT OF HYPER-VIGILANCE?

Supporting yourself coming out of hyper-vigilance involves adopting practices that promote a sense of safety, relaxation, and overall well-being. Here are some best practices:

Mindfulness and Grounding Techniques: Practice mindfulness and grounding exercises to bring your awareness to the present moment. Techniques such as deep breathing, progressive muscle relaxation, or sensory grounding can help alleviate anxiety.

Establishing a Routine: Create a daily routine that includes activities promoting a sense of stability and predictability. Consistency can contribute to a feeling of safety, reducing the need for constant vigilance.

Gradual Exposure: Gradually expose yourself to situations that trigger hyper-vigilance, starting with less challenging scenarios. Over time, as you build confidence, you can progressively face more triggering situations with a sense of control.

Boundaries: Set and communicate clear boundaries in your relationships and daily life. Knowing your limits and expressing them helps create a sense of safety and control over your environment.

Self-Care Practices: Prioritize self-care practices, including activities that bring you joy, relaxation, and fulfillment. This may include hobbies, exercise, spending time in nature, or engaging in activities that promote a positive emotional state.

Professional Support: Seek support from mental health professionals, particularly those experienced in trauma. Therapy, counseling, or support groups can provide tools and strategies to address hyper-vigilance and its underlying causes.

Cognitive-Behavioral Techniques: Explore cognitive-behavioral techniques with a therapist to identify and challenge negative thought patterns contributing to hyper-vigilance. This may involve reframing distorted beliefs and developing healthier perspectives.

Education and Understanding: Learn more about hyper-vigilance, its triggers, and its impact. Understanding the nature of this response can empower you to navigate it more effectively and reduce its hold on your daily life.

Relaxation Practices: Incorporate relaxation practices into your routine, such as meditation, progressive muscle relaxation, or guided imagery. These practices can help activate the body's relaxation response, counteracting the heightened arousal associated with hyper-vigilance.

Safe Spaces: Identify and create safe spaces where you can retreat when feeling overwhelmed. Having designated areas or activities that provide comfort and security can be essential in managing hyper-vigilance.

Journaling: Journaling can be a helpful tool to express and process your thoughts and emotions. Reflecting on your experiences and tracking progress can provide valuable insights into your journey.

Patience and Self-Compassion: Be patient with yourself during the recovery process. Cultivate self-compassion, recognizing that healing takes time and acknowledging the progress you make along the way.

Remember, the journey out of hyper-vigilance is unique to each individual. It's important to tailor these practices to your specific needs and consult with mental health professionals for personalized guidance and support.

WHY IS IT IMPORTANT FOR SOMEONE THAT IS SUPPORTING A VICTIM OF FAMILY CULT ABUSE TO UNDERSTAND HYPER-VIGILANCE?

Understanding hyper-vigilance is crucial for someone supporting a victim of family cult abuse for several reasons:

Validation of Survivor's Experience: Recognizing and understanding hyper-vigilance validates the survivor's experience. It acknowledges the impact of trauma and reinforces that hyper-vigilance is a common response to the challenging and potentially dangerous environment of a family cult.

Avoiding Triggers: Knowledge of hyper-vigilance helps support providers identify potential triggers that might intensify the survivor's anxiety or distress. This understanding enables them to create environments that minimize triggering stimuli.

Empathetic Communication: Understanding hyper-vigilance allows support providers to communicate with empathy. They can approach discussions and interactions with sensitivity, avoiding language or behaviors that might inadvertently contribute to the survivor's heightened state of alertness.

Creating a Safe Environment: Hyper-vigilance often stems from a heightened need for safety. Support providers can contribute to the survivor's healing by creating an environment that feels safe, trustworthy, and non-threatening. This includes respecting boundaries and demonstrating consistent support.

Facilitating Coping Strategies: Knowledge of hyper-vigilance enables support providers to assist survivors in developing and implementing coping strategies. This may involve helping the survivor recognize triggers, teaching grounding techniques, and promoting relaxation methods to manage anxiety.

Trauma-Informed Support: Adopting a trauma-informed approach is essential. Understanding hyper-vigilance as a trauma response allows support providers to navigate their role with greater sensitivity, recognizing that certain behaviors are adaptive responses to past trauma.

Promoting Trust and Patience: Hyper-vigilance can affect a survivor's ability to trust others. Support providers who understand this aspect can approach the relationship with patience, recognizing that building trust may take time and consistent support.

Encouraging Professional Help: If hyper-vigilance is significantly impacting the survivor's daily life, encouraging them to seek professional help from therapists or mental health professionals who specialize in trauma is crucial.

Long-Term Support: Hyper-vigilance may persist as survivors navigate their healing journey. Understanding this long-term aspect of recovery helps support providers offer sustained, patient assistance and avoids unrealistic expectations for immediate resolution.

In summary, a comprehensive understanding of hyper-vigilance equips support providers to offer empathetic, informed assistance to survivors of family cult abuse. It contributes to the creation of a supportive and healing environment that respects the survivor's experiences and helps facilitate their journey towards recovery.

HYPER-AROUSAL

Hyper-arousal refers to a state of increased psychological and physiological alertness and responsiveness to stimuli. It is often associated with heightened stress, anxiety, or arousal levels. In this state, individuals may experience an exaggerated "fight or flight" response, where the body and mind are prepared for potential threats. Key features of hyper-arousal can include:

Increased Heart Rate: The heart rate accelerates as part of the body's preparation for action.

Heightened Sensitivity: Senses become more acute, and individuals may be more reactive to stimuli in their environment.

Rapid Breathing: Breathing may become quicker as the body takes in more oxygen to support increased energy demands.

Tense Muscles: Muscles may tense up as a result of heightened stress, contributing to feelings of physical tension.

Difficulty Relaxing: Individuals in a state of hyper-arousal may find it challenging to relax or calm themselves.

Irritability: Increased irritability or a shorter temper is common in a hyper-aroused state.

Sleep Disturbances: Hyper-arousal can disrupt sleep patterns, leading to difficulties falling asleep or maintaining a restful sleep.

Impaired Concentration: The heightened state of alertness may make it difficult for individuals to concentrate on tasks or stay focused.

Hyper-arousal is often associated with trauma-related disorders, such as post-traumatic stress disorder (PTSD). Individuals who have experienced trauma may be more prone to hyper-arousal as part of their body's response to perceived threats. It's important to note that while hyper-arousal is a natural response in certain situations, persistent or excessive hyper-arousal can have negative effects on mental and physical well-being. Seeking support from mental health professionals can be beneficial for individuals experiencing chronic hyper-arousal, especially in the context of trauma.

FREQUENTLY ASKED QUESTIONS AND ANSWERS

WHY DO CHILDREN OF FAMILY CULT LEADERS/MEMBERS EXPERIENCE HYPER-AROUSAL? (THIS CAN AND TYPICALLY DOES INCLUDE ADULT CHILDREN)

Children of family cult leaders/members may experience hyper-arousal for several reasons, often stemming from the unique and challenging environment within a cult:

Constant Threat Perception: Cults often create an atmosphere of fear and control. Children may develop a heightened sense of threat perception as they are exposed to the cult's teachings, which may include apocalyptic scenarios, punishment for disobedience, or persecution by outsiders.

Psychological Manipulation: Children within cults are subjected to psychological manipulation and indoctrination. The constant reinforcement of specific beliefs and the fear of consequences for deviating from them can contribute to a state of chronic hyper-arousal.

Authoritarian Control: Authoritarian control within family cults restricts children's autonomy and fosters an environment of strict rules and obedience. The constant scrutiny and fear of punishment can lead to a heightened state of alertness.

Isolation and Limited Social Interaction: Cults often isolate their members, including children, from the outside world. Limited social interaction and exposure to diverse perspectives can contribute to a hyper-aroused state, as children may perceive the outside world as a potential threat.

Fear of Consequences: Children in family cults may fear severe consequences for themselves or their families if they do not adhere to the cult's rules. This fear can create a persistent state of hyper-arousal as they navigate their daily lives within the cult.

Role Expectations and Conditioning: Cults often assign specific roles and expectations to individuals, including children. The pressure to conform to these roles, coupled with the fear of punishment for non-compliance, can contribute to a constant state of alertness.

Traumatic Experiences: Children in family cults may be exposed to traumatic experiences, such as witnessing abusive behaviors, extreme rituals, or violence. These experiences can lead to a heightened state of arousal as the child's nervous system responds to perceived threats.

Uncertain Future: Cults may instill a sense of uncertainty about the future, emphasizing catastrophic events or the need for constant preparation. Children growing up in such an environment may develop chronic anxiety and hyper-arousal about what lies ahead.

Limited Personal Autonomy: Children within family cults often have limited personal autonomy. The lack of control over their own lives and decisions can contribute to feelings of helplessness and persistent hyper-arousal.

It's important to recognize that hyper-arousal in children within family cults is a result of the specific dynamics and manipulative tactics employed by the cult leaders.

WHAT ARE SOME BEST PRACTICES TO HELP COME OUT OF HYPER-AROUSAL AFTER LEAVING THE FAMILY CULT?

Coming out of hyper-arousal after leaving a family cult involves a combination of self-awareness, coping strategies, and professional support. Here are some best practices to help navigate this process:

Self-Reflection and Awareness: Develop self-awareness by reflecting on triggers and stressors that contribute to hyper-arousal. Recognize the patterns of heightened arousal to better understand and manage them.

Mindfulness and Grounding Techniques: Practice mindfulness and grounding exercises to anchor yourself in the present moment. Techniques such as deep breathing, progressive muscle relaxation, or guided imagery can help regulate arousal levels.

Establish Routine and Structure: Create a daily routine that provides structure and predictability. Consistent routines can contribute to a sense of stability and reduce the anxiety associated with uncertainty.

Regular Physical Activity: Engage in regular physical exercise, as it can help release pent-up energy and contribute to emotional well-being. Activities like walking, jogging, or yoga can be beneficial.

Healthy Sleep Hygiene: Prioritize good sleep hygiene by establishing a regular sleep schedule and creating a calming bedtime routine. Quality sleep is essential for overall emotional regulation.

Professional Support: Seek the guidance of mental health professionals experienced in trauma and cult recovery. Therapists can provide coping strategies, support, and a safe space for processing experiences.

Connect with Supportive Communities: Connect with individuals who have experienced similar challenges. Support groups or online communities can offer understanding, validation, and shared coping strategies.

Educate Yourself: Learn about the effects of cult dynamics, trauma, and recovery. Understanding the psychological aspects of your experience can empower you in the recovery process.

Set Realistic Goals: Establish achievable short-term and long-term goals. Celebrate small victories and acknowledge progress, fostering a sense of control and accomplishment.

Emotional Expression: Express emotions through creative outlets, journaling, or talking with a trusted friend. Processing and acknowledging emotions can contribute to emotional regulation.

Limit Exposure to Triggers: Identify and minimize exposure to triggers that contribute to hyper-arousal. This may involve setting boundaries with certain people, environments, or activities that evoke distressing emotions.

Practice Self-Compassion: Be kind to yourself during the recovery process. Recognize that healing takes time, and progress may involve setbacks. Practice self-compassion and patience.

It's important to tailor these practices to your individual needs and seek professional guidance when necessary. Recovery from hyper-arousal involves a combination of self-care, external support, and ongoing self-reflection.

As you navigate this journey, remember that healing is a gradual process, and accessing appropriate resources can contribute to a more balanced and fulfilling life outside the family cult environment.

WHAT CAN HYPER-AROUSAL LOOK LIKE TO YOUR SUPPORT SYSTEM ONCE YOU HAVE LEFT THE FAMILY CULT?

When someone who has left a family cult is experiencing hyper-arousal, their support system may observe various signs and behaviors that indicate this heightened state of physiological and psychological alertness. These signs can manifest in different ways:

Increased Anxiety: The individual may exhibit heightened levels of anxiety, with noticeable signs such as restlessness, nervousness, and a constant sense of worry.

Hyperactivity: There may be an increase in physical activity, restlessness, or an inability to sit still. The person might appear as though they are constantly on edge or in motion.

Irritability: Hyper-arousal can lead to heightened irritability. The individual may react more strongly to stressors or triggers, becoming easily agitated or frustrated.

Difficulty Relaxing: The person may struggle to relax and unwind. Attempts at relaxation may be met with restlessness, making it challenging to find moments of peace.

Insomnia or Sleep Disturbances: Hyper-arousal can interfere with sleep, leading to difficulties falling asleep, staying asleep, or experiencing restful sleep.

Increased Startle Response: The individual may display an exaggerated startle response, reacting more intensely to unexpected noises or stimuli.

Hyper-vigilance: There might be a heightened state of hyper-vigilance, where the person is excessively alert and aware of their surroundings, always anticipating potential threats.

Rapid Breathing: An increased respiratory rate may be noticeable, with faster and shallower breathing patterns reflecting the heightened arousal.

Muscle Tension: Hyper-arousal can lead to increased muscle tension. The person may feel tense, with stiffness or discomfort in various parts of the body.

Impaired Concentration: Difficulty concentrating and staying focused is common. The individual may struggle to complete tasks or engage in activities that require sustained attention.

Avoidance Behaviors: There may be a tendency to avoid situations or triggers that intensify the hyper-arousal. This avoidance can limit the person's engagement in certain activities or social interactions.

Mood Swings: Hyper-arousal may contribute to mood swings, with the person experiencing sudden shifts between different emotional states.

It's crucial for the support system to approach the individual with understanding, empathy, and patience. Creating a safe and non-judgmental space allows the person to express their feelings and seek appropriate assistance, such as therapy or counseling, to address the underlying causes of hyper-arousal.

Recognizing these signs enables the support system to provide meaningful support in the individual's journey toward healing and recovery from the effects of the family cult experience.

SELF-HARM

Self-harm refers to the intentional act of causing harm or injury to oneself as a way of coping with emotional pain, stress, or overwhelming feelings. It is essential to approach this topic with sensitivity and understanding. Common methods of self-harm include cutting, burning, hitting, or other forms of self-inflicted injury.

Self-harm is often associated with underlying emotional distress, mental health conditions, or a difficulty expressing and coping with intense emotions. It is crucial to recognize self-harming behaviors as a sign of significant emotional pain and seek professional help for the individual involved.

If you or someone you know is struggling with self-harm, it's important to reach out to mental health professionals, friends, or family for support. There are resources available to provide assistance, understanding, and guidance in navigating the challenges associated with self-harm.

FREQUENTLY ASKED QUESTIONS AND ANSWERS

WHY CAN PEOPLE THAT ARE IN FAMILY CULT RECOVERY SUFFER FROM SELF HARM?

People in family cult recovery may be at an increased risk of self-harm due to the complex and challenging nature of their experiences within the cult. Here are several factors that could contribute to self-harming behaviors in individuals recovering from a family cult:

Trauma and Emotional Distress: Many individuals leaving family cults have experienced trauma, emotional abuse, and intense stress. Coping with the emotional aftermath of these experiences may lead to self-harm as a maladaptive way of managing overwhelming feelings.

Coping Mechanism from Cult-Induced Guilt: Cults often instill deep feelings of guilt and shame in their members, making them believe they are inherently flawed. Individuals in recovery may struggle with these ingrained beliefs, and self-harm might be a way to cope with or punish themselves for perceived wrongs.

Loss of Identity and Purpose: Leaving a family cult can result in a profound loss of identity and purpose, as cults often dictate members' beliefs and roles. Coping with this loss and navigating the process of self-discovery may lead to emotional turmoil and self-harming behaviors.

Challenges in Rebuilding Relationships: Rebuilding relationships outside the cult, especially if there is significant isolation from family and friends, can be challenging. Loneliness and difficulty forming connections may contribute to self-harming behaviors.

Difficulty Expressing Emotions: Individuals raised in family cults may have been discouraged or punished for expressing emotions openly. Learning to navigate and express emotions in a healthy way is a crucial aspect of recovery, and self-harm might be an attempt to cope with unexpressed or overwhelming feelings.

Struggles with Autonomy: Recovering from a family cult often involves reclaiming autonomy and making independent choices. This process can be overwhelming, and self-harm might be a way of dealing with the stress and uncertainty associated with newfound freedom.

It's important to emphasize that self-harming behaviors are not a solution, and seeking professional help is crucial. Mental health professionals who specialize in trauma and cult recovery can provide the necessary support and guidance for individuals struggling with self-harm during the family cult recovery process. Encouraging open communication, fostering a supportive environment, and connecting with appropriate resources are vital steps in promoting healing and well-being.

HOW TO RECOGNIZE SOMEONE MAY BE STRUGGLING WITH SELF HARM OR SELF HARM TENDENCIES?

Unexplained Cuts or Bruises: Noticeable wounds, cuts, or bruises, particularly in areas that are not easily visible, such as wrists or thighs.

Wearing Covering Clothing Unseasonably: Consistently wearing long sleeves or pants, even in warm weather, to conceal possible self-inflicted injuries.

Isolation and Withdrawal: Withdrawing from social interactions, avoiding friends or family, and spending excessive time alone.

Signs of Emotional Distress: Observable signs of emotional distress, such as frequent mood swings, increased irritability, or expressions of sadness.

Changes in Behavior: Noticeable changes in behavior, including increased secrecy, avoiding discussions about feelings, or a sudden shift in personality.

Difficulty Handling Stress: Expressing difficulty in managing stress or overwhelming emotions. Self-harm can be a way to cope with intense feelings.

Frequent Excuse-Making: Providing explanations or excuses for injuries that seem inconsistent or unlikely, especially when pressed for details.

Presence of Sharp Objects or Tools: Discovery of sharp objects like razors, knives, or other tools that could be used for self-harm, especially in personal belongings.

Signs of Depression or Anxiety: Symptoms of depression or anxiety, such as changes in sleep patterns, loss of interest in activities, or persistent feelings of hopelessness.

Difficulty Maintaining Eye Contact: Avoiding eye contact, particularly when questioned about potential self-harming behaviors.

Expressing Feelings of Guilt or Shame: Verbalizing feelings of guilt, shame, or unworthiness. Individuals struggling with self-harm may carry a heavy emotional burden.

Sudden Change in Friendships: A sudden change in social circles or distancing from friends who may notice and inquire about self-harming behaviors.

It's important to approach the situation with empathy and non-judgmental support. If you suspect someone is struggling with self-harm tendencies, encourage them to seek professional help from a mental health provider.

Open communication and expressing concern in a caring manner can be crucial in providing support during difficult times.

HOW TO SEEK HELP FOR SELF HARM OR SELF HARM TENDENCIES.

If you or someone you know is struggling with self-harm or self-harm tendencies, seeking help is crucial. Here are steps to take:

Speak Openly and Honestly: If you are experiencing self-harm tendencies, consider talking openly with someone you trust, such as a friend, family member, or mental health professional. Express your feelings and concerns honestly.

Professional Help: Reach out to a mental health professional, such as a therapist, counselor, or psychiatrist. They can provide specialized support and guidance tailored to your situation.

Confide in a Trusted Person: If you are concerned about someone else, approach them with empathy and express your concern. Encourage them to talk about their feelings and consider seeking professional help.

Connect with Support Groups: Consider joining support groups where individuals share similar experiences. This can provide a sense of community and understanding.

Develop a Safety Plan: Work with a mental health professional to develop a safety plan outlining strategies to cope with distressing emotions and alternatives to self-harm.

Remove Means for Self-Harm: Temporarily remove or secure any objects that could be used for self-harm, such as sharp objects or medications.

Encourage Professional Assessment: If you suspect someone is at risk, encourage them to seek a professional assessment. Offer to assist in finding a mental health provider or accompany them to appointments.

Educate Yourself: Learn more about self-harm and mental health conditions to better understand what you or your loved one may be experiencing. Knowledge can empower you to make informed decisions.

NATIONAL SUICIDE PREVENTION LIFELINE

In the United States, the National Suicide Prevention Lifeline can be reached at 1-800-273-TALK (1-800-273-8255). This hotline provides free and confidential support for individuals in crisis or anyone concerned about someone who may be at risk of suicide. It's available 24/7, and the call is routed to the nearest crisis center in the Lifeline's national network.

BDSM

(Bondage, Discipline/Dominance, Submission/Sadism, Masochism)

BDSM stands for Bondage and Discipline, Dominance and Submission, and Sadism and Masochism. It refers to a variety of consensual sexual practices and activities that involve power dynamics, role-playing, and the exchange of control and sensation between partners.

In BDSM, individuals may take on roles such as dominant (the person who takes control) or submissive (the person who relinquishes control), and activities may include bondage (restraint with ropes, cuffs, or other devices), discipline (punishment or control), domination (exerting power or authority), submission (surrendering control or authority), sadism (deriving pleasure from inflicting pain), and masochism (deriving pleasure from receiving pain).

It's important to note that BDSM is based on mutual consent, trust, and communication between partners, and it should always be practiced safely and responsibly. Consent is key, and any activities involving BDSM should be negotiated and agreed upon by all parties involved.

BDSM can be a consensual and enjoyable form of sexual expression for those who participate, but it's not for everyone, and individuals should only engage in activities that they are comfortable with and have thoroughly discussed with their partners.

FREQUENTLY ASKED QUESTIONS AND ANSWERS

WHY DO MANY FORMER FAMILY CULT MEMBERS TURN TO BDSM AS A SELF-THERAPY?

Engaging in BDSM (Bondage, Discipline/Dominance, Submission/Sadism, Masochism) practices as a form of self-therapy for many former family cult members can be attributed to several factors:

Empowerment and Control: BDSM allows individuals to explore and reclaim a sense of control over their bodies and experiences. For those who have experienced manipulation and control within a family cult, engaging in consensual BDSM activities can be empowering.

Reclaiming Personal Agency: Former cult members often grapple with a sense of loss of personal agency. BDSM provides a consensual context where individuals can actively participate in, negotiate, and consent to various activities, helping to reclaim a sense of autonomy.

Exploration of Boundaries: BDSM practices often involve explicit negotiation of boundaries and consent. Former cult members may use BDSM as a means to explore and redefine their personal boundaries in a safe and consensual environment.

Catharsis and Release: BDSM activities can provide a cathartic release of emotions and stress. Engaging in consensual acts, particularly those involving power dynamics, may offer a healthy outlet for emotions associated with past traumas.

Building Trust and Communication: BDSM emphasizes clear communication and trust between participants. For individuals coming from a background of manipulation and deceit within a family cult, engaging in BDSM can be an avenue to build trust and enhance communication skills.

Physical and Emotional Healing: Engaging in BDSM activities can facilitate physical and emotional healing. It allows individuals to reconnect with their bodies, redefine sensations, and create positive associations with touch and intimacy.

Community and Support: The BDSM community often provides a supportive and non-judgmental environment. Former family cult members may find solace and understanding within this community, fostering a sense of belonging and acceptance.

Reframing Concepts of Power: BDSM challenges traditional notions of power and authority. For former cult members who may have experienced distorted power dynamics, participating in consensual power play within BDSM can offer a healthy reevaluation of these concepts.

Building Positive Relationships: Engaging in BDSM can be a way to explore and establish healthy, consensual relationships. This can be particularly valuable for individuals who have faced challenges in forming positive connections due to their experiences in a family cult.

It's important to note that BDSM as self-therapy is a personal choice, and not everyone who leaves a family cult will choose or find solace in these practices. Additionally, individuals considering BDSM should prioritize informed consent, communication, and the establishment of boundaries to ensure that these activities are consensual, safe, and supportive of their healing journey.

Professional counseling and support remain crucial elements for those recovering from the trauma associated with family cult experiences.

BOUNDARIES

Healthy boundaries refer to the emotional, physical, and interpersonal limits that individuals establish to protect their well-being, maintain self-respect, and foster positive relationships. These boundaries create a framework for how individuals interact with others and navigate various aspects of life. Here are key aspects of healthy boundaries:

Self-Awareness: Healthy boundaries start with self-awareness. Understanding one's own needs, values, and limits is essential for establishing boundaries that align with personal well-being.

Clear Communication: Clearly communicate personal boundaries to others. Effective communication involves expressing needs, stating limits, and articulating expectations to ensure mutual understanding.

Consistency: Consistency in enforcing boundaries is crucial. It helps build trust and ensures that others understand and respect the established limits over time.

Respect for Others' Boundaries: Healthy boundaries involve not only setting limits for oneself but also respecting the boundaries of others. This reciprocal respect forms the basis of positive and mutually beneficial relationships.

Balancing Empathy and Self-Care: While it's important to be empathetic and considerate of others, maintaining healthy boundaries requires balancing this with self-care. Individuals need to prioritize their well-being without feeling guilty.

Flexibility: Healthy boundaries are flexible and can adapt to different situations and relationships. Flexibility allows individuals to navigate varying circumstances while still upholding their core values and limits.

Saying No When Necessary: Setting healthy boundaries often involves the ability to say no when necessary. It's a crucial aspect of self-advocacy and prevents individuals from overcommitting or compromising their well-being.

Recognizing Manipulative Behaviors: Being aware of manipulative behaviors and recognizing when someone is attempting to violate personal boundaries is important. Healthy boundaries act as a protective mechanism against manipulation or coercion.

Protecting Emotional Space: Emotional boundaries safeguard one's emotional space and autonomy. This can involve setting limits on the type and intensity of emotional involvement in various relationships.

Understanding Limits: Recognizing personal limits in terms of time, energy, and emotional capacity is essential. Understanding when to step back or take a break allows for sustainable and healthy interactions.

Self-Advocacy: Establishing healthy boundaries is a form of self-advocacy. It involves speaking up for oneself, asserting needs, and taking actions that align with personal well-being.

Building Healthy Relationships: Healthy boundaries contribute to the development of positive and respectful relationships. They create a foundation for trust, open communication, and mutual support.

Empowering Autonomy: Setting and maintaining boundaries empower individuals to exercise autonomy and control over their lives. It reinforces the idea that personal choices and decisions are valid and respected.

Seeking Support: Seeking support from friends, family, or professionals can be crucial in maintaining healthy boundaries. Discussing boundaries with others can provide insights, encouragement, and guidance.

Establishing and maintaining healthy boundaries is an ongoing process that evolves with self-discovery and life experiences. It is a fundamental aspect of self-care and contributes to the creation of fulfilling and respectful relationships.

The concepts of hard, flexible, and no boundaries refer to different approaches individuals take in establishing and maintaining their personal boundaries in relationships and interactions. Here's an overview of the distinctions:

Hard Boundaries:

Hard boundaries involve setting strict and firm limits in various aspects of life. Individuals with hard boundaries are clear about what they will and will not tolerate, and they communicate these limits unequivocally. *Characteristics should include:*

Clear and Explicit: Hard boundaries are explicit and clearly communicated. There is little room for interpretation or negotiation.

Rigidity: There is a level of inflexibility, and individuals with hard boundaries are less likely to make exceptions or compromise on their established limits.

Protective: Hard boundaries often serve as a protective mechanism, shielding individuals from situations or behaviors that could potentially be harmful or detrimental.

Flexible Boundaries:

Flexible boundaries involve setting limits that are adaptable based on different situations and relationships. Individuals with flexible boundaries can adjust their limits depending on circumstances. *Characteristics should include:*

Adaptability: Flexible boundaries allow for adaptation to different contexts, relationships, and scenarios. There is room for negotiation and compromise.

Balance: There is a balance between maintaining personal autonomy and being responsive to the needs and expectations of others.

Communication: Individuals with flexible boundaries communicate openly about their needs and are willing to discuss and adjust their limits as circumstances evolve.

No Boundaries:

No boundaries, also known as porous or weak boundaries, refer to a lack of clear limits or an inability to establish and maintain personal boundaries effectively. Some *characteristics* include:

Difficulty Saying No: Individuals with no boundaries may struggle to say no, even when it's in their best interest.

Overextension: There is a tendency to overextend oneself, often accommodating others at the expense of personal well-being.

Vulnerability to Exploitation: Without clear boundaries, individuals may be more vulnerable to manipulation or exploitation by others.

It's important to note that finding the right balance in setting boundaries is a personal and dynamic process. Healthy boundaries can incorporate elements of both flexibility and firmness, depending on the context. The key is to establish boundaries that align with one's values, promote well-being, and contribute to positive and respectful interactions in various relationships.

FREQUENTLY ASKED QUESTIONS AND ANSWERS

WHY ARE BOUNDARIES IGNORED WITHIN A FAMILY CULT?

In a family cult, boundaries are often ignored due to the manipulative and controlling dynamics inherent in such groups. Several factors contribute to this phenomenon:

Authoritarian Leadership: Family cults typically have a central figure or leader who exerts authoritarian control. This leader may demand absolute loyalty and obedience, disregarding the personal boundaries of family members.

Manipulation and Coercion: Cult leaders often use manipulation and coercion tactics to ensure compliance. Family members may feel pressured to ignore their own boundaries in favor of meeting the leader's expectations.

Isolation: Family cults often isolate members from external influences and differing perspectives. This isolation reduces exposure to alternative viewpoints and reinforces the leader's control over the narrative, making it easier to dismiss individual boundaries.

Fear of Consequences: Members of a family cult may fear severe consequences, such as ostracism or punishment, if they assert their boundaries. This fear discourages individuals from expressing their autonomy and asserting personal limits.

Emotional Manipulation: Emotional manipulation within family cults can create a sense of guilt or obligation that discourages individuals from setting and enforcing boundaries. Cult leaders may use emotional tactics to exploit familial ties and loyalty.

Cult Identity Supersedes Individuality: The identity of individuals within a family cult is often subsumed by the cult's collective identity. This can lead to a suppression of individual needs, desires, and boundaries in favor of conforming to the cult's ideology.

Cult Indoctrination: Members are indoctrinated into a specific belief system that discourages questioning or resisting the cult's authority. This indoctrination may lead individuals to subjugate their personal boundaries in service of the cult's agenda.

Power Imbalance: Family cults often perpetuate a significant power imbalance between the leader and followers. This power dynamic makes it challenging for individuals to assert their boundaries, as the consequences may be severe.

Groupthink: Groupthink, a psychological phenomenon where group members prioritize harmony and conformity over critical thinking, is prevalent in family cults. This collective mindset may suppress individual dissent and boundary-setting.

Psychological Manipulation Tactics: Techniques such as gaslighting, mind control, and thought-stopping are commonly used within family cults. These tactics can undermine an individual's ability to recognize and assert their boundaries.

Conditional Love and Acceptance: Family cults often condition love, acceptance, and belonging on compliance with the cult's expectations. This conditional nature discourages individuals from asserting boundaries that may lead to rejection.

Addressing boundary violations within a family cult requires recognizing the manipulative tactics at play, promoting critical thinking, and fostering environments that encourage autonomy and individuality. Breaking free from such dynamics often involves seeking support from external sources, including mental health professionals, to navigate the complex process of reclaiming one's autonomy and setting healthy boundaries.

WHY DO VICTIMS OF FAMILY CULTS STRUGGLE WITH BOUNDARIES?

Victims of family cults often struggle with boundaries due to the pervasive and manipulative dynamics inherent in these groups. Several factors contribute to this struggle:

Authoritarian Control: Family cults are typically led by authoritative figures who exert control over every aspect of members' lives. This authoritarian structure discourages individual autonomy and the assertion of personal boundaries.

Guilt and Shame Tactics: Cult leaders frequently employ guilt and shame tactics to manipulate and control members. Victims may internalize these feelings, making it challenging to establish and maintain healthy boundaries.

Fear of Consequences: Members fear severe consequences for challenging or setting boundaries. This fear can range from emotional and psychological manipulation to threats of physical harm or isolation, making individuals hesitant to assert their needs.

Cultural and Religious Indoctrination: Family cults often embed their beliefs within a cultural or religious context. This indoctrination can instill a sense of duty and obligation, making it difficult for victims to prioritize their own well-being over the demands of the cult.

Isolation: Cults typically isolate members from external influences, limiting exposure to alternative perspectives and healthy relationship models. This isolation impedes the development of interpersonal skills, including the ability to establish boundaries.

Blurred Family and Cult Lines: In family cults, the boundaries between familial relationships and the authority of the cult leader are often blurred. Victims may struggle to differentiate between healthy familial interactions and the control exerted by the cult.

Manipulative Love-Bombing: Cult leaders often engage in love-bombing, showering members with excessive affection and praise to create dependency. Victims may associate setting boundaries with risking the loss of this conditional love and approval.

Psychological Manipulation: Victims are subjected to various forms of psychological manipulation, including gaslighting and mind control. This manipulation erodes their sense of self and autonomy, making it challenging to establish clear boundaries.

Childhood Indoctrination: Many victims are born into family cults, experiencing indoctrination from an early age. This early conditioning can deeply influence their understanding of relationships and hinder the development of healthy boundaries.

Trauma Bonding: Victims may develop strong emotional ties to the cult, even in the face of abuse. This trauma bonding can create a sense of loyalty and allegiance, making it difficult to break free and establish boundaries.

Dependency on Cult Community: Family cults often form a tight-knit community that becomes the primary social support for members. Victims may fear losing this sense of belonging and community if they assert their autonomy through boundary-setting.

Overcoming these challenges requires a comprehensive approach, including therapy, education, and a supportive network. Victims of family cults often benefit from professional guidance to untangle the complex web of psychological manipulation and develop the skills needed to establish and maintain healthy boundaries.

WHAT ARE SOME WAYS YOU CAN CREATE HEALTHY BOUNDARIES AFTER LEAVING A FAMILY CULT?

Creating healthy boundaries after leaving a family cult is a crucial aspect of reclaiming personal autonomy and well-being. Here are some ways to establish and maintain healthy boundaries:

Self-Reflection: Take time for self-reflection to understand your values, needs, and personal limits. Identify areas where you feel comfortable and where you need to set boundaries.

Educate Yourself: Learn about healthy boundaries and consent. Understanding the importance of boundaries in relationships and how they contribute to your well-being is empowering.

Seek Professional Support: Consider seeking support from therapists, counselors, or support groups specializing in recovery from cult experiences. Professional guidance can be instrumental in navigating the challenges of boundary-setting.

Gradual Boundary Setting: Start by setting small, manageable boundaries and gradually progress. This might include asserting your preferences, expressing your opinions, or establishing limits on certain behaviors.

Communication Skills: Develop effective communication skills to express your boundaries clearly and assertively. Practice open and honest communication with others about your needs and expectations.

Learn to Say No: Practice saying no without guilt. Recognize that setting boundaries is a healthy form of self-care, and it's okay to prioritize your well-being.

Establish Emotional Boundaries: Clearly define emotional boundaries, such as limiting discussions about your past cult experiences or setting boundaries around intrusive questioning. Communicate these boundaries with those you interact with.

Identify Triggers: Identify situations or behaviors that trigger discomfort or anxiety. Knowing your triggers allows you to set boundaries around these specific areas to protect your mental and emotional well-being.

Build a Support System: Surround yourself with a supportive network of friends, family, or individuals who understand your journey. A strong support system can provide encouragement as you navigate the process of setting boundaries.

Practice Self-Care: Prioritize self-care activities that promote your physical, emotional, and mental well-being. Taking care of yourself reinforces the importance of maintaining healthy boundaries.

Boundaries with Family: If you choose to maintain contact with family members from the cult, clearly communicate your boundaries. Be firm in asserting what behaviors are unacceptable and what you need for a healthy relationship.

Explore Personal Interests: Engage in activities and explore interests that are solely your own. This helps establish a sense of individuality and reinforces your ability to make independent choices.

Set Technological Boundaries: Consider setting boundaries regarding communication through technology. Control who has access to your personal information and establish guidelines for online interactions.

Be Patient with Yourself: Understand that setting and enforcing boundaries is a process that takes time. Be patient with yourself and acknowledge the progress you make along the way.

Celebrate Achievements: Celebrate milestones in boundary-setting. Acknowledge and celebrate the moments when you successfully assert your boundaries, reinforcing positive behavior.

Remember that establishing healthy boundaries is a personal and ongoing process. It's about creating a balance that promotes your well-being while maintaining respectful relationships with others.

CONSENT

Consent is a voluntary, informed, and mutual agreement between individuals to engage in a specific activity. It is a fundamental aspect of respectful and ethical interactions, particularly in personal, social, and intimate relationships. Key components of consent include:

Voluntary: Consent must be given willingly, without any form of coercion, pressure, or manipulation. It is a choice made freely by all parties involved.

Informed: Individuals must have a clear understanding of the nature of the activity for which consent is given. This includes awareness of potential risks, consequences, and the specific details of what is being agreed upon.

Mutual: Consent involves agreement from all parties involved. It is a shared understanding and agreement that each participant is willing to engage in the activity.

Affirmative: Consent is affirmative and explicit. It is communicated through clear and positive actions or words, indicating a conscious decision to participate in the activity.

Reversible: Consent is not a one-time agreement; individuals have the right to change their minds at any point. It can be withdrawn at any stage, and all parties should respect this decision without pressuring or coercing the other.

Specific: Consent is specific to the activity agreed upon. It does not imply consent for other activities, and each new activity requires a separate, explicit agreement.

Context-Dependent: The context in which consent is given is crucial. Factors such as power dynamics, intoxication, and age may influence the ability to provide informed and voluntary consent.

Communication: Open and honest communication is essential for obtaining and giving consent. Individuals should feel comfortable discussing their boundaries, preferences, and any concerns related to the activity.

Enthusiastic: Enthusiastic consent implies that individuals express genuine eagerness and desire to engage in the activity. It goes beyond mere acquiescence and reflects an active and positive agreement.

Respectful: Consent requires respect for the autonomy and boundaries of all parties involved. It ensures that everyone's comfort and well-being are prioritized.

Consent is a continuous process that should be sought and maintained throughout the duration of an activity. It is a shared responsibility for all individuals involved, and active communication is crucial to ensuring that boundaries are respected. Consent is a cornerstone of healthy relationships and plays a vital role in promoting trust, communication, and mutual respect.

FREQUENTLY ASKED QUESTIONS AND ANSWERS

WHAT IS INVOLUNTARY CONSENT?

The term "involuntary consent" is contradictory because consent, by its nature, is a voluntary and willing agreement. Involuntary actions and consent are mutually exclusive concepts. Consent must be given freely, without coercion, manipulation, or any form of force.

If an individual is coerced, pressured, threatened, or manipulated into agreeing to something, it cannot be considered true consent. Involuntary actions that appear as consent may result from external factors that compromise an individual's ability to make genuine, autonomous decisions.

It's essential to recognize the importance of genuine, voluntary consent in all interactions, especially in personal, intimate, or professional relationships. Any form of involuntary agreement is a violation of personal autonomy and ethical standards.

If there are concerns about coercion or manipulation, it is crucial to prioritize open communication, respect for boundaries, and the well-being of all individuals involved.

WHY IS CONSENT IGNORED WITHIN A FAMILY CULT?

In a family cult, consent is often ignored due to the manipulative and coercive dynamics that exist within such groups. Several factors contribute to the disregard for consent within family cults:

Authoritarian Control: Family cults typically have a central authority figure, often the leader or a select few, who holds immense power and control. This authoritarian structure can lead to a culture where individual consent is overridden in favor of obedience to what the leader dictates.

Manipulation and Coercion: Cult leaders may use manipulation and coercion tactics to enforce compliance with their ideologies. This can include emotional manipulation, guilt-tripping, or threats, all of which erode an individual's ability to give genuine, voluntary consent.

Isolation and Dependence: Family cults often isolate members from external influences, making individuals highly dependent on the cult for their social, emotional, and sometimes even physical needs. This dependence can make it challenging for individuals to assert their own boundaries and freely give or withhold consent.

Cult Indoctrination: Members of family cults are often subjected to intense indoctrination, where the cult's beliefs and practices become deeply ingrained. This indoctrination can result in individuals feeling obligated to comply with the group's expectations, regardless of personal consent.

Fear of Consequences: Members within family cults may fear severe consequences, such as ostracism, punishment, or threats to their well-being, if they refuse to comply with the wishes of the cult leader. This fear can coerce individuals into giving consent against their true desires.

Blurred Boundaries: Family cults often blur the lines between familial relationships and the authority of the cult leader. This can result in a distorted understanding of consent, where familial loyalty and obedience to the leader take precedence over individual autonomy.

Power Imbalance: The power dynamics within family cults create significant imbalances. The leader or key figures wield disproportionate power, making it difficult for individuals to freely express their desires or withhold consent without fear of reprisal.

Exploitation of Trust: Cult leaders may exploit the trust that family members place in each other. This exploitation can involve leveraging family bonds to manipulate individuals into giving consent or engaging in activities they might otherwise reject.

Cultural Indoctrination: Some family cults embed their practices within a cultural or religious framework. This cultural indoctrination can lead individuals to believe that compliance with the group's expectations is a moral or spiritual duty, further eroding the concept of voluntary consent.

Addressing the issue of ignored consent within family cults requires an understanding of the coercive tactics at play, raising awareness about healthy boundaries and consent, and providing individuals with avenues for seeking support and education outside the confines of the cult. Breaking free from such dynamics often involves external assistance, such as counseling or intervention, to help individuals regain control over their autonomy and decision-making.

WHY DO VICTIMS OF FAMILY CULTS STRUGGLE TO UNDERSTAND CONSENT?

Victims of family cults often struggle to understand consent due to the pervasive dynamics of control, manipulation, and distorted interpersonal relationships within these groups. Several factors contribute to this struggle:

Authoritarian Control: Family cults are typically characterized by authoritarian control, with a central leader dictating members' actions and decisions. This control undermines individual agency, making it difficult for victims to grasp the concept of voluntary and mutual consent.

Manipulation and Coercion: Cult leaders often use manipulation and coercion tactics to enforce compliance. Victims may have experienced situations where their choices were overridden, making it challenging to differentiate between genuine consent and coerced acquiescence.

Conditional Love and Approval: Cult leaders often link love and approval to compliance with their directives. Victims may associate giving consent with the hope of receiving love or avoiding punishment, rather than understanding it as a voluntary and equal agreement.

Cultural and Religious Indoctrination: Family cults often embed their beliefs within a cultural or religious context. Victims may be taught that questioning or challenging the leader's authority is morally wrong, creating a skewed understanding of personal autonomy and consent.

Fear of Repercussions: Victims may fear severe consequences, such as emotional manipulation, isolation, or punishment, for refusing to comply with the wishes of the cult leader. This fear can cloud their ability to freely give or withhold consent.

Guilt and Shame: Cult leaders employ guilt and shame tactics, making victims feel responsible for any negative outcomes within the cult. This guilt and shame can create confusion around the concept of consent, as victims may feel compelled to comply regardless of their personal desires.

Limited Exposure to Healthy Relationships: Cults often isolate members from external influences, limiting exposure to healthy relationship models. Victims may lack the knowledge and experience to recognize and engage in consensual interactions.

Distorted Boundaries: The blurred boundaries within family cults, where familial and cult dynamics intertwine, can contribute to a distorted understanding of interpersonal relationships. Victims may struggle to establish clear boundaries, making it challenging to navigate the nuances of consent.

Trauma Bonding: Victims may develop strong emotional bonds with the cult, even if it involves abusive practices. This trauma bonding can cloud their ability to recognize and assert personal boundaries, including the concept of consent.

Psychological Exploitation: Psychological exploitation within the cult may undermine victims' confidence in their own judgment. This exploitation can affect their ability to discern and communicate consent in interpersonal relationships.

Overcoming these challenges often requires professional support, education on healthy relationships and consent, and a gradual process of rebuilding personal autonomy. Therapy and counseling play crucial roles in helping victims untangle the complex web of manipulation and control, empowering them to understand and practice consensual interactions outside the family cult environment.

HOW TO BECOME COMFORTABLE WITH CONSENT AFTER LEAVING A FAMILY CULT?

Becoming comfortable with consent after leaving a family cult involves a process of self-discovery, education, and building healthy relationships. Here are some steps to help you navigate this journey:

Understand Consent: Educate yourself about what consent means. Recognize that it's a voluntary, informed, and mutual agreement between individuals. Familiarize yourself with the principles of affirmative, enthusiastic, and reversible consent.

Reflect on Personal Boundaries: Take time to reflect on your personal boundaries. Identify what feels comfortable and uncomfortable for you in various situations. This self-awareness forms the foundation for establishing and respecting boundaries.

Learn about Healthy Relationships: Educate yourself about the characteristics of healthy relationships. Understand the importance of communication, respect, and mutual understanding in creating a safe and consensual environment.

Engage in Communication Skills: Develop effective communication skills to express your needs, desires, and boundaries. Practice open and honest communication in your interactions with others, fostering an environment where consent is valued.

Set Gradual Boundaries: Begin by setting gradual and clear boundaries in different aspects of your life. This could include friendships, romantic relationships, or even casual interactions. Start with small steps and progressively build your comfort level.

Establish Trust: Cultivate trust in your relationships. Trust is a fundamental component of consensual interactions. Surround yourself with individuals who prioritize open communication and mutual respect.

Seek Supportive Relationships: Connect with individuals who understand your background and are supportive of your journey. Having a strong support system can provide encouragement as you navigate relationships and consent.

Participate in Consent Workshops: Attend workshops or seek educational resources on consent. Many organizations offer programs that focus on understanding and practicing healthy consent. This can be particularly helpful in gaining practical insights.

Explore Personal Desires: Take the time to explore your own desires and preferences. Understand what brings you joy and satisfaction in relationships. This self-exploration contributes to a clearer understanding of your boundaries and the importance of consent.

Practice Self-Advocacy: Develop the ability to advocate for yourself. This includes expressing your boundaries, saying no when needed, and asserting your preferences. Learning to prioritize your needs contributes to a healthier approach to consent.

Be Patient with Yourself: Understand that the process of becoming comfortable with consent is unique to each individual. Be patient with yourself, and recognize that it's okay to take the time you need to navigate this aspect of your personal growth.

Therapeutic Support: Consider seeking therapeutic support from professionals experienced in trauma recovery or relationships. A therapist can provide guidance tailored to your specific experiences and help you navigate the complexities of consent.

Remember that your journey towards comfort with consent is personal and ongoing. It involves continuous self-discovery, learning, and forming connections with supportive individuals. By prioritizing communication, education, and self-advocacy, you can build relationships that are consensual, respectful, and aligned with your values.

AUTONOMY

Healthy autonomy refers to the ability of an individual to assert independence, make self-directed decisions, and navigate life with a sense of self-responsibility. Here are key characteristics that define what healthy autonomy looks like:

Self-Awareness: Individuals with healthy autonomy have a clear understanding of their own identity, values, and beliefs. They are self-aware and can articulate what is important to them.

Self-Direction: Autonomy involves the capacity to make informed decisions based on personal values, goals, and preferences. Individuals with healthy autonomy actively participate in shaping their own lives.

Emotional Regulation: Autonomy includes the ability to regulate emotions effectively. Individuals with healthy autonomy can navigate their emotional landscape, express feelings constructively, and cope with challenges.

Assertiveness: Autonomy involves assertiveness—communicating one's needs, preferences, and boundaries in a clear and respectful manner. This allows individuals to advocate for themselves in various situations.

Boundary Setting: Healthy autonomy includes the skill of setting and maintaining appropriate boundaries. Individuals can define limits that protect their well-being while respecting the boundaries of others.

Goal Setting and Pursuit: Autonomous individuals set and pursue personal goals aligned with their values. They have a sense of purpose and direction in their lives, working toward objectives that are meaningful to them.

Interdependence: Autonomy doesn't mean isolation. Healthy autonomy involves maintaining independence while also recognizing the importance of interdependence in relationships. Individuals can navigate healthy connections without compromising their independence.

Problem-Solving Skills: Autonomous individuals possess problem-solving skills. They can navigate challenges, learn from experiences, and adapt their approach to overcome obstacles.

Prioritizing Well-Being: Autonomy includes prioritizing self-care. Individuals with healthy autonomy recognize the importance of physical, emotional, and mental well-being and take intentional steps to nurture themselves.

Resilience: Autonomy involves resilience in the face of setbacks. Individuals with healthy autonomy can bounce back from challenges, learning and growing from adversity.

Open-Mindedness: Autonomous individuals are open-minded and consider alternative perspectives. While they make independent decisions, they are receptive to new ideas and information.

Accountability: Autonomy includes a sense of responsibility for one's actions. Autonomous individuals take accountability for their choices and understand the consequences of their decisions.

Freedom of Expression: Healthy autonomy allows for the expression of individuality. Individuals feel free to express their unique qualities, preferences, and creativity without fear of judgment.

Continuous Growth: Autonomy involves a commitment to continuous personal growth. Individuals with healthy autonomy seek opportunities for learning, self-improvement, and personal development.

In essence, healthy autonomy is about having the freedom to be oneself, make choices aligned with personal values, and navigate life with a sense of purpose and resilience. It fosters a balance between independence and connection, contributing to a fulfilling and authentic life.

FREQUENTLY ASKED QUESTIONS AND ANSWERS

WHY DO VICTIMS OF FAMILY CULTS STRUGGLE TO ASSERT PERSONAL AUTONOMY?

Victims of family cults often struggle to assert personal autonomy due to the intricate web of psychological, emotional, and social dynamics inherent in these groups. Several factors contribute to this struggle:

Authoritarian Control: Family cults are typically led by authoritative figures who exert control over every aspect of members' lives. This authoritative control suppresses individual autonomy and conditions victims to comply with the leader's demands.

Guilt and Shame Tactics: Cult leaders commonly use guilt and shame as tools for manipulation. Victims may internalize these feelings, making it challenging to assert their autonomy without experiencing overwhelming emotional distress.

Fear of Consequences: Victims often fear severe consequences for challenging the authority of the cult leader or asserting their independence. These consequences may include emotional manipulation, isolation, or threats, creating a significant barrier to autonomy.

Cultural and Religious Indoctrination: Family cults often embed their beliefs within a cultural or religious context. Victims may be taught that questioning or asserting autonomy is morally wrong, leading to internal conflicts when attempting to break free from the cult's control.

Isolation: Cults isolate members from external influences and alternative perspectives. This isolation limits victims' exposure to different ways of thinking, making it difficult for them to conceptualize and pursue personal autonomy.

Psychological Manipulation: Victims are subjected to various forms of psychological manipulation, including gaslighting and mind control. This manipulation distorts their perception of reality, undermining their confidence in asserting personal autonomy.

Trauma Bonding: Victims may develop strong emotional ties to the cult, even if it involves abusive practices. This trauma bonding can create a sense of loyalty and dependency, making it challenging to break free and assert individual autonomy.

Dependency on Cult Community: Family cults often form a tightly knit community that becomes the primary social support for members. Victims may fear losing this sense of belonging and community if they assert their autonomy, leading to resistance against breaking away.

Conditioned Submission: Victims are often conditioned from an early age to submit unquestioningly to the authority of the cult leader. This conditioning hinders the development of independent thought and the ability to assert personal autonomy.

Limited Critical Thinking Skills: Cults discourage critical thinking and independent decision-making. Victims may lack the skills necessary to assess situations objectively and assert their autonomy confidently.

Overcoming these challenges requires a multifaceted approach, including therapy, education, and a supportive community. Professional guidance helps victims untangle the psychological complexities created by the family cult, empowering them to rebuild their sense of self and assert personal autonomy.

The process often involves gradually reclaiming independence, building a support network, and developing the skills needed to navigate life outside the cult's influence.

WHAT ARE SOME HEALTHY WAYS TO ESTABLISH PERSONAL AUTONOMY AFTER LEAVING A FAMILY CULT?

Establishing personal autonomy after leaving a family cult is a significant and empowering journey. Here are some healthy ways to foster and strengthen your sense of personal autonomy:

Self-Reflection: Engage in self-reflection to understand your values, beliefs, and personal goals. Explore your identity independently from the influences of the family cult.

Education and Information: Seek education on a variety of subjects to broaden your perspectives. Exposure to diverse information empowers you to make informed decisions based on your own understanding.

Therapeutic Support: Consider engaging in therapy or counseling to process your experiences and develop coping mechanisms. A mental health professional can provide guidance in reclaiming your autonomy.

Connect with Supportive Communities: Connect with communities or support groups that understand the challenges of leaving a family cult. Shared experiences and support can be instrumental in rebuilding a sense of self.

Set Personal Goals: Identify and set personal goals that align with your values and aspirations. These goals can be both short-term and long-term, giving you a sense of purpose and direction.

Cultivate Independence: Gradually cultivate independence in various aspects of your life. This might include making decisions about your daily routine, finances, and personal choices.

Develop Critical Thinking: Cultivate critical thinking skills to question and analyze information independently. Encourage a mindset that values curiosity and a willingness to explore new ideas.

Explore New Interests: Explore hobbies and interests that were discouraged or restricted within the family cult. This allows you to discover and develop aspects of yourself that may have been suppressed.

Expand Social Networks: Build diverse social connections outside the family cult. Establishing relationships with people who respect your autonomy and individuality contributes to personal growth.

Practice Decision-Making: Practice making decisions independently, starting with small choices and gradually moving to more significant ones. Learning to trust your judgment is a key aspect of reclaiming personal autonomy.

Establish Boundaries: Clearly define and communicate your personal boundaries. This includes emotional, physical, and psychological boundaries. Advocate for what makes you comfortable and respect the boundaries of others.

Mindfulness and Self-Awareness: Cultivate mindfulness and self-awareness practices. This helps you stay attuned to your own thoughts, emotions, and needs, fostering a deeper understanding of yourself.

Celebrate Personal Achievements: Acknowledge and celebrate your achievements, no matter how small. Recognizing your accomplishments reinforces a positive sense of self and reinforces your ability to effect change.

Healthy Self-Care Practices: Prioritize self-care practices that contribute to your well-being. This may include physical exercise, meditation, adequate sleep, and activities that bring joy and relaxation.

Embrace a Growth Mindset: Embrace a growth mindset that views challenges as opportunities for learning and development. This perspective encourages resilience and adaptability.
Reclaiming personal autonomy is a gradual process that involves self-discovery, resilience, and a commitment to your own well-being. Be patient with yourself, and seek support from those who understand and respect your journey.

PARENTAL ENMESHMENT

Parental enmeshment within a family cult describes a dynamic where boundaries between parent and child become blurred, leading to an unhealthy and overly dependent relationship. This enmeshment often serves the cult's agenda, reinforcing control and loyalty. Several characteristics typify parental enmeshment within a family cult:

Emotional Fusion: Enmeshed parents may become emotionally fused with their child, relying on them for emotional support and validation. This fusion reinforces the child's dependence on the parent and the cult for a sense of identity.

Lack of Boundaries: Clear boundaries between parent and child are absent, with the child's thoughts, emotions, and actions closely intertwined with those of the parent. This lack of separation hinders the child's development of individual identity.

Control Through Emotional Manipulation: Enmeshed parents may use emotional manipulation to maintain control over the child. This can involve guilt, emotional blackmail, or creating a sense of obligation tied to the cult's doctrines.

Isolation from External Relationships: Enmeshment often results in the isolation of the child from external relationships, including friendships or connections outside the family cult. This isolation reinforces dependence on the parent and the cult for social and emotional support.

Suppression of Independence: Children in enmeshed relationships within a family cult may find it challenging to assert their independence or develop autonomous thoughts. The cult's ideologies may be ingrained to the extent that the child's identity is subsumed by the collective beliefs.

Loyalty Above Individual Needs: Enmeshed relationships prioritize loyalty to the cult above the child's individual needs. This loyalty is enforced through emotional manipulation and a sense of obligation, further binding the child to the cult's influence.

An enmeshed parent-child relationship within a family cult introduces a web of complexities that can profoundly impact individuals involved. Here are some intricacies of such relationships:

Blurred Boundaries: Enmeshment blurs the boundaries between parent and child, making it challenging to differentiate individual identities. This lack of separation impedes the child's development of autonomy and a distinct sense of self.

Dependency and Fear: The child often becomes emotionally and, in some cases, financially dependent on the enmeshed parent. Fear of consequences for asserting independence or questioning the family cult's beliefs can be deeply ingrained.

Emotional Manipulation: Enmeshed relationships involve emotional manipulation as a means of control. Parents may use guilt, shame, or conditional affection to keep the child compliant with the cult's doctrines.

Isolation from External Support: The enmeshed dynamic isolates the child from external relationships, preventing the formation of supportive connections outside the family cult. This isolation reinforces dependency on the parent and the cult for emotional and social needs.

Suppression of Individual Expression: The family cult's ideologies often take precedence over the child's individual thoughts, feelings, and beliefs. Expressing dissent or pursuing personal goals outside the cult's framework may be actively discouraged.

Psychological Impact: Enmeshed relationships can lead to profound psychological consequences, including anxiety, depression, low self-esteem, and difficulties forming healthy relationships outside the family cult.

Cultural Shock upon Exiting: Breaking away from an enmeshed parent-child relationship within a family cult can lead to a cultural shock when individuals are suddenly exposed to alternative perspectives and ways of life. Adjusting to a more independent and diverse environment can be overwhelming.

Guilt and Loyalty Struggles: Even when individuals recognize the unhealthy nature of the enmeshment, feelings of guilt and struggles with loyalty may arise. Breaking free often involves confronting these emotions and redefining one's sense of loyalty and belonging.

FREQUENTLY ASKED QUESTIONS AND ANSWERS

WHAT IS FINANCIAL ENMESHMENT WITHIN A FAMILY CULT?

Financial enmeshment within a family cult refers to a dynamic where a parent exerts control over a child's financial resources, often using economic dependence as a means to reinforce loyalty and compliance within the cult. This form of manipulation can have profound consequences for the child's autonomy and financial independence:

Financial Control: Enmeshed parents within a family cult may tightly control the child's finances, managing their income, expenses, and overall financial decisions. This control serves to keep the child dependent on the parent and the cult for financial support.

Economic Isolation: Parents may discourage or prohibit the child from pursuing education, employment, or financial opportunities outside the confines of the cult. This isolation prevents the child from developing financial independence and exploring alternative paths.

Exploitation of Resources: Children in financially enmeshed relationships may be used to generate income for the family or the cult. This could involve the child contributing earnings, inheritance, or assets to support the group's activities.

Conditional Financial Support: Financial assistance is often conditional upon the child's adherence to the cult's beliefs and rules. Any deviation may result in the withdrawal of financial support, creating a powerful incentive for compliance.

Lack of Financial Education: Enmeshed children may be deprived of financial education and literacy, hindering their ability to make informed decisions about their money. This lack of knowledge further reinforces dependence on the parent and the cult.

Financial Blackmail: Parents may use financial resources as a form of emotional blackmail, manipulating the child's loyalty by threatening to withhold financial support or access to resources if they question or challenge the cult's authority.

WHAT DO ENMESHED PARENTS LOOK LIKE TO SOMEONE THAT IS NOT FAMILIAR?

Enmeshed parents display behaviors characterized by an excessive closeness or over-identification with their children, often blurring boundaries between parent and child roles. Here are some signs of enmeshed parenting for someone not familiar:

Lack of Boundaries: Enmeshed parents struggle to establish clear boundaries between themselves and their children. There is a limited recognition of individuality, and personal space is often invaded.

Over-Involved in Child's Life: Enmeshed parents may be excessively involved in every aspect of their child's life, from decision-making to daily activities. They may have difficulty letting the child navigate their own experiences.

Emotional Fusion: Emotional boundaries are blurred, leading to emotional fusion between parent and child. The parent's emotions may become intertwined with the child's, making it challenging for the child to develop a separate emotional identity.

Dependency: Enmeshed parents may encourage or foster dependency in their children, making it difficult for them to become independent and make decisions on their own.

Limited Individual Autonomy: The child's autonomy is restricted, as enmeshed parents may exert control over their choices, friendships, and even career decisions. The child's identity is often intertwined with the parent's expectations.

Lack of Privacy: Enmeshed families may have little respect for privacy. Parents might intrude into the child's personal space, read their diaries, or engage in conversations that breach the child's need for confidentiality.

Difficulty with Healthy Separation: Enmeshed parents may resist or find it challenging to accept their child's need for healthy separation and independence. This can lead to guilt or emotional manipulation when the child attempts to establish their own life.

Shared Identity: Parents may project their own unfulfilled aspirations onto the child, creating a shared identity where the child is expected to fulfill the parent's dreams rather than pursue their own.

Guilt and Manipulation: Emotional manipulation, often involving guilt, can be prevalent in enmeshed relationships. Children may feel guilty for asserting their independence or pursuing individual goals.

Impaired Decision-Making: Enmeshed parents may make decisions for the child without considering their wishes or involving them in the process. This can hinder the child's ability to develop decision-making skills.

It's important to note that enmeshed parenting can have lasting effects on a child's emotional and psychological well-being. Healthy parent-child relationships involve fostering independence, respecting boundaries, and allowing children to develop their own identities. Recognizing enmeshed patterns is a crucial step toward establishing healthier family dynamics.

WHAT ARE SOME STEPS FOR ADULT CHILDREN TO BREAK FREE FROM PARENTAL ENMESHMENT AND FAMILY CULTS?

Breaking free from parental enmeshment and family cults is a challenging process that requires careful consideration and support. Here are some steps adult children can take:

Seek External Support: Reach out to friends, family members, or support groups outside the cult to establish connections and build a support system. Consult with mental health professionals who specialize in cult recovery and enmeshment dynamics.

Educate Yourself: Gain knowledge about enmeshment, cult dynamics, and the impact of such relationships on mental health. Understanding the patterns is a crucial step toward breaking free.

Establish Boundaries: Identify and communicate clear boundaries with parents and other cult members. This may involve limiting contact, setting emotional boundaries, and asserting your right to make independent choices.

Develop Independence: Cultivate your independence by making decisions for yourself. This includes career choices, personal beliefs, and lifestyle decisions that align with your authentic self.

Therapeutic Intervention: Engage in therapy with professionals experienced in cult recovery and enmeshment issues. Therapy can provide a safe space to explore emotions, gain clarity, and develop coping strategies.

Connect with Support Groups: Join support groups for individuals who have left cults or experienced enmeshment. Sharing experiences and insights with others who have gone through similar situations can be empowering.

Establish a New Social Network: Build connections with people who share diverse perspectives and beliefs. Developing a broader social network helps counter the isolating effects of cults and enmeshment.

Practice Self-Care: Prioritize self-care activities that promote your well-being, such as exercise, mindfulness, and engaging in hobbies. Cultivate a positive and nurturing environment for yourself.

Challenge Distorted Beliefs: Question and challenge any distorted beliefs instilled by the cult or enmeshment. Develop critical thinking skills and explore alternative perspectives to reshape your worldview.

Legal and Financial Independence: Work towards achieving legal and financial independence. This may involve securing employment, managing finances, and establishing legal autonomy to reduce dependencies.

Create a Safety Plan: If there are concerns about safety or potential retaliation, create a safety plan. This may involve securing a safe place to stay, informing trusted individuals about your situation, and seeking legal advice if necessary.

Allow Yourself Time to Heal: Understand that breaking free from enmeshment and cult dynamics is a gradual process. Allow yourself time to heal, and be patient with the emotional challenges that may arise during this journey.

It's important to note that breaking free from family cults and enmeshment may involve complex emotional and psychological processes. Seeking professional guidance and support is crucial, and individuals are encouraged to reach out to organizations specializing in cult recovery for assistance.

To all those who have experienced or are still enduring the trauma of fundamental Christian family cults, your resilience is recognized, and your pain is acknowledged with deep compassion. As you navigate the path of healing and self-discovery, may you find strength in your journey and support in those who understand.

Remember, your experiences are valid, and seeking help from trusted individuals or mental health professionals can be a crucial step toward reclaiming your well-being. You are not alone, and your courage in facing these challenges is truly commendable.

CHAPTER 5

LEAVING

....

Trigger Warning: Sensitive Content

This content may contain information or discussions that could be distressing or triggering for some individuals. Topics may include but are not limited to trauma, abuse, violence, or other potentially upsetting subject matter. Reader discretion is advised. If you find that you are emotionally impacted by such content, it is recommended to seek support or refrain from reading further. Your well-being is important

Leaving a fundamental Christian family cult can be a profoundly challenging journey. The difficulties stem from the tightly knit community dynamics, strict doctrinal beliefs, and often isolation from the outside world. Individuals face emotional and psychological struggles as they grapple with questioning long-held convictions, navigating strained family relationships, and rebuilding their identity outside the confines of the cult. Despite the hardships, breaking free is necessary for personal growth, autonomy, and the pursuit of a more authentic life.

FREQUENTLY ASKED QUESTIONS AND ANSWERS

WHY IS IT SO DIFFICULT TO LEAVE A FAMILY CULT?

Leaving a family cult can be an exceptionally challenging and complex process due to a combination of psychological, social, and logistical factors. Here are some reasons why individuals may find it difficult to leave a family cult:

Psychological Manipulation: Cult leaders often employ sophisticated techniques of psychological manipulation, such as gaslighting, love-bombing, and fear tactics. These tactics create a warped reality for members, making it difficult for them to trust their own perceptions or question the leader's authority.

Isolation: Cults often isolate members from external influences, including friends, extended family, and other support networks. This isolation makes it harder for individuals to access alternative perspectives or seek help from those outside the cult.

Dependency: Cults foster a sense of dependency on the group or leader for emotional, social, and sometimes even practical needs. Leaving means severing ties with a familiar and often the only support system known to the individual.

Fear of Consequences: Cult members may fear severe consequences for leaving, ranging from social ostracism to threats of harm. The fear of losing family, friends, or facing divine retribution can be a powerful deterrent.

Cultural and Religious Indoctrination: Cults often use cultural or religious justifications to reinforce their authority and discourage members from leaving. The belief that leaving the cult equates to abandoning one's faith or betraying a divine plan can be a significant barrier.

Loss of Identity: Cults often shape the identity of their members, defining their purpose, values, and worldview. Leaving the cult may result in a profound loss of identity, leaving individuals uncertain about their beliefs and sense of self.

Financial Dependence: In some cases, cult members may be financially dependent on the group or leader. Leaving may involve not only emotional and social consequences but also financial instability.

Manipulation of Guilt and Shame: Cults use guilt and shame as powerful tools to control members. Individuals may feel guilty about questioning the cult's teachings or leaving, especially if they have been led to believe that doing so is morally wrong.

Lack of Information: Cults control the information that members receive, limiting exposure to alternative perspectives. The lack of information about life outside the cult makes it challenging for individuals to envision a different, more positive future.

Trauma Bonding: Individuals within a cult may develop a form of trauma bonding with the group or leader. Despite the negative experiences, the emotional connection formed within the cult can create a reluctance to sever ties.

WHY ARE ADULT CHILDREN OF FAMILY CULTS OFTEN UNABLE TO BREAK AWAY FROM THE CULT?

Adult children of family cults often face significant challenges when attempting to break away from the cult. Several factors contribute to their difficulty in leaving:

Psychological Manipulation: Cult leaders employ sophisticated psychological manipulation techniques to control their members. Adult children may have been conditioned from a young age to believe that leaving the cult is not only morally wrong but also results in severe consequences, such as divine punishment or personal failure.

Fear of Retribution: Cults instill a deep fear of retribution for those who attempt to leave. Adult children may fear losing their families, facing social isolation, or being subjected to psychological or physical harm if they choose to break away.

Isolation from External Support: Cults thrive on isolating their members from external influences, making it challenging for adult children to access support networks outside the cult. This isolation limits their exposure to alternative perspectives and reinforces dependence on the cult community.

Financial Dependence: Many adult children in family cults are financially dependent on the cult community. Leaving may mean losing financial support, housing, or other resources, making it difficult to establish independence.

Emotional Manipulation: Cult leaders often manipulate the emotions of their followers, creating a deep emotional bond. Adult children may experience guilt, shame, or a sense of obligation, making it emotionally challenging to break away from the only community they have known.

Cultural and Identity Ties: Cults often create a unique culture and identity for their members. Adult children may struggle to break away due to a strong attachment to this identity, fearing the loss of a sense of purpose or belonging outside the cult.

Limited Education and Life Skills: Children raised within a cult may have limited exposure to education and life skills necessary for independent living. This lack of preparation can be a significant barrier when considering leaving the cult.

Fear of Divine Consequences: Cults often instill a deep-seated fear of divine consequences for leaving the group. Adult children may genuinely believe that leaving will lead to spiritual damnation or punishment.

Cognitive Dissonance: Adult children may experience cognitive dissonance, where their beliefs and desires to leave conflict with the indoctrination received in the cult. Resolving this internal conflict is a complex and challenging process.

Social Pressure and Shunning: The fear of being shunned by family and friends within the cult community can be a powerful deterrent. Adult children may fear losing their entire social support system, making it difficult to break away.

Breaking free from a family cult is a complex and often gradual process that involves overcoming psychological, emotional, and practical barriers. Providing support, resources, and a non-judgmental environment can be crucial for adult children seeking to leave such environments.

WHY IS IT NECESSARY TO GO LOW OR NO CONTACT WITH YOUR FAMILY CULT?

Going low or no contact with a family cult is often necessary for several reasons, as it can contribute to the well-being and recovery of individuals who have experienced the harmful effects of cult dynamics. Here are some reasons why this approach is considered essential:

Protecting Mental Health: Family cults often employ manipulative and coercive tactics that can lead to severe mental health consequences. Going low or no contact is a crucial step to protect individuals from ongoing psychological harm and promote mental well-being.

Breaking Manipulative Influence: Cults thrive on maintaining influence and control over their members. Going low or no contact disrupts the cult's ability to manipulate individuals through coercive tactics, allowing survivors to regain autonomy over their thoughts and decisions.

Establishing Personal Boundaries: Low or no contact helps survivors establish and maintain clear personal boundaries. Cults often infringe upon individuals' boundaries, and establishing distance is a way to reclaim control over one's personal space and choices.

Avoiding Triggering Environments: Remaining in contact with the family cult may expose individuals to triggering environments, reminders of past trauma, and ongoing pressure to conform. Going low or no contact minimizes exposure to these triggers, facilitating the recovery process.

Preventing Emotional Manipulation: Family cults may attempt emotional manipulation, guilt-tripping, or shaming to maintain control over individuals. Going low or no contact reduces the opportunity for such manipulative tactics to be employed.

Protecting Physical Safety: In extreme cases, family cults may pose physical threats to individuals who attempt to leave or distance themselves. Going low or no contact can be essential for protecting physical safety and avoiding potential harm.

Fostering Independence: Cults often foster dependency on the group and its leaders. Going low or no contact is a crucial step toward fostering independence, enabling survivors to make decisions based on their own values and preferences.

Reclaiming Identity: Family cults may suppress individual identities, promoting a collective identity centered around cult teachings. Going low or no contact allows survivors to reclaim their unique identity outside the confines of the cult's influence.

Facilitating Healing and Recovery: Distance from the cult environment provides survivors with the necessary space and freedom to focus on healing and recovery. It allows for a gradual process of rebuilding one's life without constant interference.

Avoiding Recurrent Trauma: Staying in contact with the family cult may expose individuals to recurrent trauma, hindering the recovery process. Going low or no contact minimizes the risk of ongoing traumatic experiences associated with the cult.

Protecting Relationships Outside the Cult: Maintaining contact with the family cult can strain relationships with those outside the cult. Going low or no contact allows survivors to nurture healthy connections with friends, extended family, and support networks.

Disrupting Mind Control: Family cults often employ mind control techniques to shape members' beliefs and behaviors. Going low or no contact disrupts these mind control mechanisms, allowing survivors to engage in independent thought and critical analysis.

While going low or no contact is a significant step, it's essential to recognize that each individual's circumstances are unique. Professional support, such as counseling or therapy, can provide guidance and help survivors navigate the complexities of detaching from a family cult while prioritizing their mental and emotional well-being.

WHAT DO ADULT CHILDREN WITHIN A FAMILY CULT FACE IF THEY ARE UNABLE TO LEAVE THE CULT?

Adult children within a family cult who are unable to leave may face various challenges and consequences:

Continued Psychological Manipulation: Remaining within the cult subjects adult children to ongoing psychological manipulation. Cult leaders may intensify efforts to control their thoughts, beliefs, and behaviors, further reinforcing the indoctrination.

Limited Autonomy and Decision-Making: Adult children within the cult may have limited autonomy and decision-making power. Their choices, including life partners, careers, and personal beliefs, may be heavily influenced or dictated by the cult leaders.

Social Isolation: Cults often isolate their members from the outside world. Adult children who stay within the cult may experience social isolation from friends and family outside the group, limiting their exposure to diverse perspectives.

Financial Dependence: Remaining within the cult may perpetuate financial dependence on the cult community. Adult children may continue relying on the cult for housing, financial support, and other resources.

Cultural and Identity Stagnation: Adult children who stay within the cult may face a lack of personal and cultural growth. Their identity and worldview may remain stagnant, shaped exclusively by the teachings of the cult.

Marriage and Family Dynamics: Cult leaders often control marriage and family dynamics within the group. Adult children may be pressured to marry within the cult, limiting their ability to form relationships based on personal choice and compatibility.

Fear of Consequences: Fear of divine consequences or retribution may persist for those who remain in the cult. This fear can contribute to ongoing anxiety, guilt, or feelings of unworthiness.

Restricted Educational Opportunities: Educational opportunities may be limited for adult children within a cult. Access to diverse educational experiences and critical thinking skills may be stifled, impacting their personal and professional development.

Health and Well-being Challenges: The lack of access to independent healthcare and support systems outside the cult can lead to challenges in maintaining overall health and well-being.

Continued Emotional Manipulation: Emotional manipulation within the cult may persist, affecting the mental and emotional health of adult children. Feelings of guilt, shame, and unworthiness may persist as they conform to the cult's expectations.

Breaking away from a family cult is a complex process, and those who remain face ongoing challenges. It requires a combination of internal realization, external support, and a willingness to confront the psychological and emotional barriers created by the cult environment. Providing resources and assistance to those seeking to leave is crucial for their well-being and autonomy.

DECONSTRUCTION OF INDOCTRINATION

Indoctrination deconstruction after leaving a family cult is a process of dismantling the deeply ingrained beliefs, ideologies, and thought patterns that were instilled during cult membership. It involves critical examination, questioning, and reevaluation of one's worldview. Here's what indoctrination deconstruction may look like:

Questioning Beliefs: Individuals begin to question the beliefs and doctrines instilled by the cult. This involves critically examining the teachings and assessing their validity, logic, and ethical implications.

Research and Education: Engaging in independent research and education becomes a key component. Individuals seek information from diverse sources, explore different perspectives, and gain a more comprehensive understanding of the world.

Identifying Manipulation Tactics: Recognizing the manipulation tactics employed by the cult is crucial. This includes understanding how fear, guilt, control, and misinformation were used to shape beliefs and behaviors.

Challenging Cognitive Distortions: Cults often instill cognitive distortions that support their narrative. Individuals work to identify and challenge these distorted thought patterns, fostering a more balanced and rational mindset.

Dealing with Cognitive Dissonance: The process involves confronting cognitive dissonance – the discomfort arising from holding conflicting beliefs. This can be emotionally challenging but is a necessary step in aligning one's beliefs with evidence and personal values.

Seeking Mental Health Support: Consulting with mental health professionals, especially those experienced in cult recovery, provides valuable support. Therapists can assist in processing the emotional impact of indoctrination and guide individuals through the deconstruction process.

Engaging in Critical Thinking: Cults discourage critical thinking and independent reasoning. Deconstructing indoctrination involves honing critical thinking skills, learning to question information, and distinguishing between fact and belief.

Understanding Behavioral Conditioning: Cults often use behavioral conditioning techniques to enforce conformity. Individuals recognize and work to overcome patterns of behavior that were conditioned within the cult environment.

Reevaluating Core Values: Reevaluating and establishing one's core values independently of the cult's influence is a fundamental aspect. This involves identifying personal values and ethics based on individual experiences and reflection.

Exploring Different Worldviews: Exposure to diverse worldviews and perspectives becomes a part of the deconstruction process. This includes engaging with people from various backgrounds, cultures, and belief systems.

Building Autonomy: Reclaiming autonomy and personal agency is central to deconstructing indoctrination. Individuals learn to make decisions based on their own judgment rather than relying on external authority figures.

Embracing Uncertainty: The deconstruction process often involves grappling with uncertainty. Individuals learn to tolerate ambiguity, accepting that not all questions may have clear-cut answers.

Rebuilding Relationships: Cults often control and manipulate interpersonal relationships. Deconstruction includes rebuilding connections with family, friends, and others based on genuine and mutual respect.

Forgiveness and Self-Compassion: Forgiving oneself for beliefs and actions while under the influence of the cult is part of the deconstruction process. Cult survivors cultivate self-compassion as they navigate the complexities of their journey.

Integration and Moving Forward: Successful indoctrination deconstruction involves integrating newfound beliefs and perspectives into one's identity. It is a process of moving forward with a more authentic sense of self and a renewed connection to the broader world.

Indoctrination deconstruction is a gradual and often challenging process. Take your time and don't be harsh on yourself.

FREQUENTLY ASKED QUESTIONS AND ANSWERS

WHAT IS THE IMPORTANCE OF GETTING MENTALLY, PHYSICALLY, AND EMOTIONALLY EVALUATED AFTER LEAVING A FAMILY CULT?

Getting mentally, physically, and emotionally evaluated after leaving a family cult is crucial for several reasons. Here are the key importances of undergoing these evaluations:

Assessment of Trauma: Cult experiences often involve psychological and emotional trauma. Professional evaluations can help identify and assess the extent of trauma, providing a foundation for targeted therapeutic interventions.

Diagnosis and Treatment of Mental Health Conditions: Cult survivors may develop or exacerbate mental health conditions such as anxiety, depression, or post-traumatic stress disorder (PTSD). Evaluations can lead to accurate diagnoses and facilitate appropriate treatment plans.

Identification of Emotional Impact: Leaving a family cult can evoke a range of emotions, including guilt, shame, fear, and confusion. Emotional evaluations help individuals understand and navigate these complex feelings, promoting emotional well-being.

Validation of Experiences: Cult survivors may face skepticism or disbelief about their experiences. Professional evaluations provide a validation of the psychological and emotional impact of cult involvement, fostering a sense of validation and understanding.

Detection of Physical Health Issues: Cult environments may neglect physical well-being, and individuals leaving cults may have unaddressed health concerns. Physical evaluations help detect and address any medical issues that may have arisen during or after cult involvement.

Identification of Cognitive Distortions: Cult experiences often involve manipulation and cognitive distortions. Mental health evaluations can identify distorted thought patterns and aid in the development of healthier cognitive processes.

Support for Recovery Planning: Comprehensive evaluations provide the information needed to create personalized recovery plans. This may include therapeutic approaches, coping strategies, and other interventions tailored to the individual's specific needs.

Prevention of Long-Term Consequences: Untreated mental health issues or unresolved trauma can lead to long-term consequences. Early evaluations and interventions can help prevent the escalation of psychological and emotional difficulties.

Establishment of Baseline Health: Evaluations serve as a baseline for understanding an individual's current mental, emotional, and physical health. This baseline is valuable for tracking progress over time and adjusting interventions as needed.

Creation of a Supportive Network: Professional evaluations can help individuals connect with appropriate support networks, including therapists, support groups, and mental health professionals with expertise in cult recovery.

Self-Discovery and Identity Reconstruction: Cult involvement often stifles personal identity. Evaluations can be instrumental in the self-discovery process, helping individuals reconstruct their identities and values outside the cult environment.

Safety Planning: In cases where individuals have experienced abuse or are at risk of harm, evaluations can inform safety planning measures. This includes addressing immediate concerns and implementing strategies to ensure ongoing safety.

Empowerment and Autonomy: Going through evaluations empowers individuals to take control of their well-being. Understanding one's mental, emotional, and physical health fosters a sense of autonomy and self-advocacy.

In summary, mental, physical, and emotional evaluations after leaving a family cult provide a holistic understanding of an individual's well-being, laying the groundwork for effective and personalized recovery strategies. Seeking professional help ensures that the recovery process is guided by expertise and tailored to the unique needs of each survivor.

WHAT CAN SOMEONE COMING OUT OF A FAMILY CULT EXPECT FINANCIALLY?

The financial situation of someone coming out of a family cult can vary widely depending on the specific circumstances of their cult experience and their individual resources. Here are some factors to consider:

Financial Independence: Many family cults control their members financially, which can limit access to personal funds and assets. Upon leaving, individuals may need to establish financial independence, including securing employment or accessing savings.

Educational Gaps: Some family cults restrict access to mainstream education or provide limited educational opportunities. Individuals leaving the cult may face challenges in terms of educational gaps and may need to pursue further education or training to enhance their employability.

Limited Work Experience: Cult members may have limited work experience outside the cult environment. Transitioning into the workforce and building a resume may require time and effort.

Property and Assets: Depending on the cult's structure, individuals may or may not have access to personal property and assets. Legal assistance may be needed to reclaim any possessions or financial assets that were controlled by the cult.

Emotional and Psychological Impact on Career: The emotional and psychological impact of cult experiences can affect an individual's ability to pursue and maintain employment. Mental health support may be essential in addressing these challenges.

Legal Issues: Some individuals leaving family cults may encounter legal challenges, especially if the cult controlled legal matters such as property ownership or financial transactions. Legal assistance may be required to resolve any issues.

Debt and Financial Obligations: Cults may incur debt on behalf of their members or limit financial independence. Individuals leaving may need to assess and address any debts or financial obligations associated with their cult involvement.

Support Systems: Establishing a support system, both emotionally and practically, is crucial. Friends, family members, or support groups can provide assistance during the financial transition.

Budgeting and Financial Literacy: Cult members may have limited exposure to financial management outside the cult's control. Learning basic budgeting skills and financial literacy becomes important in managing personal finances.

Employment Challenges: Depending on the nature of the cult's restrictions, individuals may face challenges in explaining their background or dealing with potential biases when seeking employment. Networking and professional support can help overcome these challenges.

Housing and Living Arrangements: Individuals may need to secure housing and cover living expenses. This may involve finding affordable housing, understanding lease agreements, and managing day-to-day expenses.

Government Assistance Programs: Depending on the individual's situation and location, government assistance programs may be available to provide financial support, especially if there are concerns about immediate needs like housing or food.

WHAT ARE SOME POINTS TO CONSIDER WHEN ESCAPING A FAMILY CULT?

Escaping a family cult is a challenging and sensitive process that requires careful planning and support. If you or someone you know is seeking to leave a family cult, consider the following steps:

Build a Support System: Connect with individuals outside the cult who can provide emotional support and guidance. Cultivate relationships with friends, extended family, or people who share similar values outside the cult.

Educate Yourself: Learn about the tactics used by cults to control members. Understand the psychological and emotional dynamics involved in cult environments.

Seek Professional Help: Consult with mental health professionals experienced in dealing with cult-related trauma. Reach out to organizations that specialize in providing support to individuals leaving cults.

Secure Financial Independence: Establish financial independence by saving money discreetly or seeking employment outside the cult's influence. Open a personal bank account in your name and ensure that you have access to your financial resources.

Create a Safety Plan: Plan your exit carefully, taking into account potential risks and safety concerns. Choose a time to leave when you are less likely to be closely monitored.

Document Abuses or Manipulation: Keep a record of any abuses or manipulative tactics used within the cult. Document instances of coercion, control, or any behavior that may be relevant if legal action is necessary.

Establish a Temporary Safe Haven: Identify a safe place to go, such as a friend's house, a shelter, or a supportive community organization. Have a bag with essential items ready for a quick departure.

Educate Yourself about Legal Rights: Understand your legal rights regarding leaving the cult, especially if you are a minor. Consult with legal professionals or organizations that specialize in cult-related issues.

Contact Cult Awareness Organizations: Reach out to organizations that specialize in cult awareness and exit counseling. Seek guidance on the most effective ways to leave and recover from the cult experience.

Plan for Emotional Support: Join support groups or therapy sessions specifically designed for individuals leaving cults. Engage with individuals who have successfully left similar situations for insights and guidance.

Maintain Boundaries: Set clear boundaries with cult members, especially those who may try to persuade you to stay. Be prepared for attempts at persuasion, manipulation, or emotional pressure.

Protect Your Online Presence: Secure your online presence to prevent monitoring by the cult. Change passwords and adjust privacy settings on social media. Consider creating new online accounts if necessary.

Remember that leaving a family cult is a complex process, and professional assistance and emotional support are crucial. If you are in immediate danger, contact local authorities or organizations that specialize in cult intervention for assistance.

CONSERVATORSHIP

A conservatorship is a legal arrangement where a court appoints an individual or entity to manage the personal and/or financial affairs of another person, known as the conservatee. This legal relationship is typically established when the court determines that the conservatee is unable to make certain decisions for themselves due to incapacity or vulnerability.

There are two main types of conservatorship:

Conservatorship of the Person: In this type, the appointed conservator is responsible for making decisions related to the conservatee's personal care, health, and living arrangements. This can include decisions about medical treatment, housing, and daily activities.

Conservatorship of the Estate: In this type, the appointed conservator manages the conservatee's financial affairs. This can involve handling income, paying bills, managing investments, and making financial decisions on behalf of the conservatee.

FREQUENTLY ASKED QUESTIONS AND ANSWERS

WHAT A CONSERVATORSHIP IS AND HOW IT CAN BE USED AGAINST THEM WHEN ESCAPING THEIR FAMILY CULT?

Understanding why a conservatorship may be used against someone escaping a fundamental Christian family cult is crucial for several reasons:

Control Mechanism: Family cults often rely on strict control mechanisms to maintain authority over their members. Initiating a conservatorship is a way for cult leaders to extend this control legally, even after a member has attempted to leave. It becomes a tool to restrict the individual's autonomy.

Legal Leverage: Conservatorship provides legal leverage, granting control over the person's personal and financial matters. Cult leaders may use this legal authority to influence major life decisions, ensuring that the individual remains under the cult's influence and conforming to its doctrines.

Preventing Independence: Escaping a family cult often involves seeking independence and making decisions outside the cult's influence. Cult leaders may use conservatorship to impede this process, limiting the individual's ability to live independently and make choices contrary to the cult's teachings.

Retaliation and Punishment: Leaving a family cult is often viewed as an act of defiance or betrayal. Initiating a conservatorship can be a form of retaliation and punishment, imposing legal consequences for the individual's decision to break away and deterring others from doing the same.

Financial Manipulation: Conservatorship often involves control over finances. Cult leaders may exploit this financial control to induce dependency, making it challenging for the individual to sustain themselves outside the cult without the leader's approval.

Isolation and Control: Conservatorship contributes to the isolation and dependency that family cults seek to instill in their members. By legally tethering the individual to the cult, leaders can maintain a level of influence and control even if the person physically leaves the cult environment.

Legal Maneuvering: Cult leaders may exploit legal systems and procedures to their advantage. Initiating conservatorship proceedings allows them to engage in legal maneuvering, potentially using the legal system to harass, intimidate, or control the individual.

Fear of Exposure: Family cults may fear that individuals who leave could expose the cult's inner workings, abusive practices, or fraudulent activities. Conservatorship can be used to control the narrative and prevent such information from coming to light.

Maintaining Group Unity: Conservatorship may be seen as a way to maintain unity within the cult. By asserting legal control, cult leaders may believe they can force the individual back into the fold, using legal mechanisms to reverse their decision to leave and preventing potential defections.

Legal Justification: Cult leaders may use legal proceedings to justify their actions as legitimate and in the best interest of the individual. This legal veneer can be employed to mask the underlying coercive and manipulative nature of the cult's influence.

Understanding these dynamics helps individuals escaping family cults prepare for potential legal challenges and safeguards their autonomy.

Seeking legal advice and building a support network are crucial steps to navigate the complexities associated with conservatorship and ensure the protection of one's rights and well-being.

WHAT IS THE TYPICAL PROCESS OF ESTABLISHING A CONSERVATORSHIP?

Petition for Conservatorship: An interested party, such as a family member, friend, or concerned individual, files a petition with the court to request the establishment of a conservatorship. The petitioner provides evidence supporting the need for conservatorship, often including details about the conservatee's incapacity.

Court Evaluation: The court conducts an evaluation, which may include assessments by medical professionals or other experts, to determine the conservatee's capacity to make decisions. This evaluation helps the court assess whether a conservatorship is warranted.

Court Hearing: A court hearing is scheduled where the petitioner presents evidence, and the court decides whether to grant the conservatorship. If granted, the court then appoints a conservator.

Conservator's Responsibilities: The appointed conservator assumes the responsibilities specified by the court. These may include making decisions on behalf of the conservatee, reporting regularly to the court, and acting in the best interests of the conservatee.

Conservatorships are intended to provide protection for individuals who are deemed unable to care for themselves or manage their affairs. However, they also involve a significant restriction of the conservatee's autonomy. In recent years, concerns have been raised about the potential for abuse or misuse of conservatorships, prompting discussions about reforming these legal arrangements. It's important to note that conservatorship laws and procedures may vary by jurisdiction.

WHY SHOULD SOMEONE UNDERSTAND WHAT A CONSERVATORSHIP IS AND HOW IT CAN BE USED AGAINST THEM WHEN ESCAPING THEIR FAMILY CULT?

Understanding why a conservatorship may be used against someone escaping a fundamental Christian family cult is crucial for several reasons:

Control Mechanism: Family cults often rely on strict control mechanisms to maintain authority over their members. Initiating a conservatorship is a way for cult leaders to extend this control legally, even after a member has attempted to leave. It becomes a tool to restrict the individual's autonomy.

Legal Leverage: Conservatorship provides legal leverage, granting control over the person's personal and financial matters. Cult leaders may use this legal authority to influence major life decisions, ensuring that the individual remains under the cult's influence and conforming to its doctrines.

Preventing Independence: Escaping a family cult often involves seeking independence and making decisions outside the cult's influence. Cult leaders may use conservatorship to impede this process, limiting the individual's ability to live independently and make choices contrary to the cult's teachings.

Retaliation and Punishment: Leaving a family cult is often viewed as an act of defiance or betrayal. Initiating a conservatorship can be a form of retaliation and punishment, imposing legal consequences for the individual's decision to break away and deterring others from doing the same.

Financial Manipulation: Conservatorship often involves control over finances. Cult leaders may exploit this financial control to induce dependency, making it challenging for the individual to sustain themselves outside the cult without the leader's approval.

Isolation and Control: Conservatorship contributes to the isolation and dependency that family cults seek to instill in their members. By legally tethering the individual to the cult, leaders can maintain a level of influence and control even if the person physically leaves the cult environment.

Legal Maneuvering: Cult leaders may exploit legal systems and procedures to their advantage. Initiating conservatorship proceedings allows them to engage in legal maneuvering, potentially using the legal system to harass, intimidate, or control the individual.

Fear of Exposure: Family cults may fear that individuals who leave could expose the cult's inner workings, abusive practices, or fraudulent activities. Conservatorship can be used to control the narrative and prevent such information from coming to light.

Maintaining Group Unity: Conservatorship may be seen as a way to maintain unity within the cult. By asserting legal control, cult leaders may believe they can force the individual back into the fold, using legal mechanisms to reverse their decision to leave and preventing potential defections.

Legal Justification: Cult leaders may use legal proceedings to justify their actions as legitimate and in the best interest of the individual. This legal veneer can be employed to mask the underlying coercive and manipulative nature of the cult's influence.

Understanding these dynamics helps individuals escaping family cults prepare for potential legal challenges and safeguards their autonomy. Seeking legal advice and building a support network are crucial steps to navigate the complexities associated with conservatorship and ensure the protection of one's rights and well-being.

WHY IS A CONSERVATORSHIP A REAL FEAR TO SOMEONE LIVING IN A FUNDAMENTAL CHRISTIAN FAMILY CULT?

A conservatorship can be a real fear for someone living in a fundamental Christian family cult. It is often threatened within some family cults as a manipulation tactic to instill a fear of leaving the cult and its use as a repercussion. Here are a few examples of areas someone might be faced with under a conservatorship:

Control and Obedience: Fundamental Christian family cults often emphasize strict control and obedience to authority figures. A conservatorship allows leaders or parents within the cult to extend this control legally, influencing major life decisions of the individual who may be attempting to leave.

Restriction of Autonomy: Conservatorship restricts an individual's autonomy, granting legal authority over personal and financial matters. In a cult environment, where conformity is paramount, this restriction can be a powerful tool to limit the individual's ability to make independent decisions.

Escape Suppression: Cult leaders may perceive a member's desire to leave as a threat to the cult's cohesion. Initiating a conservatorship is a means to suppress attempts to escape, ensuring the individual remains under the influence and control of the cult.

Financial Manipulation: Conservatorship often involves control over finances. In a cult setting, financial manipulation can be used to induce dependency, making it challenging for the individual to sustain themselves outside the cult without the leader's approval.

Isolation and Dependency: Conservatorship contributes to the isolation and dependency cults seek to instill. By legally tethering the individual to the cult, leaders can maintain a level of influence and control even if the person physically leaves the cult environment.

Retaliation for Leaving: Leaving a fundamental Christian family cult is often considered an act of defiance. Conservatorship can be used as a form of retaliation, punishing the individual for choosing to depart and deterring others from doing the same.

Fear of Social Repercussions: Conservatorship may be wielded as a means to control the narrative and prevent the individual from speaking out against the cult. Fear of social repercussions, including shunning or isolation from family and community, can be a powerful deterrent.

Legal Manipulation: Cult leaders may exploit legal systems to their advantage. Initiating conservatorship proceedings allows them to engage in legal manipulation, potentially using the legal system to their advantage and complicating the individual's efforts to break free.

Perceived Spiritual Duty: In a religious context, cult leaders may claim a perceived spiritual duty to enforce conservatorship. They may assert that it is their obligation to guide and control the lives of their followers, using religious doctrine to justify legal measures.

Fear of Losing Children: In family cults, leaders may use conservatorship to retain control over children who attempt to leave. This fear of losing children to the influence of the outside world can be a powerful motivator for leaders to initiate legal proceedings.

The fear of conservatorship within a fundamental Christian family cult reflects the broader pattern of control, manipulation, and coercion that characterizes such environments. Individuals facing this fear may need legal assistance, support networks, and resources to navigate the complexities of leaving a cult while safeguarding their autonomy and well-being.

WHAT CAN YOU AND YOUR SUPPORT SYSTEM DO TO HELP PROTECT YOUR FREEDOM, IF YOUR FAMILY CULT THREATENS OR MOVES FORWARD WITH A CONSERVATORSHIP AGAINST YOU?

If your family cult threatens or moves forward with a conservatorship against you, taking proactive steps, both individually and with your support system, can help protect your freedom. Here are actions you and your support system can consider:

Seek Legal Counsel: Immediately consult with an attorney specializing in conservatorship and family law. A legal professional can provide guidance on your rights, help you understand the legal landscape, and assist in formulating a strategy to protect your freedom.

Document Everything: Keep detailed records of all interactions with the family cult. Document threats, coercive tactics, and any attempts to control or manipulate you. This documentation can serve as valuable evidence in legal proceedings.

Assert Your Autonomy: Emphasize your ability to make independent and informed decisions about your life. Gather evidence that showcases your self-sufficiency, responsible decision-making, and overall capacity to care for yourself.

Secure Financial Independence: If possible, establish financial independence by opening personal bank accounts, securing your financial documents, and ensuring your financial affairs are separate from the family cult's control.

Notify Authorities if Necessary: If you feel your safety is at risk, consider notifying local authorities or law enforcement about the situation. Provide them with relevant information and documentation, and seek advice on protective measures.

Build a Support Network: Strengthen your support network by connecting with friends, other family members, or support groups who understand your situation. Share information about the conservatorship threat, and ensure they are aware of the potential challenges you may face.

Educate Your Support System: Educate your support system about the specifics of conservatorship laws in your jurisdiction. This knowledge will empower them to provide informed assistance and collaborate effectively with legal professionals.

Create a Safety Plan: Develop a safety plan with your support system to address potential risks associated with the conservatorship threat. This plan may include measures for physical safety, emotional well-being, and legal protection.

Alternative Living Arrangements: Explore alternative living arrangements to reduce the impact of the conservatorship on your daily life. This may involve staying with supportive friends, family members, or seeking refuge through relevant organizations.

Advocate for Your Autonomy: Work closely with your support system to advocate for your autonomy during legal proceedings. Provide them with any necessary information and enlist their support in emphasizing your capacity to make independent decisions.

Stay Informed and Involved: Stay actively involved in legal proceedings. Attend court hearings, cooperate with your attorney, and stay informed about any developments. Being engaged in the process is essential for protecting your rights.

Network with Advocacy Organizations: Connect with advocacy organizations specializing in cult recovery and conservatorship issues. They may offer resources, guidance, and assistance in navigating the legal challenges associated with leaving a family cult.

Maintain Emotional Resilience: Cultivate emotional resilience to cope with the stress and uncertainty of the situation. Lean on your support system for emotional support, and consider seeking counseling or therapy to help navigate the emotional impact of the conservatorship threat.

Consider Protective Orders: If there are concerns about harassment or potential harm, explore the possibility of obtaining protective orders to ensure your safety.

Remember, facing a conservatorship threat is a complex and sensitive situation. Seeking professional advice, building a strong support network, and taking proactive measures can contribute to protecting your freedom and well-being. In addition to specific actions related to conservatorship threats, a support system can play a vital role in assisting someone leaving a fundamental Christian family cult. Here are additional ways a support system can provide help:

Emotional Support: Offer a non-judgmental and empathetic space for the individual to express their emotions. Leaving a family cult can be emotionally challenging, and having a supportive environment is crucial for mental well-being.

Create a Safe Haven: Provide a safe haven for the individual to stay temporarily. This could involve offering accommodations, whether at a friend's place or another supportive environment, to ensure they have a secure place as they transition.

Connect with Cult Survivor Support Groups: Help the individual connect with cult survivor support groups or organizations. These groups can offer valuable insights, shared experiences, and resources for those leaving similar situations.

Assist with Practical Matters: Offer practical assistance with daily tasks, such as finding housing, securing employment, or managing finances. Leaving a family cult often involves rebuilding one's life, and practical support can ease the transition.

Educate on Cult Dynamics: Educate the individual and the support system about cult dynamics, manipulation tactics, and recovery processes. Understanding these aspects can contribute to a more informed and supportive environment.

Encourage Independence: Encourage and support the individual in reclaiming their independence. Help them build confidence in making decisions, setting goals, and shaping their own life outside the constraints of the cult.

Facilitate Professional Counseling: Encourage the individual to seek professional counseling or therapy. Cult recovery often involves addressing complex psychological and emotional challenges, and professional support can be invaluable.

Assist in Rebuilding Social Connections: Help the individual rebuild social connections outside the cult. This can involve introducing them to new social circles, communities, or friends who share common interests and values.

Provide Information on Legal Rights: Offer information about legal rights and resources. Understanding legal protections can empower the individual to make informed decisions and navigate potential legal challenges associated with leaving a family cult.

Support Educational Pursuits: Support any educational pursuits the individual may have. Whether pursuing further studies or acquiring new skills, education can be a key component of rebuilding one's life after leaving a cult.

Encourage Healthy Coping Mechanisms: Promote healthy coping mechanisms and self-care practices. This could include exercise, mindfulness, or engaging in activities that bring joy and fulfillment.

Maintain Open Communication: Foster open communication within the support system. Regular check-ins and discussions can help address evolving needs and challenges as the individual navigates life outside the family cult.

Help Navigate Spiritual Exploration: If the individual is open to it, assist in navigating their spiritual exploration. This may involve connecting with supportive religious or spiritual communities that prioritize personal growth and autonomy.

Be Patient and Understanding: Understand that the recovery process is unique to each individual. Be patient and provide ongoing support as the person adapts to their newfound freedom and constructs a life independent of the cult.

A comprehensive support system that addresses emotional, practical, and social aspects is essential for someone leaving a fundamental Christian family cult. Tailoring assistance to the individual's specific needs and respecting their autonomy is key to fostering a positive recovery journey.

WHY DO SO MANY FAMILY CULT LEADERS MEET THEIR CHILDREN THAT CHOOSE TO LEAVE OR ESCAPE THE CULT WITH A CONSERVATORSHIP?

Family cult leaders may attempt to use conservatorship as a means of maintaining control over their children who choose to leave or escape the cult for several reasons:

Control and Power: Conservatorship grants the cult leader legal authority over the individual's personal and financial affairs. This control reinforces the leader's power and ensures continued dominance even after the individual has left the cult.

Retaliation and Punishment: Cult leaders may view a child's decision to leave as an act of defiance or betrayal. Initiating conservatorship proceedings can be a way to retaliate against the individual, imposing legal consequences and punishments for their departure.

Preventing Independence: Conservatorship restricts the individual's autonomy and ability to make independent decisions. Cult leaders, seeking to prevent the establishment of an independent life outside the cult, may use conservatorship as a tool for continued influence.

Financial Control: By gaining control over the individual's finances through conservatorship, cult leaders can exert economic leverage. This financial control may limit the individual's ability to sustain themselves outside the cult, making them more susceptible to manipulation.

Isolating the Individual: Conservatorship can contribute to the isolation of the individual who has left the cult. It limits their ability to seek support, make legal decisions, or engage with the outside world, reinforcing the cult's influence.

Legal Maneuvering: Cult leaders may exploit legal systems and procedures to their advantage. Initiating conservatorship proceedings allows them to engage in legal maneuvering, potentially using the legal system to harass, intimidate, or control the individual.

Reclaiming the Member: Some cult leaders may see conservatorship as a way to reclaim a wayward member. By asserting legal control, they may believe they can force the individual back into the fold, using legal mechanisms to reverse their decision to leave.

Perceived Spiritual Duty: In some cases, cult leaders may justify conservatorship as a perceived spiritual duty. They may genuinely believe that they have a divine mandate to exert control over the lives of their followers, even those who choose to leave.

Fear of Exposure: Cult leaders may fear that individuals who leave the cult could expose its inner workings, abusive practices, or fraudulent activities. Conservatorship can be used to control the narrative and prevent such information from coming to light.

Maintaining Family Image: Conservatorship may be used to maintain a facade of a united and obedient family. Cult leaders, particularly concerned with appearances, may go to great lengths to control the actions and choices of those who have left to protect the cult's image.

It's important to note that conservatorship laws and procedures vary, and the success of such attempts depends on legal systems and jurisdictions. Individuals facing these situations may benefit from seeking legal advice and support to protect their rights and navigate the complexities associated with leaving a family cult.

A LETTER TO THE READER FROM THE AUTHOR IN PERSONAL REGARDS, ON THE SUBJECT OF "LEAVING":

Dear Reader,

Anytime I am asked to share my story, it is often met with shock and amazement. But the question I get asked the most, I would like to address one final time: Why did it take you so long to leave?

This question has no one simple answer and it comes in many layers. It took me 39 years, 3 months, and 14 days to finally have the ability and means to leave/escape my Fundamentalist Christian Family Cult.

I could tell you of the many times I tried to leave my parents home (where I was forced to live), escape, and go no contact with my cult leader parents and how I was brought back by physical force and kept there by fear for years on end.

I could tell you of year after year, since the time of my birth, what it was to have my will and spirit broken by physical force and spiritual guilt. I can account for every time that I was put into physically submissive positions to affirm their superiority, and held there until I was in every way broken.

I could tell you how my mother would (and did) brag to anyone, of how she trained me like a dog. "Kids are smarter than dogs, but the techniques in training work the same." She would snap her fingers and I would instantly show up at her side, like a fear driven puppy. The fear of not obeying her commands, often can still bring me to tears to this day. The punishments she would choose to inflict on me at any time if I did not fall to her feet in complete submission, had no limits.

I could tell you of all the physical and sexual abuse I endured in the name of God up until the day I was finally able to escape once and for all. Yes, I can account for each and every time.

I could tell you about how my mother "heard the voice of God" directly and the unspeakable things she did with that "power" within our home.

I could tell you about all of the isolation that I endured. The loneliness of being an only child living a majority of my life with only the company of my mother and father. My parents chose to cut ties and went no contact with both of their entire families when I was the ages of 9 (my mother's family) and 14 (my father's family), based on their rigid value system, and limited relationships and time with "outsiders" from then on.

I could tell you about how my personal relationships were limited, controlled, and monitored to the point that no one could endure my parents, even for the love they might have bore me. No relationship of any kind lasted more than six months.

I could tell you about how any person that was brought into the family by my mother under the guise of "friendship," was always thought of more as a recruit by her. Once this person would see through the control and restrictions that they would be placed under, they would generally leave and cut off all communication with us.

On the rare occasion they were not the kind of person to leave when things got intense, my mother would flip on them if they failed to comply after a few minor infractions. That person would then be completely cut off by her (and subsequently the family), and subjected to a smear campaign to everyone closest to them.

I could tell you about the intense indoctrination I received as a homeschooler and the further isolation this caused in my life. I had no classmates, no friends, no one my own age to play with, no one to grow up with, and share a history with. I have no keepers of my history, aside from the parents that abused and isolated me from the world.

I could tell you about the immense gaps in my education. The "Creationist" approved curriculum I received was greatly lacking in basic education that would be useful in any modern world. I have taken great lengths over the years to re-educate myself in these gaps, but the struggles these gaps created are countless and still continue.

However, in contrast, I could tell you about the unnecessary information I received within my education that was taught to be "critical". An example of this is the complete understanding of the firmament and how it applies to our world through Christ, not science. This line of education was in no way useful in preparing me for the "real world" and what lay ahead.

I could tell you about the years of financial enmeshment that crippled me from having any money of my own that wasn't watched daily, taken from me, as well as all spending accounted for.

I could tell you about how my physical person was monitored 24/7 in some shape or form, from the moment I was born until the day I left. This included never having the ability to lock ANY door, and at a minimum all doors must remain cracked at ALL times.

I could tell you of all of times I was medically neglected, to my longterm detriment. It was the belief of my Family Cult, that the power of prayer, the laying of hands, calling upon God through my mother to heal directly, and through naturalistic medicine.

I could tell you of all the times I went to the police to beg for assistance, and being turned away with non-belief and dismissal. Thinking of the words one officer used still makes me cringe,"That's crazy, they are your parents. You need a counselor, not a cop."

I could tell you about all of these things, but you could see it as merely a list of my abuse and trauma. Yet it still doesn't answer the question of "Why didn't I leave sooner?". It simply comes down to not having the means and ability to leave. But by answering that question, I could invalidate the difference between a Family Cult, and heavily enmeshed, abusive parents.

Please allow me to explain, growing-up in an non-cult, but abusive situation, you typically have the means and help necessary to leave that situation when you become legally emancipated or of legal age. But in stark contrast, someone growing up within a Family Cult, is typically isolated in the extreme they have no outside connections from the cult.

Typically there are severe educational gaps that makes it very difficult to get or maintain a job (in most cases, especially if you are female). Typically all financial accounts are shared with the leader(s) and/or all money is controlled by the leader(s).

Typically all physical movements are tracked in multiple forms. This may include physical tracking devices, constantly having someone with you, having you followed, or tracked, etcetera.

The most pivotal point to be made is if you do try to leave, you are typically brought back by any means possible, up to and including physical and legal force, despite your age. I have not mentioned the forced marriages and procreation that most are saddled with from extremely young age in the name of God, and their nearly impossible chances of escape they have.

This book is my testament as to why I was not able to leave sooner. It breaks down not only my experience, but the experiences of so many other victims and survivors as well. It is the testament to all of the lost children of Family Cults, born into a situation that they are not allowed to leave. I mourn for all of those children, and the adults they were forced to become, or will become.

I mourn for the 39 years, 3 months, and 14 days of a life not fully lived. I mourn for the person I was. When I finally escaped, it was only with the help of one person I was able to connect with, in secret.

It was with this person's help, I was able to not only escape, but they offered me protection my parents; who came at me with full force trying to find my exact location and serve me with a conservatorship.

I am happy to report, they were unsuccessful in all of their attempts. This journey took almost a year to guarantee my safety and ability to stay free. I now live a peaceful life, under a new name, new state, and new career. I have deconstructed my past, attended many intensive therapy sessions, continue therapy weekly, and I feel I have healed enough from my past to move forward. I am now 41 years old, a partner, a parent, a friend, a victims advocate, an author, and most importantly, a survivor.

Thank you, my dear Reader for hearing my story and expanding your mind to understand the tragedy that is most stories of Fundamental Christian Family Cult victims. We were children, born into this, and it is not a life we chose. Please always keep that in mind when someone might share their story with you.

This book, in all of its personal experience poured into it, is intended to help guide those on their journey to freedom, and to the great people that support us along this life-changing journey. I commend you all for your bravery and celebrate with you on every step along the way.

- Kenogi

CHAPTER 6

THE SUPPORT SYSTEM

....

Trigger Warning: Sensitive Content

This content may contain information or discussions that could be distressing or triggering for some individuals. Topics may include but are not limited to trauma, abuse, violence, or other potentially upsetting subject matter. Reader discretion is advised. If you find that you are emotionally impacted by such content, it is recommended to seek support or refrain from reading further. Your well-being is important.

LETTER TO THE READER FROM THE SUPPORT PERSON

Hello Reader,

You can call me AP. I am, and have been, Kenogi's support person. I have been a part of their life since the last year of them living with their parents. I will not lie to you, and tell you that this road is easy. It is definitely not. I have seen how deep the enmeshment is, and how deep it goes.

When I first began talking to Kenogi, they had what I call "dead eyes." You could see in the eyes that there was no internal happiness. The external "happiness" was at best a mask they wore, at worst it was absolutely fake. They were a zombie, that just moved along each day as needed. An automaton. Their eyes told a story that was much older than they were.

It was almost as though I was staring at a long dead person who had given up many years before. If someone were to bring back the dead, their eyes would have more life than I saw in Kenogi's eyes from the day I met them.

We started out as work friends, who became friends over text and phone calls, and eventually a romantic partner. When our relationship became friends over phone calls, we used FaceTime for our calls. There were times that we would be talking and their mother would walk in and invite themselves to our conversations. I was cordial, friendly, and on my best behavior. After these phone calls, their mother would say that we were talking to each other too much. "It's weird," "Nobody should want to talk to YOU on the phone that much," among other demeaning things.

While their mother would never say anything to me about how she felt, she would definitely try to put on her best "I'm a good Christian woman, who is friendly to everybody" face. She would talk to me almost as though she held a higher station in life than she actually did. As a man who group up in the south, my cordiality was purely out of my southern upbringing of "respect your elders." I never liked her, as she seemed incredibly fake, and the disdain I had for her began even before I knew the extent of what she was doing to Kenogi.

Kenogi's household seemed very "showy" to me. The videos I'd see of the home made it look very sterile. Almost like everything was setup as though it was a house on the market ready to be sold, and was done up like a family home. The beds were neatly made, the house was very bland looking from a decorative state. Everything looked like an IKEA store fake bedroom, kitchen, or living space.

Early in our conversations over the phone, I began to notice that there were components of their life that I found odd. For example, not being able to close and lock the bathroom door while they were using the bathroom, or in the shower or bath.

There was one day, very early in our FaceTime calls that Kenogi had experienced a very rough day. I suggested that they take a bubble bath and participate in some self-care. Kenogi explained that they did not have any bubble bath, so I advised them to go to a local store and purchase some, and while they were at it, pick up a candle. This was the first time that I introduced the idea of "self-care" to Kenogi, it would not be the last.

I advised them to take a self-care night, and that they needed to light the candle, turn off the lights, set the candle on the bathtub, and climb in. Just lay there and relax. As our relationship progressed, there were more and more instances of me doing this. Advising them to take a bubble bath, having them take self-care days or nights.

We also began having "movie nights." We would be on the phone watching a movie through the internet together. We would do this at least once a week, kind of a virtual date night, so to speak. This became a ritual that we would do together to help with self-care. It helped Kenogi to relax and forget about the hell that they were living through.

I continued to provide different ways for Kenogi to take self-care moments, hours, days, etc. This became especially prevalent when their mother received a diagnosis that required Kenogi to take time off of work to assist in their mother's healthcare.

After taking this leave of absence from work, I noticed that the abusive nature of their mother became more…visibly out in the open. Kenogi had to sleep in the living room where their mother was comfortable. They had to get up at all hours of the night to give meds, clean wounds, and get snacks. They had to bathe their mother. They were belittled for the food they would make because their mother couldn't eat whatever it was that she initially requested. Kenogi was sleeping at best 3-5 hours a night, at worst, 45 minutes to an hour.

As this was happening, our relationship was becoming closer and more romantic. Their mother was limiting our interactions, both in the literal "don't talk to them" sense and in her constant need for attention.

Kenogi had not been allowed to seek therapy for any issues that had occurred in their past, and their mother believed that therapy was hog-wash and would destroy the "family unit". Kenogi and I had to hatch a plan that would assist them in getting the therapy that they needed.

We began plotting ways to get them therapy. The eventual way that we were able to get them into therapy was that Kenogi needed someone to help them get through this difficult time where they were having to care for their mother. It was "too stressful" for them to take care of on their own, and they needed assistance from someone that wasn't in the situation. Their mother begrudgingly agreed to allow this to happen… though she berated them daily for this.

This therapy is part of what eventually assisted Kenogi in getting out of the home, for good. Kenogi initially began therapy to assist with figuring out their life and current mental state. But, Eye Movement Desensitization and Reprocessing (EMDR) therapy began here for them. They unlocked a lot of past, long locked away memories.

This brought a new stress to our relationship, for both of us. Watching Kenogi struggle through this was as emotionally heartbreaking for me, as it was strengthening to me and them. This gave Kenogi a new outlook on how to address their past. It assisted in recovering from past trauma, by knowing just how horrible it was.

We discussed every session, we discussed what had happened, what memories were unlocked, and how we would navigate this world together. We knew that no matter how horrific this trauma was, that together we would be able to navigate through it, and I informed them that I would be there to help them with the navigation.

Kenogi also got into martial arts for a short while at this same time. This was meant to assist in getting past the traumas of their past by relieving the stress and emotions in a healthy (while somewhat violent) way, in a safe space. Kenogi would go through their EMDR session during the morning or afternoon, and then go to the martial arts class in the evenings.

The martial arts night of the week was always an incredibly difficult night. There was one night where they had been having an incredibly stressful week. Between their mother, the household chores that they were required to complete, and the constant barrage of "Help me do XYZ thing" that they were receiving from their mother. Which actually meant "Hey, do this thing I'm telling you to do, so that I can tell you that it's wrong, and make you do it a different way, even though I've always told you to do it this way."

I was supposed to go to a party on this night, but the party would start before they would be out of martial arts. I chose to stay home until after they were out. I did this because every night when they would go to martial arts, they would call me and cry about how much of a struggle it was. The martial arts brought up a lot of bad memories that they were working through during this.

I advised Kenogi to call me as soon as they were out, if they needed me. Initially, they argued with me that I would be at the party, and that they didn't want to disturb my fun. I told them that I didn't care, if they needed me, call me.

After it was over, they called me. I had not told them I was not going to go to the party until after I heard from them, so they were incredibly surprised by this. I talked to them until they got home, and we said goodbye in their garage. I then went to the party, but continued messaging them throughout the night, constantly checking in.

I discussed with Kenogi, after their mother had healed enough, that they should get out, take a trip, take care of their mental health, in nature, as I knew this was their solace. They agreed that this would be good, because they'd always enjoyed being in nature, and missed their hikes that they used to take. So, they decided to take a trip where they could be surrounded by nature.

At one point their mother invited themselves on a trip that Kenogi had planned and then ruined the trip, forcing them to go home 5 days early. Kenogi planned several more trips for short periods no more than a few days at a time. I advised them to tell their mother that they were not invited, and to stay at home. I was very involved in supporting them in breaking away from what I suspected was a lifetime of people pleasing, and I deeply wanted to assist them on standing on their own two feet.

When Kenogi came to my area to visit, they stayed in a home they rented for the week. We planned a movie night with a couple of my friends. Kenogi met me at the theater, hopped into my car, and we went to pick up my friends. During this, Kenogi was very worried that their mother was tracking where they were. They disabled the tracker on their phone and awaited the phone calls from their mother, which happened several times.

If Kenogi didn't answer the call the first time, their mother would call over and over until they answered. Literally, their mother would hang up after a few rings, and call right back. Eventually, Kenogi would answer, say they were doing something else, their mother would be satisfied, and end the call.

When it came almost time for the movie, Kenogi texted their mom and said that they were about to go into the movie, and would call her back later when they arrived back at the rental. Their mother didn't like it, but accepted this. After the movie was over, and they left, they had to call their mother back.

This was the beginning of me noticing how often their mother would check in on them. It was the first time that I'd seen in person, just how often Kenogi was having to "check-in." If more than a couple of hours went by without a voice or text check-in, the phone would ring. Every night at 9pm, Kenogi had to call and check-in, tell their mother that they were headed to bed, and say "good night," perform their "prayer ritual" as a family, and then could continue on with their evening.

I visited Kenogi one day and stayed through the evening at the home they had rented. Their mother called during the day, and Kenogi told her that we were sitting around talking and listening to music, or watching videos. All completely benign things. The next morning, their mother called and said that they had to stop talking to me because I was...a few words that I will not repeat here.

Their mother and I had spoken the night before and she goaded me into a conversation about several topics that could be controversial. I stayed cordial, I mildly debated the topics, and asked for sources when provided information that I was not familiar enough with to debate. I was given the common responses of "look it up yourself." So, I tried to find them, then with a brief glance of things, I would attempt to respond, but admitted my lack of information provided me a bit of a disadvantage on the topic.

By this point, I knew the type of person she was, and knew that she was trying to get me to start a fight. However, my southern training, and my debate skills, kept me very calm throughout. If I'm being honest, I kind of enjoyed watching her flounder during the conversation, and watching her try to get me mad or flustered. It was a bit of a high for me to keep my cool, and show her that she wasn't as smart about the topics she was trying to talk about as she may have thought.

To be fair, I realize that this could come off as me becoming the support person in a vindictive way. That was definitely not the case. I was already the support person for Kenogi at this point, and my cockiness was more a culmination of the experience that I had already been in with Kenogi and finally actually having an opportunity to have a "real" conversation with their mother.

Instead of being allowed to enjoy the rest of their trip, Kenogi was forced into a position at this point to create an escape plan. Their mother went into a narcissistic rage about the two of us spending time together. Kenogi became afraid of the hell that we had unleashed together, and was afraid to go back home.

Originally, Kenogi was only going to be there for a week. Luckily, fate was on our side at this point and there was a significant weather event. This gave the perfect cover for Kenogi to stay for another week, and gave us time to plan their escape…together. Kenogi and I began the process of them being able to escape the only life they'd known, with the only "support" system they'd ever known. It was at this moment, that I officially took on the role of support system. Or, at a minimum, that's when I made a knowing choice to become the support system.

When Kenogi initially started planning their escape, it was under the guise of getting into nature to get closer to God. However, it was about getting somewhere safe, somewhere that they could start a new life away from them. They just had to play their cards right, and they would finally be out.

They began getting secret credit cards to help them with their escape. They would have nothing when they left, no money, no furniture, no bed to sleep on, but they would have a home to put this stuff in. They got the credit cards, rented the first affordable place that they could, and began filling it with things to just live.

Kenogi had it all planned out, get out of the house, get in somewhere safe, and begin life anew. During this time, I was kept a secret. Whenever their mother would call, Kenogi would step outside, talk to her for 5-10 minutes, and then come back in, or I'd be outside and have to be dead quiet until they were off the phone.

I would hear the belittling, the "you can't get right with God if you're leaving all of the time, going here or there," conversations. It was a lot of the stressful conversations that Kenogi was having previously, in their shared family home, but just over the phone this time.

There was a plan, and everything was going according to plan, until it wasn't. As fate tends to do, it stepped in and ruined the "plan" that was in place. Kenogi had been forbidden to talk to me, because if they were trying to get closer to God, they didn't need any distractions.

Late one night, Kenogi and I were talking in their new home. They had played the part very well of hiding our conversations before moving out. During our conversation, something happened, and their mother called. There was a fight, which led to them cutting contact with their family. Their mother berated them for 5-10 minutes, but by this point, Kenogi had begun to find their voice. Kenogi told their mother that they are grown, and will talk to whomever they please, and ended the call to their father yelling "F*** that b****, hang up on them."

When Kenogi called me back, we discussed this, and discussed a way for them to stay safe in their situation. They had already turned off long before this moment, the tracking that was on the phone. But, this fight, led to them going deeper into hyper-vigilance to stay protected.

They carried their pistol with them everywhere. They never left their dog home alone. They would lock the doors with a hotel door lock in the deadbolt. Every sound made them jump, every shadow scared them, and there was nothing I felt I could do to make it better.

This began Kenogi's journey to freedom. Kenogi did go back one more time, to gather as much stuff as they could fit in their car, along with a trusted third-party, and that was the last time their old "support system" was ever seen. It was not however, then end of the journey for Kenogi, or myself.

While they were close enough to me, it was still a 30-45 minute drive for me to get there. They would not know if their parents were coming, and it would be far too long before I'd be able to get to them. What could happen in that 30-45 minutes? I became hyper-vigilant too.

I would worry about them daily. I couldn't just drop work and rush over there. I couldn't keep them safe 24/7. Their parents called doctors, friends, and other people trying to track Kenogi down. Through some of these people, we found out that they'd hired a private investigator.

"Someone" called one of these people claiming to be Kenogi's brother, and trying to find them. Kenogi does not have any brothers. Professionals who were involved in the situation advised Kenogi that their parents were trying to get a conservatorship against them, as they were harassing them to the point legal actions were taken against their parents. This threat and many others were made.

At one point, a tracking device, that was unknowingly hidden in Kenogi's backpack, made a noise and they found it. They had (prior to this) started to slightly come out of hyper-vigilance, but this sent it back into overdrive. It was beginning to seem for every one step forward, we would be forced back by thirty steps.

I would come over on the weekends, stay from Friday to Sunday. We would cook together, grill out, hang out with neighbors, but as soon as I would leave, the hyper-vigilance would kick in again for both of us. Neither of us felt they were fully safe. They would see a car that looked like their parent's car, and would go into panic.

There were little things that Kenogi would do, that confused me. Just things that their training had taught them was the correct thing to do. I remember a conversation we had in a grocery store parking lot one time. Kenogi was driving, and they parked in the far back of the parking lot. For context, I have back problems, and generally have to use a wheelchair in the grocery store.

I asked Kenogi why they parked in the "back 40," when there were plenty of spaces near the front. They paused, thought about it for a moment, and realized it was because they'd been trained to park there for "safety" reasons.

Which, when explained, they realized didn't really make sense. It was because if you park at the front, someone could attack you easier and you wouldn't be safe. But logically, if you're parked in the front, you're more likely to be helped by a stranger than if you're far away from the door.

We would run across other things like this all the time over the next year. Random things from their "trainings" that made no sense from a safety perspective, but were trained as safety related things.

We have worked together on the "de-programming" process. Over this chapter, you will read about what you as the support person will need to know and do. We've learned all of these things together, and I hope that our process will help you.

I will see you on the other side of the chapter, for my after-thoughts.

– AP

FREQUENTLY ASKED QUESTIONS AND ANSWERS

HOW ARE PEOPLE COMING FROM A FAMILY CULT THAT WERE HOMESCHOOLED VIEWED?

The perception of children in Christian Fundamental Family Cults that have been homeschooled can vary widely in society, with opinions often shaped by cultural, religious, and ideological differences. It's important to recognize that these perceptions are not universal, and individuals within these families can have diverse experiences. It is important to understand how we are perceived in society, before anyone can support someone in recovery of a Family Cult. Here are some common perspectives:

Positive Views:

Values and Morality: Some people view children in Christian fundamentalist homeschooling families positively, seeing them as being raised with strong moral and religious values. The emphasis on character development and ethical principles is often appreciated by those who share similar beliefs.

Family Bonding: Supporters of homeschooling may see the close family bonds that often result from homeschooling as a positive aspect. The opportunity for parents to actively participate in their children's education and the fostering of a tight-knit family unit are viewed favorably by some.

Academic Achievement: In some cases, homeschooled children from Christian fundamentalist families are recognized for academic achievements. The personalized attention and tailored curriculum may contribute to success in certain academic areas.

Negative Views:

Social Isolation: Critics often express concern about the social isolation of homeschooled children in Christian fundamentalist families. Limited exposure to diverse perspectives, cultures, and ideas may be seen as hindering social development.

Lack of Diversity: Homeschooling within a Christian fundamentalist context may be criticized for providing a narrow view of the world. The absence of exposure to a variety of beliefs and lifestyles may be considered detrimental to a child's understanding of diversity.

Potential for Indoctrination: There are concerns about the potential for indoctrination, where children may be taught a specific worldview without exposure to alternative perspectives. Critics argue that this can limit critical thinking skills and discourage independent thought.

Gender Roles: Some view the reinforcement of traditional gender roles within Christian fundamentalist homeschooling as restrictive, potentially limiting opportunities and choices for girls and boys based on predetermined roles.

Limited Access to Comprehensive Education: Critics may argue that homeschooling in these contexts might not provide a well-rounded education, especially in areas such as science, history, or sex education, where materials are filtered through a specific ideological lens.

Religious Intolerance: Concerns about religious intolerance may arise, particularly if the curriculum emphasizes exclusivity and promotes a worldview that is intolerant of other religious beliefs or secular perspectives.

Public opinion regarding children of Christian fundamentalist homeschoolers is often shaped by broader debates about educational choices, religious freedom, and the balance between parental rights and the well-being of the child. It's essential to approach these discussions with sensitivity and an understanding of the diverse experiences within such families.

HOW TO PERSONALLY PREPARE BEFORE SUPPORTING SOMEONE COMING OUT OF A FUNDAMENTAL CHRISTIAN FAMILY CULT?

Supporting someone coming out of a fundamental Christian family cult requires careful preparation and a compassionate approach. Here's how to personally prepare:

Educate Yourself: Learn about the dynamics of cults, particularly those rooted in fundamentalist Christianity. Understand the tactics used, the psychological impact on individuals, and common challenges faced during and after leaving.

Cult Recovery Resources: Familiarize yourself with resources on cult recovery. This includes books, articles, documentaries, and support organizations that specialize in helping individuals transition out of cult environments.

Cult Expert Consultation: Consider consulting with cult recovery experts or mental health professionals experienced in dealing with the aftermath of cult involvement. Their insights can guide your approach and provide valuable information on recovery dynamics.

Nonjudgmental Attitude: Cultivate a nonjudgmental attitude. Recognize that the person may have had unique experiences shaped by their cult involvement, and approach conversations with empathy rather than judgment.

Active Listening Skills: Develop active listening skills. Allow the person to share their experiences without interruption, and validate their emotions. Avoid rushing to provide solutions; sometimes, they might need a listening ear more than advice.

Respect Autonomy: Understand and respect their autonomy. Recognize that they may need to make decisions for themselves, even if those decisions differ from what you might choose.

Cultural Sensitivity: Be culturally sensitive to the religious background of the individual. Avoid derogatory language about their former beliefs and instead focus on understanding their journey.

Foster Trust: Build trust gradually. Individuals leaving cults may have experienced betrayal and manipulation, so it's important to foster an environment where trust can be rebuilt over time.

Establish Boundaries: Set clear boundaries for yourself. Understand the emotional toll supporting someone through cult recovery may take on you, and be prepared to seek your support when needed.

Prepare for Emotional Intensity: Recognize that the recovery process can be emotionally intense. Be prepared for fluctuations in mood, potential triggers, and the need for patience during challenging moments.

Avoid Triggers: Identify potential triggers for the individual and avoid using language or engaging in activities that may be triggering. This may include refraining from discussions that could evoke memories of their cult experience.

Self-Education on Trauma: Educate yourself on trauma and its effects. Understand how trauma impacts mental health and be prepared to offer support that acknowledges the trauma without re-traumatizing.

Know Available Resources: Familiarize yourself with available resources and support networks for cult survivors. This includes mental health professionals, support groups, and organizations specializing in cult recovery.

Mindfulness Practices: Incorporate mindfulness practices into your routine. This can help you stay grounded, maintain emotional balance, and approach situations with a calm and compassionate mindset.

Regular Self-Reflection: Engage in regular self-reflection. Consider your own biases, beliefs, and reactions to ensure that your support remains unbiased and respectful of the individual's autonomy.

Be Open to Learning: Be open to learning from the person's experiences. They are the expert on their own journey, and their insights can help you understand the nuances of recovery from a fundamental Christian family cult.

Remember that supporting someone through cult recovery is a nuanced and ongoing process. Personal preparation involves continuous learning, empathy, and a commitment to fostering a safe and supportive environment for the individual's healing journey.

WHAT ARE SOME BEST PRACTICES WHEN SUPPORTING SOMEONE WHO IS RECOVERING FROM A FUNDAMENTAL CHRISTIAN FAMILY CULT?

Supporting someone recovering from a fundamental Christian family cult requires a thoughtful and empathetic approach. Here are some best practices to consider:

Listen Actively: Practice active listening without judgment. Allow the individual to share their experiences, feelings, and thoughts at their own pace.

Validate Their Experiences: Validate their emotions and experiences. Recognize that recovery from a cult involves unique challenges, and acknowledging their journey is a crucial aspect of support.

Respect Autonomy: Respect their autonomy. Understand that the recovery process is personal, and individuals need to make decisions for themselves, even if those decisions differ from what you might choose.

Provide a Safe Space: Create a safe and nonjudgmental space for open communication. Encourage them to express their thoughts and feelings without fear of criticism.

Educate Yourself: Educate yourself on the dynamics of cults, the psychological impact of cult involvement, and the challenges faced during recovery. This knowledge will help you better understand their experiences.

Be Patient: Be patient and understanding. Recovery is a gradual process, and individuals may experience emotional highs and lows as they navigate their journey.

Offer Practical Support: Offer practical support in daily life, such as helping with tasks, providing a listening ear, or assisting with logistical challenges as they rebuild their lives.

Encourage Professional Help: Encourage them to seek professional help from therapists or counselors experienced in trauma and cult recovery. Professional support can be instrumental in the healing process.

Respect Boundaries: Respect their boundaries. Understand that recovering individuals may need space or have specific limits on discussions related to their cult experiences.

Avoid Triggering Language: Be mindful of your language to avoid using triggering terms or phrases related to their past involvement in the cult.

Celebrate Milestones: Celebrate milestones in their recovery journey. Recognize and applaud their achievements, whether big or small, as they move forward in rebuilding their lives.

Encourage Social Connections: Encourage social connections outside the cult environment. Support their efforts to build relationships with individuals who share similar experiences or those who offer understanding and empathy.

Promote Self-Care: Emphasize the importance of self-care. Encourage activities that promote physical, emotional, and mental well-being, such as exercise, mindfulness, and relaxation techniques.

Be a Consistent Presence: Be a consistent and reliable presence in their life. Consistency can provide stability and reassurance during the often tumultuous process of recovery.

Provide Information on Cult Recovery Groups: Share information about cult recovery groups or support networks. Connecting with others who have gone through similar experiences can be immensely beneficial.

Empowerment and Choice: Empower them to make their own choices. Help them rebuild a sense of agency and autonomy in decision-making.

Encourage Educational Pursuits: Support educational pursuits outside the cult doctrine. Encourage the exploration of diverse perspectives and knowledge that align with their interests.

Normalize Emotions: Normalize a range of emotions. Understand that feelings of confusion, anger, or sadness are part of the recovery process, and it's okay to experience them.

Engage in Mutual Learning: Engage in mutual learning. Cultivate an environment where both you and the recovering individual can share insights and perspectives, fostering understanding and growth for both parties.

Stay Informed on Cult Recovery Resources: Stay informed about available cult recovery resources, including books, websites, and organizations that offer support. This knowledge can be valuable in guiding the recovery journey.

Remember that every individual's recovery journey is unique, and flexibility in your approach is key. Being a supportive presence involves adapting to their needs, providing encouragement, and fostering an environment conducive to healing and personal growth.

WHAT ARE SOME OF THE ABUSES SOMEONE YOU ARE SUPPORTING MIGHT HAVE EXPERIENCED WHILE IN THEIR FUNDAMENTAL CHRISTIAN FAMILY CULT?

Individuals recovering from a fundamental Christian family cult may have experienced various forms of abuse within the cult environment. The nature and extent of abuse can vary, but here are some common forms of abuse that survivors might have endured:

Psychological and Emotional Manipulation: Cult leaders often employ manipulative tactics to control members, including guilt-tripping, fear-based control, and emotional coercion.

Isolation: Individuals may have been isolated from friends and family outside the cult, limiting their exposure to external perspectives and support systems.

Authoritarian Control: Leaders exerting strict control over various aspects of members' lives, including personal choices, relationships, and even thoughts.

Spiritual Abuse: Exploitative use of religious or spiritual beliefs to manipulate and control individuals, often leading to feelings of guilt, shame, or fear.

Physical Abuse: In extreme cases, there may be instances of physical abuse, including corporal punishment or violence as a means of enforcing compliance.

Financial Exploitation: Members might have been pressured to contribute significant amounts of money to the cult, sometimes beyond their financial means.

Arranged Marriages: Control over members' romantic relationships, including arranged marriages that may not align with personal preferences or desires.

Gender-Based Oppression: Imposition of strict gender roles, where women are often subjugated and limited in their roles within the family and community.

Control Over Information: Restriction of access to information, controlling what members can read, watch, or learn to maintain a narrow worldview aligned with cult teachings.

Censorship and Punishment for Dissent: Punishment or ostracization for questioning the cult's teachings, expressing doubt, or considering leaving the group.

Shunning: Practices of shunning or isolating members who do not conform to the cult's expectations, leading to profound feelings of abandonment.

Conditional Love and Acceptance: Love and acceptance being conditioned on adherence to the cult's rules, doctrines, and expectations, creating an environment where members fear rejection.

Child Exploitation: Exploitation of children for labor, indoctrination, or other purposes, with little regard for their well-being.

Sexual Abuse: In some instances, survivors may have experienced sexual abuse within the cult, often perpetrated by leaders or other members.

Loss of Autonomy: Deprivation of personal autonomy, with decisions about education, career, and personal life being dictated by cult leaders.

Pressure to Conform: Intense pressure to conform to the cult's beliefs and practices, fostering an environment where individuality and critical thinking are discouraged.

It's crucial to approach survivors of cults with sensitivity and understanding, recognizing the complexity of their experiences. Recovery often involves addressing the trauma resulting from these forms of abuse, seeking professional support, and rebuilding a sense of autonomy and self-worth. If you are supporting someone who has experienced abuse in a fundamental Christian family cult, encouraging them to seek professional help from therapists experienced in trauma recovery is essential.

WHAT ARE SOME BEHAVIORS YOU MIGHT WITNESS FROM SOMEONE WHO IS RECOVERING FROM FUNDAMENTAL CHRISTIAN FAMILY CULTS?

Recovery from a fundamental Christian family cult is a complex process that manifests in various ways. Individuals may exhibit a range of behaviors as they navigate the challenges associated with leaving such an environment. Here are some common behaviors you might witness in someone recovering from a fundamental Christian family cult:

Identity Exploration: Engaging in a process of self-discovery as they explore their beliefs, values, and personal identity outside the constraints of the cult's doctrines.

Questioning Beliefs: Actively questioning and reevaluating the religious beliefs and doctrines they were indoctrinated with, often leading to a shift in perspectives.

Emotional Rollercoaster: Experiencing intense emotional highs and lows, including periods of anger, sadness, confusion, and joy as they grapple with the complexities of their past.

Social Withdrawal: Initially withdrawing from social interactions as they navigate feelings of isolation and reevaluate their relationships outside the cult environment.

Difficulty Trusting Others: Struggling with trust issues, as the cult experience may have involved betrayal or manipulation by people they once considered trustworthy.

Fear of Judgment: Feeling a heightened fear of judgment from outsiders due to the stigma often associated with leaving religious cults.

Guilt and Shame: Experiencing feelings of guilt and shame related to their past involvement in the cult, as well as any actions they took or were compelled to take while within it.

Loss of Faith Crisis: Going through a crisis of faith and grappling with existential questions about spirituality, morality, and the purpose of life.

Difficulty Setting Boundaries: Struggling with setting and enforcing personal boundaries, as cult environments often blur the lines between individual autonomy and group control.

Deprogramming Anxiety: Experiencing anxiety related to the deprogramming process, which involves dismantling deeply ingrained beliefs and behaviors acquired during cult involvement.

Isolation and Alienation: Feeling isolated or alienated from family members who may still be involved in the cult or from those who may not fully understand their experiences.

Rebuilding Relationships: Working to rebuild relationships with friends and family outside the cult, often requiring patience, understanding, and open communication.

Cautious Exploration: Engaging cautiously in new experiences, relationships, and belief systems, as they navigate a world beyond the confines of the cult.

Navigating Triggers: Coping with triggers that remind them of their cult experience, which may evoke strong emotional reactions and require supportive interventions.

Educational Pursuits: Pursuing education and information to fill gaps in knowledge and develop a more well-rounded understanding of the world.

Advocacy and Support Seeking: Becoming an advocate for cult awareness and seeking support from others who have experienced similar journeys.

Building Autonomy: Gradually building a sense of autonomy and self-determination, making choices based on personal values rather than external influence.

Recovery Milestones: Celebrating recovery milestones, whether big or small, as they progress along their journey of healing and self-discovery.

It's important to approach individuals recovering from fundamental Christian family cults with empathy, patience, and nonjudgmental support. Each person's experience is unique, and the behaviors they exhibit are part of a complex process of rebuilding their lives outside the confines of the cult environment.

WHY DO VICTIMS OF FAMILY CULTS SEEK CONSTANT REASSURANCE: "YOU ARE NOT MAD AT THEM," AFTER LEAVING THEIR FAMILY CULT?

Victims of family cults seeking constant reassurance that "You are not mad at them" after leaving the cult can be attributed to various psychological and emotional factors:

Conditioned Fear of Rejection: Cults often use tactics that instill a deep fear of rejection in members. Individuals leaving a family cult may carry this fear into their post-cult life, seeking reassurance to alleviate concerns of being rejected or abandoned.

Cult-Induced Guilt and Anxiety: Cults frequently employ guilt and anxiety as control mechanisms. Even after leaving, individuals may struggle with lingering feelings of guilt and anxiety, seeking reassurance to confirm that they are not the target of anger or resentment.

Uncertainty in Relationships: Leaving a family cult often means navigating new relationships and dynamics outside the controlled environment. Individuals may seek reassurance as they grapple with uncertainties about how to interpret and navigate interpersonal relationships.

Rebuilding Trust: Cults can erode trust, and individuals leaving may struggle with trusting others due to past experiences. Seeking reassurance about not being mad is an attempt to rebuild trust and ensure the stability of relationships in the aftermath of the cult.

Fear of Abandonment: Cults commonly use the fear of abandonment as a tool for control. Individuals leaving may seek reassurance to counteract this fear, wanting confirmation that their departure from the cult does not translate into abandonment in their new relationships.

Self-Doubt and Cognitive Confusion: Leaving a family cult often involves a process of reevaluating belief systems and overcoming cognitive confusion. Seeking reassurance about not being mad may stem from a place of self-doubt and a need for external validation to navigate these cognitive challenges.

Trauma Bonds and Emotional Dependence: Emotional bonds formed within the cult may create a sense of emotional dependence. Seeking reassurance can be an attempt to maintain emotional connections and prevent feelings of isolation, even if those connections were toxic.

Lingering Manipulation: Manipulative tactics employed in cults can leave lasting effects. Individuals may seek reassurance to confirm that they are not falling victim to manipulation or that their actions are not being interpreted as hostile.

Cognitive Dissonance: Leaving a family cult often involves grappling with cognitive dissonance—conflicting beliefs and emotions. Seeking reassurance helps individuals reconcile this dissonance and align their understanding of relationships with their evolving beliefs.

Transition to Autonomy: The transition to an autonomous life after leaving a family cult can be challenging. Seeking reassurance is a way for individuals to navigate this transition, gain validation, and establish a secure foundation for their newfound independence.

WHAT CAN BE EYE OPENING FOR SOMEONE THAT IS SUPPORTING SOMEONE IN FAMILY CULT RECOVERY, THAT DOES NOT HAVE A RELIGIOUS BACKGROUND?

Supporting someone recovering from a fundamental Christian family cult can be eye-opening for a non-religious person, revealing aspects of the experience that may be shocking or unfamiliar. Here are some things a non-religious supporter might discover:

Intensity of Belief Systems: The intensity and absoluteness of the belief systems within the cult may be shocking. Members may have been taught to see the world through a narrow, black-and-white lens, leaving little room for nuance or alternative perspectives.

Authoritarian Control: The level of authoritarian control exercised by cult leaders can be surprising. Individuals may have been subjected to strict rules, with their personal choices, relationships, and even thoughts tightly regulated by the cult's leadership.

Emotional Manipulation Tactics: Non-religious supporters may be shocked by the emotional manipulation tactics employed within the cult. Techniques such as guilt-tripping, love-bombing, and fear-based control can have a profound impact on individuals' emotional well-being.

Fear of Hell and Damnation: The fear of hell and damnation as a consequence of disobedience or questioning the cult's teachings may be startling. This fear can have a lasting psychological impact on survivors.

Isolation and Shunning: The practice of isolation and shunning can be shocking. Cult members may have been cut off from friends and family outside the cult, contributing to a sense of isolation and abandonment.

Rigid Gender Roles: The imposition of rigid gender roles within the cult, with limited roles for women and strict expectations for men, may be surprising. Non-religious supporters may find it challenging to comprehend the extent of these gender-based restrictions.

Repression of Critical Thinking: The deliberate repression of critical thinking and independent inquiry can be unsettling. Cult members may have been discouraged from questioning beliefs, fostering an environment where dissent is not tolerated.

Crisis Doctrines: The promotion of crisis doctrines, predicting imminent apocalyptic events or catastrophic consequences, may come as a shock. Such doctrines create a heightened sense of urgency and fear among cult members.

Pressure for Reproduction: The emphasis on large families and procreation, often justified by specific interpretations of religious texts, may be surprising. Non-religious supporters may find it difficult to understand the pressure placed on individuals to have numerous children.

Conditional Love and Acceptance: The concept of conditional love and acceptance within the cult community may be jarring. Individuals may feel that their worth is contingent on their adherence to the cult's doctrines, leading to a constant fear of rejection.

Limited Access to Information: The restricted access to information and the control over educational resources can be unexpected. Cult members may have been shielded from diverse perspectives and alternative sources of knowledge.

Post-Cult Identity Crisis: Non-religious supporters might be surprised by the identity crisis individuals face after leaving the cult. Survivors may grapple with rebuilding a sense of self and understanding their place in a world vastly different from the one they knew.

Supporting someone recovering from a fundamental Christian family cult involves recognizing and empathizing with the unique challenges posed by the interplay of intense religious beliefs, control mechanisms, and the aftermath of leaving such an environment.

WHAT ARE SOME OF THE DIFFICULTIES THAT SOMEONE MIGHT FACE AS A SUPPORT SYSTEM FOR SOMEONE IN FUNDAMENTAL CHRISTIAN FAMILY CULT RECOVERY?

Supporting someone in fundamental Christian family cult recovery can be challenging, and individuals providing support may encounter various difficulties. Here are some common challenges they might face:

Limited Understanding: Understanding the complexities of life within a family cult can be challenging for those who haven't experienced it. Supporters may struggle to grasp the full extent of the psychological, emotional, and social challenges the individual faced.

Cultural and Religious Differences: Cultural and religious differences between the supporter and the individual in recovery may pose challenges. Beliefs, values, and practices that were central to the cult may be difficult to comprehend, leading to misunderstandings or strained interactions.

Emotional Toll on Supporters: Supporting someone through cult recovery can be emotionally draining. Supporters may experience vicarious trauma as they witness the survivor's pain, emotional struggles, and the long process of rebuilding their lives.

Balancing Empathy and Objectivity: Striking a balance between empathy and objectivity can be challenging. Supporters may feel deeply for the survivor, yet they need to maintain an objective perspective to provide effective assistance and avoid becoming overwhelmed by emotions.

Navigating Triggers and Trauma: The survivor may experience triggers or trauma-related responses that are difficult for supporters to handle. Knowing how to respond appropriately and sensitively to these challenges can be a delicate balance.

Dealing with Resistance: Individuals leaving a family cult may face internal resistance due to indoctrination. Supporters may encounter challenges when trying to introduce alternative perspectives or encourage the survivor to question ingrained beliefs.

Legal and Practical Challenges: Supporters may need to navigate legal complexities if the survivor faces threats of conservatorship or other legal repercussions after leaving the family cult. Addressing practical challenges such as housing, employment, and financial independence can also be demanding.

Coping with Limited Resources: Supporters may face challenges in finding appropriate resources or services for cult recovery. Limited awareness or availability of specialized support may hinder the effectiveness of the assistance they can provide.

Maintaining Boundaries: Establishing and maintaining healthy boundaries is crucial, as supporters may find themselves deeply involved in the survivor's life. Striking a balance between offering support and respecting the survivor's autonomy can be challenging.

Lack of Professional Guidance: Supporters may lack professional guidance on how to navigate the complexities of cult recovery. Access to therapists, counselors, or support groups with expertise in this area may be limited, leaving supporters without the necessary resources.

Patience and Persistence: The recovery process is often lengthy and nonlinear. Supporters may struggle with feelings of frustration or impatience as they witness the survivor's slow progress or setbacks.

Fear of Retaliation: There may be concerns about potential retaliation from the cult or its members. Supporters may fear personal repercussions, such as social ostracism, if they actively assist the survivor in leaving the cult.

Navigating Spiritual Exploration: If the survivor is exploring alternative spiritual or religious paths, supporters may find it challenging to navigate these changes. They may need to reconcile their own beliefs with the survivor's evolving spiritual journey.

Ensuring Self-Care: Supporting someone through cult recovery can take a toll on supporters' well-being. Balancing the needs of the survivor with their own self-care becomes crucial to prevent burnout or compassion fatigue.

Overcoming these challenges requires ongoing learning, open communication, and a commitment to supporting the survivor's autonomy and healing process. Seeking guidance from professionals with expertise in cult recovery can also be beneficial for supporters facing these difficulties.

CAN SOMEONE SUPPORTING A VICTIM OF FAMILY CULTS DEVELOP PTSD FROM EXPOSURE TO THEIR TRAUMA?

Yes, individuals supporting victims of family cults can potentially develop secondary trauma or what is commonly referred to as Vicarious Trauma, and in some cases, this can lead to symptoms similar to those seen in Post-Traumatic Stress Disorder (PTSD). Here are key points to consider:

Vicarious Trauma: Vicarious trauma is the emotional and psychological toll that exposure to the trauma of others can have on individuals, particularly those in support roles. This can occur when someone is consistently exposed to the traumatic experiences of others, such as survivors of family cults.

Empathy and Connection: Support providers who deeply empathize with the experiences of survivors may internalize their pain and suffering. This intense connection can contribute to the development of symptoms similar to PTSD.

Symptoms and Impact: Individuals experiencing vicarious trauma may exhibit symptoms such as intrusive thoughts, nightmares, heightened arousal, emotional numbing, and difficulties in interpersonal relationships. These symptoms can have a significant impact on the well-being of the support provider.

Burnout and Compassion Fatigue: Continuous exposure to the trauma of family cult survivors may lead to burnout and compassion fatigue. Support providers may feel emotionally drained, fatigued, and emotionally distant as a result of the cumulative stress.

Self-Care is Crucial: Engaging in self-care practices is essential for those supporting survivors of family cults. Establishing boundaries, seeking supervision or consultation, and taking breaks to focus on personal well-being can help mitigate the risk of vicarious trauma.

Professional Support: Professionals in supportive roles, such as therapists, counselors, or advocates, should seek their own therapeutic support. Regular supervision, consultation with colleagues, and access to their own mental health care are vital components of preventing and managing vicarious trauma.

Acknowledgment and Validation: Acknowledging the potential impact of vicarious trauma and validating the emotions of support providers are critical steps in promoting an environment that fosters well-being and resilience.

While supporting victims of family cults is essential for their healing, it's equally important for those providing support to prioritize their own mental health.

Seeking professional guidance, maintaining boundaries, and practicing self-care can contribute to the overall well-being of individuals in support roles and help prevent the development of symptoms resembling PTSD.

HOW CAN THE VICTIM ASSIST IN SUPPORTING THEIR SUPPORT SYSTEM WHILE THEY ARE IN RECOVERY?

Supporting your support system while recovering from a fundamental Christian cult involves fostering open communication, setting boundaries, and recognizing the mutual nature of the relationship. Here are some ways to support those who are supporting you:

Communicate Openly: Foster open and honest communication with your support system. Share your thoughts, feelings, and progress in recovery. Transparency helps build trust and understanding.

Educate Them: Provide information about cult dynamics, recovery challenges, and the specific issues you may face. Education helps your support system better comprehend the complexities of your experience.

Set Clear Boundaries: Establish clear boundaries to protect your well-being. Communicate your needs and limits, helping your support system understand how they can best assist you without causing undue stress.

Express Gratitude: Express gratitude for their support. Acknowledge the importance of their role in your recovery journey. A simple thank-you can go a long way in reinforcing the value of their support.

Encourage Self-Care for Them: Remind your support system to prioritize their own well-being. Recovering from a cult experience can be emotionally taxing for both you and those supporting you. Encourage them to engage in self-care activities.

Provide Resources: Share resources on cult recovery and support for friends and family. This can include books, articles, or support groups that offer insights into the recovery process and tips for assisting survivors.

Be Patient and Understanding: Cultivate patience and understanding. Recovery is a gradual process, and there may be challenges along the way. Your support system will appreciate your patience as they navigate how best to assist you.

Offer a Listening Ear: Allow your support system to express their feelings and concerns. Cult recovery can impact both survivors and their supporters emotionally. Offering a listening ear creates a space for mutual understanding.

Seek Professional Guidance: Encourage your support system to seek professional guidance if needed. Therapy or counseling can be beneficial for both survivors and their supporters, providing a space to address challenges and enhance coping mechanisms.

Share Achievements and Milestones: Celebrate achievements and milestones in your recovery journey. Sharing these moments with your support system not only keeps them informed but also reinforces the positive aspects of the recovery process.

Acknowledge Their Impact: Acknowledge the impact your support system has on your recovery. Let them know how their assistance has contributed to your progress and well-being.

Provide Regular Updates: Keep your support system informed about your recovery progress. Regular updates can help them understand the evolving nature of the recovery journey and how they can adjust their support accordingly.

Encourage Open Questions: Create an environment where your support system feels comfortable asking questions. Open dialogue helps dispel misunderstandings and promotes a more informed and supportive relationship.

Participate in Joint Activities: Engage in joint activities that strengthen your connection outside the context of recovery. Shared experiences can deepen your bond and provide moments of respite from the challenges of recovery.

Respect Their Boundaries: Respect the boundaries of your support system. Understand that supporting someone in recovery may be emotionally demanding, and they may need breaks or moments for self-care.

Remember, supporting your support system is a collaborative effort. By maintaining open communication, setting boundaries, and expressing appreciation, you create a supportive dynamic that benefits both you and those assisting you on your path to recovery from a fundamental Christian cult experience.

WHY IS COMMUNICATION SO IMPORTANT BETWEEN YOU AND YOUR SUPPORT SYSTEM WHEN IN FAMILY CULT RECOVERY?

Communication is crucial between individuals in family cult recovery and their support system for several reasons:

Validation and Understanding: Open communication allows survivors to express their experiences, emotions, and challenges.

This provides an opportunity for their support system to validate their feelings and gain a deeper understanding of the impact of cult involvement.

Building Trust: Family cult recovery often involves rebuilding trust, both in oneself and in relationships. Honest and transparent communication fosters an environment where trust can be nurtured, enabling a more secure foundation for healing.

Identifying Triggers and Needs: Through communication, survivors can articulate their triggers and specific needs during the recovery process. This information helps the support system create an environment that minimizes triggers and meets the survivor's emotional and practical needs.

Establishing Boundaries: Effective communication allows survivors to set and communicate clear boundaries. This helps both survivors and their support system understand limits and ensures a more respectful and supportive interaction.

Providing Emotional Support: Sharing thoughts and feelings facilitates emotional support. Survivors benefit from knowing they have a safe space to express themselves, reducing feelings of isolation and loneliness.

Navigating Challenges: Recovery from a family cult involves facing various challenges. Communication enables survivors and their support system to collaboratively navigate these challenges, seeking solutions and providing mutual encouragement.

Coping Strategies: Discussing coping strategies is essential. Survivors can communicate what strategies are effective for them, and their support system can learn how best to provide assistance during difficult moments.

Professional Support Coordination: Open communication allows for coordination with mental health professionals or other experts. The support system can play a role in facilitating access to appropriate resources and encouraging ongoing therapeutic interventions.

Monitoring Progress: Regular communication helps monitor the survivor's progress in recovery. Recognizing positive changes, acknowledging milestones, and addressing setbacks together contribute to a more effective support system.

Mutual Understanding: Effective communication fosters a mutual understanding between survivors and their support system. This shared understanding promotes empathy, compassion, and a collaborative approach to overcoming the challenges of family cult recovery.

Encouraging Self-Advocacy: Communication empowers survivors to express their needs and preferences. Encouraging self-advocacy helps individuals take an active role in their recovery, fostering a sense of control and autonomy.

In family cult recovery, where the impact can be profound and complex, open and respectful communication is a cornerstone for building a supportive and healing environment. It promotes a sense of safety, trust, and understanding, enhancing the overall recovery process for survivors and their support system.

WHAT IS THE BEST WAY TO CREATE A SUCCESSFUL SUPPORT SYSTEM AFTER LEAVING A FAMILY CULT?

Creating a successful support system after leaving a family cult is crucial for healing and transitioning into mainstream society. Here are steps to build an effective support system:

Connect with Non-Cult Family Members: Reach out to family members who are not part of the cult. Rebuilding connections with supportive relatives can provide a foundation for emotional and practical assistance.

Seek Professional Guidance: Consult with mental health professionals experienced in trauma and cult recovery. Therapists, counselors, or psychologists can offer tailored support and coping strategies.

Join Support Groups: Seek out support groups for individuals who have left similar cults. Sharing experiences with those who understand can provide validation and a sense of community.

Network with Cult Survivors: Connect with individuals who have successfully left family cults. Learning from their experiences, insights, and coping strategies can be valuable in navigating the challenges ahead.

Engage in Therapy or Counseling: Participate in individual or group therapy to address emotional and psychological challenges. Therapists with expertise in cult recovery can guide the healing process.

Build Friendships Outside the Cult: Cults often isolate members from the outside world. Actively seek and cultivate friendships with people who share similar interests and values beyond the cult environment.

Attend Social Events: Attend social gatherings, community events, or religious services outside the cult to expand your social circle. Building connections in diverse settings can contribute to a broader support system.

Develop Mentorship Relationships: Seek mentors or role models who can provide guidance and support. Mentors can offer insights, advice, and encouragement as you navigate your new life.

Online Support Communities: Utilize online forums and communities for cult survivors. Virtual support can be accessible and provide a platform for sharing experiences and seeking advice.

Educate Trusted Friends: Educate close friends about your experiences and the challenges you may face. Cultivate relationships with individuals who are empathetic and willing to provide emotional support.

Access Legal Support: If there are legal challenges associated with leaving the cult, consult with legal professionals. Addressing legal issues can contribute to a more stable foundation for rebuilding your life.

Set Boundaries: Establish clear boundaries with individuals who may not be supportive or who may attempt to draw you back into the cult. Prioritize your well-being and emotional health.

Participate in Workshops and Seminars: Attend workshops or seminars on cult recovery and personal development. These events provide opportunities to learn from experts and connect with others on a similar journey.

Be Patient and Consistent: Building a support system takes time. Be patient with the process, and consistently invest effort in nurturing relationships and connections.

Remember that creating a successful support system is a gradual process, and it's okay to seek help from multiple sources. Tailor your support network to your individual needs and continue to prioritize self-care throughout your recovery journey.

WHAT ARE SOME TALKING POINTS TO GO OVER WITH YOUR SUPPORT SYSTEM BEFORE YOU LEAVE A FUNDAMENTAL CHRISTIAN FAMILY CULT?

Before leaving a fundamental Christian family cult, discussing certain key talking points with your support system is crucial for mutual understanding and effective assistance. Here are important topics to address:

Reasons for Leaving: Clearly communicate your reasons for leaving the family cult. This may include discussing the manipulative tactics, restrictive practices, or emotional harm you've experienced. Help your support system understand your perspective.

Impact on Mental Health: Explain how the cult environment has affected your mental health. Discuss any anxiety, trauma, or emotional distress you may have experienced and express the importance of prioritizing your mental well-being.

Desire for Autonomy: Emphasize your need for autonomy and the desire to make independent decisions about your beliefs, lifestyle, and future. Help your support system understand that you are seeking freedom from undue influence.

Boundaries and Respect: Clearly outline the boundaries you wish to establish with the cult and its members. Stress the importance of your support system respecting these boundaries and not pressuring you to conform to the cult's expectations.

Need for Emotional Support: Communicate your need for emotional support during the transition. Describe the challenges you anticipate and express how having a supportive network will be instrumental in your recovery.

Potential Repercussions: Discuss potential repercussions you may face after leaving, such as shunning, emotional manipulation, or attempts to bring you back into the fold. Prepare your support system for these possibilities and strategize how to handle them together.

Request for Confidentiality: If applicable, request confidentiality regarding your decision to leave. Discuss the potential impact on your relationships within the cult and the importance of protecting your privacy.

Educate Them About Cult Dynamics: Provide information about cult dynamics, mind control, and coercive tactics. Help your support system understand the psychological and emotional aspects of your experience, which can aid in empathizing with your journey.

Plans for the Future: Share your plans for the future, including goals, aspirations, and the kind of support you may need as you rebuild your life outside the cult. This can give your support system a clearer understanding of how they can assist you.

Address Misconceptions: Address any misconceptions your support system may have about the cult, your decision to leave, or your beliefs. Openly discuss any fears or concerns they might have and provide reassurance where needed.

Importance of Patience: Emphasize the need for patience. Leaving a cult is a complex process, and your support system's understanding and patience will be crucial as you navigate the challenges and uncertainties ahead.

Encourage Questions and Dialogue: Encourage your support system to ask questions and engage in open dialogue. This helps dispel misunderstandings and allows for a more collaborative and supportive relationship.

Provide Resources: Share resources on cult recovery for friends and family. Books, articles, or support groups can help them gain further insights into your experience and the recovery process.

Express Gratitude: Express gratitude for their willingness to support you. Acknowledge the significance of their role in your life and recovery, fostering a sense of mutual appreciation.
By addressing these talking points, you can create a foundation for understanding, empathy, and effective support as you embark on the challenging journey of leaving a fundamental Christian family cult.

CONCLUSION TO THE READER FROM THE SUPPORT PERSON

Reader, welcome back,

Now that you understand all of the components of the support person, I want to give you my personal story. It's been a long road, with lots of learning along the way.

There will be good days, and there will be bad days, but all of the days have been worth it. I've learned as I've gone. I didn't have this book, or anything like it, to be able to follow through. I had to make mistakes, correct for mistakes, trigger my partner, and apologize for the triggers.

I've walked into an unlocked door, with Kenogi expecting me, and triggered them so badly they fell on the floor crying from fear. I've walked up behind them with them knowing I'm in the room and triggered them to tears. You live and you learn.

The biggest piece of advice I can give you is this: Rely on consent. By relying on consent you not only will avoid more triggers, but you will also create a safe space. Creating that safe space will give both yourself and the person you're supporting a sense of security and safety. You will need to protect yourself just as much as you are protecting them.

Be prepared for the fallout, the sudden outbursts of anger, and the random tears. Be compassionate towards this and be there for them. When I came into this, I was not prepared for their parents to try to hunt them down. I was warned that this could/would happen, but I misjudged this and didn't believe that it was true.

When we found out they were looking for them, I went into hyper-vigilance. I stopped caring for myself, and my sole responsibility (in my own head) was to protect them. I stopped doing things that I enjoyed (video games, hobbies, going out to movies, etc) and only protected them.

You can't let yourself do this. Make time for yourself, care for yourself, and also…let your partner care for you. I refused, for way too long, to let Kenogi reciprocate the care I was giving to them. It wasn't until they forced me to sit down, play games, and enjoy a day of solitude, that I saw what I was doing to myself. I stepped back and let them take care of me for a bit.

When I stepped out of the hyper-vigilance of protecting them, I saw what they saw, and that I wasn't caring for myself. I then began freely accepting them taking care of me. I started to feel more like myself, and began enjoying the things I'd been neglecting about myself. This made my life much easier, and made our life together much easier. At one point, I almost started to feel regret about taking on these responsibilities. I almost started to dislike myself and who I was becoming because of it. SELF CARE IS IMPORTANT. Do not neglect yourself to care for the person you are supporting.

You are going to experience a lot of trauma related triggers, you're going to experience a lot of trauma related responses, and this is ok. When it happens, address it with them, calmly. Your mental health and well-being is just as important as theirs, and DO NOT FORGET THIS.

Kenogi eventually left their first apartment and moved into a new one, much closer to me. A few months later, I joined them in the same complex. We had different apartments, but we were now close enough that I felt I could keep them much safer than I previously felt.

Kenogi and I would stay at each other's places at night, weekends were their place usually, while weekdays were at mine. We would have dinner together every night, most nights we shared a bed, while others we slept separately.

Kenogi went through two different Intensive Outpatient Therapies (IOP), one was learning about Didactics through Cognitive Processing Therapy, while the other was Cognitive Behavioral Therapy. These were some of the roughest experiences we had. Kenogi did this with only a month between each of them. The first one, in comparison to the second, was a breeze. It was almost like going to sit in a class for a few weeks.

The second IOP was starkly different. The sessions were from Monday until Thursday, and by the end of the week, they were just purely raw emotion. There was no real thought process. Watching this person I cared so much about, go through this, was hell.

Before Kenogi started the second one, I had suggested taking a little time off, but the leave of absence that they had taken was running out. If they didn't go into this IOP, they would have to go back to work, and they weren't ready for that. So, we agreed mutually that they would continue their healthcare journey, because a healthy mind is a happy mind.

The Sunday before the second IOP began was a little rough. There was fear, doubt, and a lot of tears. But, this particular Sunday, unbeknownst to us, was going to be the easiest Sunday we would have for the next 6 weeks.

Each day of IOP was worse than the previous. I was working, but suggested that Kenogi stay at my home during the week. Our apartments were incredibly close, in the same complex, and it was a quick 2 minute walk. They would sleep at my place normally, and go back to theirs in the morning when I'd begin work.

I suggested Kenogi stay at my place, because they stated that they felt incredibly safe there. My place had my smell, my comfort, and my things, all of which brought them comfort. They would sit in my bed while in IOP. I suggested that they use the weighted blanket that they'd purchased me so that they would be able to feel the comfort from that after IOP.

During the first week, they were bullied and harassed by several people who were not as far into their healing journey as Kenogi was, and didn't have supportive partners. But, Kenogi barreled on. They were finding more of their voice through the healing journey that they'd been on. They were feeling more and more like someone who could do this. However, EVERY Sunday was bad.

Every Sunday would lead to "I can't do this. I don't have the strength to go through this again." This was repeated over every week of the 6 week IOP. We would sit down, talk, they would cry, and it became incredibly frustrating for me. By the end of the IOP, I was just as happy as they were that it was done, because it meant that I wouldn't have to deal with the constant barrage of the back and forth "I can't…" or "I have to do this…" messaging that I was receiving from them.

This is the struggle that you, as the support person, are going to have to deal with. IOP is difficult for both the person you're supporting, and yourself. While you are not the victim in the scenario, you may begin to feel the victim status from what you're receiving from them. It's difficult and you must know that. There is no amount of information that I can share to explain just how difficult this will be.

My personal experience has been a lot of ups and downs of emotions. This is why you remembering your self-care routine, no matter what it is, and focusing on it, is so important. You may feel hurt of your own, along with theirs, you may feel anger towards the people who brought this pain on them, you may feel anger towards the person you're supporting for taking away some of your time. But, remember that you're supporting this person by choice, and if you don't take care of yourself, nobody else will.

For myself, the turning point of going from the negative experience back to the positive experience, was seeing Kenogi's eyes. The life had returned to them after their IOPs. It was as though I was seeing these eyes I'd looked upon for over a year, for the first time.

It was at this point that I had Kenogi look at old pictures of themselves. I had not divulged that they previously had dead eyes until around this time.
They didn't understand what I meant until I had them look at old photos, from when they were still living with their parents. The contrast that they saw was enough to make them break down.

The tears that flowed from seeing their living eyes of the day, versus their dead eyes of the past, were enough to also make me cry. We shared a moment of looking at many photos and videos of the past and comparing them to photos and videos of the present. To this day, we still will go back and look at photos from even before I knew them, and it still scares us both at the difference of the two.

When this book was in it's early stages, Kenogi was originally just going to make pamphlets. They thought each of the topics, that eventually became chapters, were just going to be short little pamphlets you'd find in your mental health professionals office, like the free leaflets you find on healthcare. We had a conversation about it, and I said that it sounded as though they were wanting to write a book. They disagreed, so I said "Ok, well write it up and we'll check back in." I have a saying, "It's your lie, I'll let you tell it." I didn't say this to them at the time, but I definitely thought it.

A couple of days later, Kenogi tells me that the first one is over 60 pages. I repeated that it sounds like they're writing a book. They again declined this, and I told them that nobody is going to think 60 pages is a pamphlet, and again told them they were writing a book. We talked for a while, and I eventually told them "Just write it. Let it be, however long it needs to be." They accepted this, and as I write this, the book is nearly 400 pages long. The healing journey for both Kenogi and myself has been long, but the bumps, twists, and turns have all been worth every bit of it. Together, we have formed an amazing bond, and I don't think either of us would trade it for the world.

You, as the support person, are going to go through much more than you can expect. This is especially true if you are a romantic partner, as I am, to the person you're supporting. As I mentioned previously, remember to take care of yourself, as this journey is as much yours as it is theirs.

Since beginning this journey, I have also started seeing a therapist. I realized my mental health was being effected by this process, and it was the best thing I could've done for my mental health. I see my therapist once a month (usually), and we discuss the current status of my relationship, what is going on in my daily life, and how I'm handling the minutia of the day. Do not neglect your personal mental health, because you won't be able to handle the normal stuff of the day as well as the struggles of the person you're supporting on your own.

In closing, thank you Reader. Thank you for going on this collective journey with us. I hope that you have the ability to get yourself out of your struggle, or that you're able to help someone else get out of theirs.

– AP

CHAPTER 7

RECOVERY

....

Trigger Warning: Sensitive Content

This content may contain information or discussions that could be distressing or triggering for some individuals. Topics may include but are not limited to trauma, abuse, violence, or other potentially upsetting subject matter. Reader discretion is advised. If you find that you are emotionally impacted by such content, it is recommended to seek support or refrain from reading further. Your well-being is important.

Recovery for someone leaving a fundamental Christian family cult is a deeply personal and multifaceted journey. Here are some aspects that may be part of the recovery process:

Identity Exploration: Individuals may need to rediscover their own beliefs, values, and identity outside of the cult's influence. This could involve questioning previously held beliefs, exploring new perspectives, and forming a sense of self that feels authentic and empowering.

Emotional Healing: Many individuals leaving cults experience emotional trauma, including feelings of guilt, shame, fear, and betrayal. Recovery often involves processing these emotions, seeking therapy or counseling, and developing healthy coping strategies for managing stress and anxiety.

Education and Empowerment: Learning about cult dynamics, manipulation tactics, and healthy boundaries can be empowering and help individuals understand their experiences within the cult. Education may also involve acquiring new skills, pursuing education or career opportunities, and gaining independence and self-sufficiency.

Support and Community: Having a supportive network of friends, family members, therapists, or fellow survivors can be invaluable during the recovery process. Support groups for survivors of cults or religious trauma can provide validation, understanding, and a sense of belonging.

Self-Discovery and Growth: Recovery from a cult experience can be an opportunity for personal growth and self-discovery. Individuals may explore new interests, passions, and beliefs, and develop a stronger sense of autonomy, agency, and purpose in life.

Healing from Spiritual Trauma: For individuals who experienced spiritual abuse or manipulation within the cult, recovery may involve finding new sources of spiritual or existential meaning and healing from religious or spiritual trauma.

Recovery from leaving a fundamental Christian family cult is a complex and ongoing process that may take time, patience, and support. It's important for individuals to prioritize self-care, seek professional help if needed, and honor their own unique journey towards healing and liberation.

SEVEN STAGES OF GRIEF

The seven stages of grief, often referred to as the "Seven Stages of Grief and Loss," were introduced by psychiatrist Elisabeth Kübler-Ross in her book "On Death and Dying" published in 1969. It's important to note that these stages are not necessarily experienced in a linear or fixed sequence, and individuals may move through them in different ways. The stages are:

Shock and Denial: The initial reaction to loss is often shock and denial. This stage involves a sense of disbelief or numbness as individuals try to process the reality of the situation. It serves as a protective mechanism to absorb the impact of the loss gradually.

Pain and Guilt: As the shock begins to wear off, the pain of the loss becomes more pronounced. This stage involves experiencing intense emotions, including guilt, regret, or self-blame. Individuals may reflect on what they could have done differently or harbor feelings of responsibility.

Anger and Bargaining: Anger can manifest as a natural response to loss. Individuals may direct their anger outward, toward others or the circumstances, as they grapple with the unfairness of the situation. Bargaining may involve attempts to negotiate or make deals to reverse or mitigate the loss.

Depression and Reflection: The depth of the loss often leads to a period of sadness and reflection. This stage involves coming to terms with the reality of the situation and facing the emotional weight of the loss. Individuals may withdraw, experience feelings of loneliness, and reflect on the impact of the loss on their lives.

The Upward Turn: Gradually, individuals may begin to see signs of improvement. The intense pain starts to subside, and a sense of acceptance emerges. This stage marks the beginning of a positive shift, as individuals find ways to cope with the loss and move forward.

Reconstruction and Working Through: In this stage, individuals actively work on rebuilding their lives. They may engage in new activities, establish routines, and develop coping mechanisms. This phase involves adapting to the changes brought about by the loss and seeking ways to move forward.

Acceptance and Hope: Acceptance does not imply forgetting or completely overcoming the loss. Instead, it signifies finding a way to integrate the loss into one's life. Individuals in this stage can envision a future that includes the impact of the loss but also holds hope and the potential for new beginnings.

It's important to recognize that grief is a highly individual experience, and not everyone will go through all these stages or in the same order. Additionally, individuals may revisit certain stages, and the process is not linear. Kübler-Ross's model has been widely influential, but it's crucial to approach grief with flexibility and an understanding of its unique nature for each person.

FREQUENTLY ASKED QUESTIONS AND ANSWERS

WHY DO RECOVERING FAMILY CULT MEMBERS EXPERIENCE THE SEVEN STAGES OF GRIEF AFTER LEAVING?

Recovering family cult members often experience the seven stages of grief after leaving due to the profound and complex nature of the transition. Leaving a family cult can be akin to losing an entire way of life, including relationships, beliefs, and a sense of identity.
Here's how the seven stages of grief may manifest in this context:

Shock and Denial: Initially, individuals leaving a family cult may experience shock and disbelief as they confront the reality of their decision. They might struggle to accept the extent of the changes and the departure from familiar beliefs and routines.

Pain and Guilt: As the shock subsides, the pain of leaving and the complexity of the emotions involved can become apparent. Recovering family cult members may grapple with guilt, questioning their decisions and feeling responsible for any perceived shortcomings or failures.

Anger and Bargaining: Anger can arise as individuals process the injustices or manipulations experienced within the family cult. This stage may involve anger directed at the cult leaders, the system, or even oneself. Bargaining could manifest as attempts to reconcile past actions or regain elements of the old life.

Depression and Reflection: Leaving a family cult often involves a deep sense of loss, leading to a period of sadness and reflection. Recovering members may confront the reality of severed relationships, isolation, and the impact of cult-induced beliefs on their well-being.

The Upward Turn: Gradually, as individuals distance themselves from the cult's influence, they may begin to see signs of improvement. This stage involves a shift toward acceptance and a recognition that positive changes are possible outside the constraints of the family cult.

Reconstruction and Working Through: Recovering family cult members actively engage in rebuilding their lives. This stage includes forming new connections, establishing personal boundaries, and developing coping mechanisms to navigate the challenges of adapting to a life beyond the cult.

Acceptance and Hope: Ultimately, the process leads to acceptance. Recovering members integrate the experience of leaving the family cult into their identity and narrative. While acknowledging the impact of the cult, they find hope in the potential for a fulfilling life outside its influence.

Again, it's essential to emphasize that these stages are not linear, and individuals may move back and forth between them. The journey of recovery is highly individual, influenced by the specific dynamics of the family cult, personal experiences, and the support available during the process. Seeking professional help and connecting with support networks can be instrumental in navigating the complexities of grief and recovery after leaving a family cult.

SELF-SOOTHING

Self-soothing refers to the intentional and conscious efforts an individual makes to comfort, calm, and regulate their own emotions. It involves engaging in activities or practices that bring a sense of relaxation, peace, and emotional stability. Self-soothing techniques are particularly valuable in managing stress, anxiety, and emotional distress. These practices vary widely and can be tailored to an individual's preferences and needs. Some common self-soothing techniques include:

Deep Breathing: Slow, intentional breathing can help activate the body's relaxation response, reducing stress and promoting calmness.

Mindfulness Meditation: Practicing mindfulness involves being present in the moment without judgment. Meditation techniques can help individuals focus their attention and alleviate anxiety.

Visualizations: Imagining calming scenes or engaging in mental imagery can create a sense of peace and distraction from stressors.

Progressive Muscle Relaxation (PMR): Systematically tensing and relaxing different muscle groups promotes physical relaxation and reduces tension.

Listening to Calming Music: Music has the power to influence emotions. Listening to soothing music can have a calming effect on the mind and body.

Engaging in a Hobby: Activities such as drawing, painting, knitting, or any hobby that brings joy and focus can serve as a form of self-soothing.

Taking a Warm Bath or Shower: The soothing effect of warm water can help relax muscles and alleviate stress.

Aromatherapy: Scents like lavender, chamomile, or other calming essential oils can be used to create a soothing environment.

Physical Exercise: Engaging in moderate physical activity, such as walking or yoga, can release endorphins and improve mood.

Reading or Watching Comforting Content: Escaping into a good book, movie, or TV show can provide a mental break and offer a sense of comfort.

Grounding Techniques: Practices like grounding exercises, where individuals focus on sensory experiences in the present moment, can help reduce anxiety.

Journaling: Writing down thoughts and feelings can provide a therapeutic outlet and help individuals process emotions.

Self-soothing is a valuable skill that individuals can develop to manage their emotional well-being. It becomes especially important for those navigating the challenges of recovery after leaving environments like family cults, where emotional distress and trauma may be prevalent.

FREQUENTLY ASKED QUESTIONS AND ANSWERS

WHEN IS IT MOST IMPORTANT TO SELF-SOOTHE?

Self-soothing is important in various situations, and its relevance can be particularly crucial during specific times, including:

High-Stress Situations: In moments of heightened stress, when emotions are intense and overwhelming, self-soothing techniques can help individuals regain control and manage their emotional responses effectively.

Conflict or Confrontation: When facing conflict or confrontation, self-soothing becomes essential to prevent impulsive reactions and promote thoughtful, measured responses. It allows individuals to navigate challenging situations with greater composure.

After Traumatic Triggers: Individuals who have experienced trauma, such as those leaving a family cult, may encounter triggers that evoke distressing memories. Self-soothing is crucial in these moments to address heightened emotions and promote a sense of safety.

Before Sleep: Establishing a self-soothing routine before bedtime can contribute to better sleep quality. This is particularly important for those who may experience sleep disturbances or anxiety related to their past experiences.

Transitioning to Independence: For individuals leaving controlling environments, like family cults, the process of transitioning to independence can be overwhelming. Self-soothing techniques assist in managing the challenges and uncertainties associated with this transition.

Moments of Isolation or Loneliness: Feelings of isolation or loneliness can trigger emotional distress. Engaging in self-soothing activities helps individuals cope with these emotions and build a sense of comfort even when alone.

During Intense Emotions: When experiencing intense emotions like anger, sadness, or anxiety, self-soothing is crucial for preventing emotional escalation and promoting emotional regulation.

Periods of Uncertainty: Times of uncertainty, such as major life changes or decision-making processes, can create stress and anxiety. Self-soothing practices offer stability and help individuals navigate uncertainty with a clearer mind.

After Negative Triggers: Exposure to negative triggers, whether in the form of memories or external stimuli, can elicit distress. Self-soothing becomes a tool for managing the aftermath of these triggers and promoting emotional well-being.

Moments of Overwhelm: When feeling overwhelmed by responsibilities, challenges, or multiple stressors, self-soothing provides a way to break down overwhelming emotions into manageable components.

Recovery from Emotional Flashbacks: Individuals who experience emotional flashbacks related to past trauma may benefit significantly from self-soothing techniques to ground themselves in the present and manage the effects of the flashback.

In essence, self-soothing is valuable during any situation where emotions are heightened or when individuals need to navigate challenges while maintaining emotional balance. Developing a personalized repertoire of self-soothing practices can enhance resilience and contribute to overall emotional well-being.

WHY IS SELF-SOOTHING SO IMPORTANT FOR YOU AND YOUR SUPPORT SYSTEM?

Self-soothing is crucial for individuals and their support systems, especially those recovering from the aftermath of family cult experiences, for several reasons:

Emotional Regulation: Self-soothing techniques help regulate emotions, allowing individuals to manage intense feelings such as anxiety, fear, or anger. This is particularly important for those who may have experienced emotional turmoil within the family cult.

Stress Reduction: The aftermath of leaving a family cult can be inherently stressful. Self-soothing practices, whether through relaxation exercises, mindfulness, or other calming activities, contribute to stress reduction, promoting overall well-being.

Enhanced Coping Skills: Cultivating self-soothing skills enhances an individual's coping mechanisms. It provides practical tools to navigate challenging situations, reducing the likelihood of feeling overwhelmed or resorting to unhealthy coping strategies.

Improved Sleep Quality: Many individuals leaving family cults struggle with sleep disturbances due to anxiety and trauma. Self-soothing techniques can positively impact sleep quality by calming the mind and promoting a more relaxed state before bedtime.

Empowerment and Autonomy: Self-soothing fosters a sense of empowerment and autonomy. It allows individuals to take an active role in their emotional well-being, reinforcing the idea that they have control over their internal state.

Connection with Support System: Teaching self-soothing techniques to a support system creates a shared language and understanding. This connection enhances communication and empathy, as both individuals and their support system work together to promote emotional well-being.

Prevention of Escalation: Self-soothing practices act as preventative measures to avoid escalation of emotional distress. By addressing minor stressors early on, individuals can prevent these stressors from intensifying into more challenging emotional states.

Increased Resilience: Regular use of self-soothing techniques contributes to the development of emotional resilience. It helps individuals bounce back from setbacks and navigate future challenges with greater ease.

Positive Coping Strategies: Engaging in self-soothing activities replaces potentially harmful coping strategies with positive alternatives. This shift is essential for individuals leaving family cults, as they transition from maladaptive coping mechanisms to healthier ways of managing stress and emotions.

Promotion of Mental Health: Prioritizing self-soothing is a fundamental aspect of maintaining mental health. It contributes to emotional balance, reduces the risk of mental health challenges, and supports ongoing recovery and healing.

Both individuals and their support systems can benefit from incorporating self-soothing practices into their routines. Whether through mindfulness exercises, relaxation techniques, or other personalized methods, self-soothing plays a vital role in creating a foundation for emotional well-being and post-traumatic recovery.

SELF-CARE

Self-care is the practice of taking deliberate actions to maintain and improve one's overall well-being. It involves activities that prioritize physical, mental, and emotional health, fostering a positive relationship with oneself. Examples include exercise, rest, mindfulness, and activities that bring joy and relaxation.

FREQUENTLY ASKED QUESTIONS AND ANSWERS

WHAT CAN SELF CARE LOOK LIKE AFTER LEAVING A FAMILY CULT?

Leaving a family cult is a challenging and courageous step, and practicing self-care is essential for your well-being during the recovery process.

Here are some best practices for self-care after leaving a family cult:

Seek Professional Support: Connect with mental health professionals experienced in trauma, cult recovery, or post-cult counseling. Their expertise can provide valuable insights and support tailored to your specific needs.

Build a Support System: Cultivate relationships with individuals outside the cult who understand and support your journey. Share your experiences with trusted friends, family, or support groups to help alleviate feelings of isolation.

Educate Yourself: Learn about the dynamics of cults, manipulation tactics, and the recovery process. Understanding the psychological aspects of your experience can empower you to navigate the challenges more effectively.

Establish Healthy Boundaries: Set clear and healthy boundaries in your relationships. Clearly communicate your needs and limitations to others, and prioritize your emotional and physical well-being.

Practice Mindfulness and Grounding Techniques: Engage in mindfulness activities and grounding techniques to stay present and manage anxiety. Activities such as deep breathing, meditation, or yoga can be beneficial for reducing stress.

Celebrate Small Achievements: Acknowledge and celebrate your progress, no matter how small. Recognize the steps you've taken towards personal growth and healing.

Engage in Self-Reflection: Reflect on your values, beliefs, and goals. Self-discovery can be a crucial part of rebuilding your identity outside the cult environment.

Physical Well-being: Prioritize your physical health by maintaining a balanced diet, regular exercise, and adequate sleep. Physical well-being contributes to mental and emotional resilience.

Engage in Creative Outlets: Explore creative activities that bring joy and self-expression. Whether it's art, writing, music, or other forms of creativity, these outlets can be therapeutic.

Set Realistic Goals: Establish realistic and achievable short-term and long-term goals. Celebrate your accomplishments along the way and recognize that recovery is a gradual process.

Connect with Cult Survivors: Join support groups or online communities for individuals who have left similar cult environments. Sharing experiences and insights with others who understand can provide validation and encouragement.

Educational Pursuits: Consider pursuing educational opportunities that align with your interests and goals. This can enhance your knowledge, skills, and overall well-being.

Counseling and Therapy: Engage in counseling or therapy to explore and address the emotional impact of your cult experience. Therapists with expertise in trauma and cult recovery can provide valuable guidance.

Cultivate Hobbies and Interests: Explore new hobbies or reignite past interests. Engaging in activities that bring you joy and fulfillment contributes to a sense of purpose and identity.

Be Patient with Yourself: Recovery is a gradual process, and it's essential to be patient and compassionate with yourself. Allow yourself the time and space needed for healing and growth.

Remember that self-care is a personal journey, and finding what works best for you may involve trial and error. Tailor these practices to your unique needs and seek professional guidance when necessary.

WHAT ARE SOME SELF CARE TECHNIQUES AND TIPS?

Self-care involves intentional actions and practices that individuals engage in to maintain and improve their overall well-being, both physically and mentally. Here are some self-care techniques:

<u>Physical Self-Care:</u>

Regular Exercise: Engaging in physical activities that you enjoy, whether it's walking, jogging, or yoga.

Adequate Sleep: Prioritizing and maintaining a consistent sleep schedule for better physical and mental health.

Healthy Nutrition: Eating a balanced diet with nourishing foods to support overall health.

Emotional and Mental Self-Care:

Mindfulness and Meditation: Practicing techniques that promote present-moment awareness and relaxation.

Journaling: Writing down thoughts and feelings as a way to process and reflect on experiences.

Therapy or Counseling: Seeking professional help to address emotional concerns and gain coping strategies.

Social Self-Care:

Maintaining Relationships: Nurturing positive connections with friends, family, or a support network.

Setting Boundaries: Establishing and communicating healthy limits in relationships to prevent burnout.

Intellectual Self-Care:

Continuous Learning: Engaging in activities that stimulate the mind, such as reading, taking courses, or learning new skills.

Problem-Solving: Developing effective problem-solving strategies to handle life challenges.

Spiritual Self-Care (Optional):

Meditation or Prayer: Connecting with a higher power or engaging in reflective practices for spiritual well-being.

Engaging in Meaningful Activities: Pursuing activities that align with personal values and contribute to a sense of purpose.

Relaxation and Leisure:

Hobbies: Spending time on activities that bring joy and relaxation, whether it's art, music, or other interests.

Unplugging: Taking breaks from technology and screens to reduce stress and promote mental clarity.

Remember, self-care is individualized, and what works for one person may differ from another. It's about finding a balance that supports your physical, emotional, and mental health.

FEELING SAFE

Several factors contribute to the difficulty individuals face in feeling safe after leaving a family cult:

Fear of Retaliation: Cults often instill fear of consequences for leaving or speaking out against the group. Individuals may fear retaliation or harm, making it challenging to feel safe even in a new environment.

Emotional Manipulation: Cults commonly use emotional manipulation to control members. Even after leaving, individuals may carry the emotional scars of manipulation, leading to a persistent sense of vulnerability and mistrust.

Cult-Induced Paranoia: Cults may cultivate a sense of paranoia, convincing members that external influences are threats. This paranoia can persist after leaving, making it difficult for individuals to feel secure in their surroundings.

Trauma Bonds: Emotional bonds formed within the cult can create a conflicted sense of safety. Individuals may have experienced both harm and a sense of belonging within the cult, leading to confusion and difficulty trusting new environments.

Lack of Social Support: Leaving a family cult often means leaving behind the primary social support structure. The absence of familiar faces and a sense of community can contribute to feelings of isolation and insecurity.

Identity Crisis: Leaving a cult often involves a significant identity crisis. Individuals may struggle to define themselves outside the context of the cult, leading to feelings of vulnerability and a lack of a stable identity.

Cultural and Religious Conditioning: Cults often use cultural or religious conditioning to create a worldview that fosters dependency. Individuals may carry this conditioning into their post-cult life, impacting their ability to feel secure in different environments.

Fear of Judgment: Leaving a cult can bring about fear of judgment from others who may not understand the dynamics of cult involvement. This fear of being judged or misunderstood can contribute to a sense of insecurity.

Difficulty Trusting Others: Cults exploit trust and often betray their members' trust. Individuals leaving may find it challenging to trust new people or institutions, hindering their ability to feel safe in relationships.

Cognitive Dissonance: Leaving a family cult involves reconciling conflicting beliefs and emotions. This cognitive dissonance can create internal turmoil, contributing to a general sense of unease and difficulty in feeling secure.

Fear of Abandonment: Cults often manipulate members by inducing a fear of abandonment. After leaving, individuals may carry this fear into their relationships, making it challenging to trust that others won't abandon them.

Overcoming these challenges typically requires a combination of therapeutic support, a supportive social network, and a gradual process of rebuilding trust and self-identity. Professional counseling can be instrumental in helping individuals navigate the psychological aftermath of leaving a family cult and develop strategies to establish a sense of safety and security in their new lives.

FREQUENTLY ASKED QUESTIONS AND ANSWERS

HOW CAN YOU HELP SOMEONE FEEL SAFE AFTER LEAVING A FAMILY CULT?

Leaving a family cult can be incredibly challenging, both emotionally and psychologically. Here are some ways I can help someone feel safe:

Validation: Provide validation for their experiences and emotions, acknowledging the difficulty of leaving a cult and the courage it took to do so.

Listening Ear: Be a non-judgmental listener, allowing them to express their thoughts and feelings without fear of criticism or rejection.

Education: Offer information about cult dynamics, manipulation tactics, and recovery strategies, empowering them with knowledge to understand their experience and navigate their healing journey.

Support Networks: Connect them with support groups, therapy resources, or online communities where they can find solidarity and understanding from others who have gone through similar experiences.

Safety Planning: Help them develop a safety plan, which may include strategies for dealing with triggers, establishing boundaries with family members still involved in the cult, and accessing resources for physical and emotional safety.

Self-Care Practices: Suggest self-care practices such as mindfulness, relaxation techniques, exercise, and creative outlets to help them cope with stress and trauma.

Rebuilding Trust: Assist in rebuilding trust in themselves and others, emphasizing their own autonomy and worthiness outside of the cult's influence.

Encouragement: Offer encouragement and support as they navigate the ups and downs of their recovery journey, celebrating their progress and resilience along the way.

As the support system, you play a crucial role in helping the victim feel safe after leaving a family cult because you provide understanding, validation, and unconditional support. You offer a sense of belonging and acceptance, which is often lacking in cult environments where conformity and obedience are emphasized.

Additionally, as the support system, you can help navigate the challenges of transitioning to life outside the cult, offer practical assistance, and provide emotional reassurance during difficult times.

WHAT ARE SOME WAYS YOU CAN HELP MAKE YOURSELF FEEL SAFE AFTER LEAVING A FAMILY CULT?

It's crucial for people leaving a family cult to understand that feeling safe and finding a sense of security is a gradual process that may take time. They may need to rebuild their support networks, establish boundaries with former cult members, and seek professional help if needed. It's also important to recognize that healing from the trauma of cult experiences can be complex and may require patience, self-compassion, and understanding.

Building a new community of supportive individuals who respect their autonomy and choices can be instrumental in the journey towards feeling safe and empowered. Here are some ways you can assist yourself in feeling safe after leaving a family cult:

Seek therapy or counseling: Process your experiences, heal from trauma, and develop coping strategies.

Educate yourself about cult dynamics: Grow your understanding of manipulation tactics, and healthy boundaries to better understand your experiences and protect yourself in the future.

Build a support network: Building a network of understanding friends, family members, or fellow survivors who can offer empathy, validation, and encouragement.

Engage in self-care practices: Using techniques such as mindfulness, meditation, exercise, and hobbies that promote emotional well-being and self-compassion.

Set boundaries with former cult members: Protect your mental and emotional health with setting healthy, but firm boundaries. This will be crucial moving forward to ensure a balanced life.

Explore new beliefs: Do not be afraid of exploring new beliefs, and/or values that interest or resonate with your authentic self. It is key to promote personal growth and fulfillment.

Seek legal advice or support if you experienced abuse or exploitation within the cult: In some cases it is important to hold perpetrators accountable and seek justice.

Take gradual steps to reintegrate into mainstream society: It is extremely important to take steps to reintegrate yourself into mainstream society. Seeking employment, and finding social activities that align with your values and goals will assist in the reintegration process.

Remember that healing is a journey, and it's okay to seek help and take things one step at a time. You deserve to feel safe, empowered, and supported as you reclaim your life after leaving a family cult.

SAFE SPACE

A safe space refers to an environment or setting where individuals feel comfortable, accepted, and free from judgment. It is a space that promotes emotional well-being, encourages open communication, and allows for self-expression without fear of criticism or harm. In a safe space, individuals can share their thoughts, feelings, and experiences without concerns about negative consequences. Key characteristics of a safe space include:

Non-Judgmental Atmosphere: Individuals in a safe space can express themselves without fear of judgment. The atmosphere is supportive and accepting of diverse perspectives.

Trust and Confidentiality: Trust is a fundamental element of a safe space. Individuals should feel confident that what they share will be treated with confidentiality and respect.

Emotional Safety: Emotional safety means that individuals feel secure in expressing their emotions, vulnerabilities, and concerns without the fear of ridicule or dismissal.

Respect for Boundaries: Safe spaces respect individuals' boundaries, ensuring that personal limits and comfort levels are acknowledged and honored.

Inclusivity: Safe spaces are inclusive and embrace diversity. They recognize and respect the unique identities, backgrounds, and experiences of each individual.

Empathy and Support: Empathy and support are essential components. Individuals in a safe space receive understanding, encouragement, and assistance when needed.

Freedom of Expression: Individuals have the freedom to express themselves authentically. This includes sharing thoughts, experiences, and opinions without fear of retaliation.

Physical Safety: In some contexts, physical safety is also considered. It ensures that individuals are protected from harm or any form of physical threat.

Safe spaces can be created in various settings, including homes, workplaces, educational institutions, and community groups. They play a crucial role in fostering emotional well-being, facilitating open communication, and supporting individuals in their personal growth and recovery journeys.

FREQUENTLY ASKED QUESTIONS AND ANSWERS

HOW CAN YOU CREATE A SAFE SPACE FOR SOMEONE YOU ARE SUPPORTING THAT IS GOING THROUGH FUNDAMENTAL CHRISTIAN CULT RECOVERY?

Creating a safe space for someone going through fundamental Christian cult recovery involves fostering an environment that promotes trust, understanding, and emotional support. Here are ways to establish a safe space:

Listen Without Judgment: Be a compassionate and non-judgmental listener. Allow them to express their thoughts, feelings, and experiences without fear of criticism or condemnation.

Validate Their Feelings: Acknowledge and validate their emotions. Let them know that their feelings are valid and understandable given their unique journey.

Respect Their Boundaries: Understand and respect their boundaries. Avoid pressuring them to share more than they are comfortable with, and be mindful of topics that may trigger distress.

Be Patient: Recovery is a gradual process. Be patient and understanding, recognizing that healing takes time. Avoid rushing or imposing expectations on their journey.

Avoid Imposing Beliefs: Refrain from imposing your own beliefs or perspectives. Instead, support them in exploring their own thoughts and feelings, respecting their autonomy in the recovery process.

Offer Emotional Support: Provide emotional support by expressing care, empathy, and reassurance. Let them know that you are there for them and committed to supporting their well-being.

Educate Yourself: Take the time to educate yourself about the dynamics of cults, recovery processes, and the challenges they may face. This knowledge can help you offer more informed and sensitive support.

Encourage Self-Expression: Encourage them to express themselves creatively or through journaling. This can be a therapeutic outlet for processing emotions and thoughts.

Respect Religious Identity: If they retain a religious identity, respect their beliefs without judgment. Recognize that their recovery may involve a reevaluation of their faith, and support them in navigating this process.

Celebrate Progress: Acknowledge and celebrate their progress, no matter how small. Recognize the steps they take toward healing and self-discovery.

Offer Practical Assistance: Provide practical assistance if needed, whether it's helping with daily tasks, accompanying them to appointments, or offering a supportive presence during challenging moments.

Connect with Support Networks: Help them connect with support networks, such as therapy groups, online communities, or counseling services specializing in cult recovery. Connecting with others who share similar experiences can be valuable.

Avoid Triggers: Be mindful of potential triggers and avoid bringing up sensitive topics without their consent. Respect their emotional vulnerabilities and create an environment that minimizes distress.

Remember that creating a safe space is an ongoing commitment, and your support can play a crucial role in their journey toward recovery.

WHAT ARE SOME WAYS YOU CAN CREATE A SAFE SPACE FOR YOURSELF?

Creating a safe space for yourself after leaving a family cult involves both physical and emotional considerations. Here are some ways to do so:

Establish Boundaries: Set clear boundaries with former cult members or anyone else who may try to influence or manipulate you. This includes limiting contact with individuals who do not respect your autonomy or choices.

Cultivate Supportive Relationships: Surround yourself with understanding and empathetic individuals who validate your experiences and provide emotional support. This could include friends, family members, therapists, or support groups for survivors of cults or trauma.

Engage in Self-Care: Prioritize activities and practices that promote your physical, mental, and emotional well-being. This could include exercise, meditation, journaling, spending time in nature, or engaging in hobbies that bring you joy and relaxation.

Create a Safe Physical Environment: Ensure that your living space feels comfortable, secure, and reflects your personal preferences and values. This might involve decorating in a way that feels nurturing and soothing, implementing safety measures, and surrounding yourself with items that bring you comfort.

Educate Yourself: Learn about cult dynamics, manipulation tactics, and healthy boundaries to better understand your experiences and empower yourself to protect against potential harm in the future.

Seek Professional Help: Consider therapy or counseling to process your experiences, heal from trauma, and develop coping strategies for navigating life outside the cult.

Practice Self-Compassion: Be gentle with yourself as you navigate the challenges of leaving a cult and rebuilding your life. Recognize that healing is a journey and allow yourself to progress at your own pace.

By prioritizing your well-being, setting boundaries, and surrounding yourself with supportive people and environments, you can create a safe space where you can heal, grow, and thrive after leaving a family cult.

TRUST ISSUES

Trust issues refer to difficulties or hesitations someone may have in relying on or confiding in others. These issues can stem from past betrayals, disappointments, or a general lack of confidence in people. Trust issues may impact relationships, making it challenging for individuals to fully open up, share vulnerabilities, or believe in the sincerity of others. Trust issues can arise from various life experiences, contributing to a heightened sense of skepticism and reluctance to trust others. Common reasons for experiencing trust issues include:

Betrayal: Previous betrayals, whether in friendships, romantic relationships, or professional settings, can lead to a diminished trust in others. A history of broken promises or dishonesty can erode one's confidence in forming new connections.

Past Trauma: Individuals who have experienced trauma, such as abuse or abandonment, may find it challenging to trust others due to fear of vulnerability and potential harm.

Lack of Consistency: Inconsistency in behavior or communication from others can create uncertainty and doubt, making it difficult for someone to trust that people will remain reliable and steadfast.

Cultural or Family Background: Upbringing and cultural influences play a role. Those raised in environments with a lack of trust or where deception is normalized may develop trust issues as a learned response to their surroundings.

Low Self-Esteem: Individuals with low self-esteem may struggle to trust others because they may doubt their own worthiness of genuine connections or fear rejection.

Fear of Vulnerability: Trust often involves vulnerability, and some individuals may avoid trusting others to protect themselves from potential emotional pain or disappointment.

Past Negative Experiences: Any negative experiences, such as being taken advantage of, manipulated, or cheated, can significantly impact one's ability to trust others in the future.

Understanding the root causes of trust issues is crucial for addressing and overcoming them. It often involves a combination of self-reflection, therapy, and gradual exposure to positive, trustworthy relationships to rebuild confidence in forming connections with others.

FREQUENTLY ASKED QUESTIONS AND ANSWERS

WHAT ARE SOME TRUST ISSUES SOMEONE MIGHT EXPERIENCE WHILE LIVING WITHIN A FUNDAMENTAL CHRISTIAN FAMILY CULT?

In a fundamentalist Christian family cult, trust issues can be complex and profound. Members may face challenges due to strict hierarchical structures, manipulation, and rigid doctrinal beliefs. Some trust issues may include:

Secrecy and Lack of Transparency: Leaders may withhold information or manipulate truths, leading to a general mistrust among members who sense a lack of openness.

Fear of Judgment: Individuals may fear judgment for questioning or expressing doubt about the cult's teachings, hindering open communication within the family.

Isolation: Cults often discourage connections outside the group, leading to isolation. Members may struggle with trusting those outside the cult due to indoctrination against external influences.

Conditional Love: Love and acceptance within the family may be contingent on adhering strictly to the cult's principles, fostering a sense of conditional trust.

Emotional Manipulation: Emotional manipulation techniques can create distrust as members may feel their emotions are being exploited or controlled.

Overcoming these trust issues may involve seeking support from mental health professionals, engaging in open dialogue with trusted individuals outside the cult, and gradually reevaluating belief systems to foster a healthier sense of trust in relationships.

WHAT ARE SOME OF THE LASTING TRUST ISSUES SOMEONE MIGHT EXPERIENCE AFTER LEAVING A FUNDAMENTAL CHRISTIAN FAMILY CULT?

The long-lasting effects of trust issues stemming from leaving a fundamentalist Christian family cult can be profound and challenging. Individuals may experience:

Difficulty Forming Relationships: The ingrained mistrust from the cult experience can make it challenging to form new relationships. Fear of betrayal or manipulation may hinder the development of trust in others.

Emotional Scars: Past manipulation and conditional acceptance within the cult can leave deep emotional scars, impacting self-esteem and confidence.

Spiritual Confusion: Leaving a rigid belief system may lead to a period of spiritual confusion, where individuals grapple with their beliefs and question trust in any form of authority, including spiritual or religious figures.

Fear of Rejection: The fear of rejection or judgment, often instilled within the cult, may persist even after leaving. This fear can affect personal and professional interactions.

Struggles with Independence: Cult environments often discourage independence and critical thinking. Individuals may find it challenging to trust their own judgment and make decisions independently.

Overcoming these long-lasting effects often involves seeking professional counseling to address psychological trauma, connecting with supportive communities or individuals, and gradually rebuilding a healthier understanding of trust and relationships. Patience and self-compassion play crucial roles in the healing process.

WHAT ARE SOME WAYS SOMEONE CAN OVERCOME TRUST ISSUES AFTER LEAVING A FUNDAMENTAL CHRISTIAN FAMILY CULT?

Overcoming trust issues after leaving a fundamentalist Christian family cult requires time, self-reflection, and intentional efforts. Here are some ways to navigate this challenging journey:

Seek Professional Help: Consider therapy or counseling to address the psychological impact of leaving a cult. A mental health professional can provide guidance, support, and coping strategies tailored to your specific situation.

Connect with Supportive Communities: Build connections with individuals who have experienced similar transitions. Support groups or online communities can offer a sense of understanding, shared experiences, and validation, fostering a supportive environment.

Reevaluate Belief Systems: Take the time to critically examine the beliefs instilled by the cult. This process involves exploring personal values, spirituality, and forming an authentic belief system that aligns with your true self.

Gradual Exposure to Trust: Start rebuilding trust in a controlled and gradual manner. Begin by trusting small aspects of daily life, and progressively extend that trust to others. This can include forming friendships, engaging in group activities, or seeking mentorship from trustworthy individuals.

Educate Yourself: Learn about manipulation techniques used by cults to better understand the dynamics at play. This knowledge can empower you to recognize and counteract any lingering effects of manipulation in your thought processes.

Practice Self-Compassion: Cultivate self-compassion and understanding. Acknowledge that overcoming trust issues is a process, and it's okay to seek support and take the necessary time for healing.

Set Boundaries: Establish healthy boundaries in relationships. Clearly communicate your needs and expectations, and be mindful of your own well-being. Learning to say "no" when necessary is an important part of rebuilding trust.

Engage in Self-Discovery: Rediscover your authentic self and interests. Cultivate a sense of individuality apart from the cult's influence, allowing you to build trust in your own identity.

Remember that overcoming trust issues is a gradual process, and seeking professional guidance is a valuable step towards healing. Patience, self-compassion, and a commitment to personal growth are essential components of this transformative journey.

WHAT ARE SOME WAYS TO SUPPORT SOMEONE WHO IS STRUGGLING WITH TRUST ISSUES AFTER LEAVING A FUNDAMENTAL CHRISTIAN FAMILY CULT?

Supporting someone struggling with trust issues after leaving a fundamental Christian family cult requires empathy, patience, and a non-judgmental approach. Here are ways to provide support:

Listen Actively: Create a safe space for them to express their feelings without judgment. Actively listen to their experiences and validate their emotions, acknowledging the difficulty of their journey.

Educate Yourself: Learn about the dynamics of cults and the psychological impact of leaving such environments. Understanding the complexities involved will enable you to offer more informed and empathetic support.

Encourage Professional Help: Suggest therapy or counseling to help them navigate the emotional challenges. A mental health professional with experience in trauma and cult recovery can provide tailored assistance.

Respect their Pace: Recognize that healing is a gradual process. Avoid pushing them to open up or make quick decisions. Respect their pace and allow them the time needed to rebuild trust at their own comfort level.

Offer Practical Assistance: Assist with practical matters, such as finding housing, employment, or resources for independent living. Practical support can alleviate stress and provide a foundation for rebuilding trust in their ability to navigate the world.

Validate Their Experience: Affirm their courage in leaving the cult and acknowledge the unique challenges they face. Validating their experience helps counteract any lingering self-doubt or guilt.

Be Patient and Persistent: Building trust takes time. Be patient and persistent in your support, demonstrating a consistent and reliable presence in their life. Show that you are committed to their well-being.

Create a Supportive Network: Encourage connections with others who have experienced similar situations. Sharing experiences with people who understand can provide a sense of community and reduce feelings of isolation.

Respect Their Beliefs: Be respectful of their evolving beliefs and spiritual journey. Avoid imposing your own beliefs and allow them the space to explore and redefine their spirituality on their terms.

Celebrate Small Progress: Acknowledge and celebrate even small steps forward. Recognizing their achievements, no matter how minor, helps build confidence and reinforces positive behaviors.

Remember that everyone's healing journey is unique. Providing unwavering support, understanding, and encouragement can play a crucial role in helping someone rebuild trust and create a healthier, more fulfilling life after leaving a fundamentalist Christian family cult.

ANGER ISSUES

Anger issues refer to difficulties in managing and expressing anger appropriately. People with anger issues may experience intense and frequent bouts of anger that interfere with their daily lives and relationships. This can manifest in various ways, such as outbursts of yelling or violence, passive-aggressive behavior, or even internalized anger leading to resentment and bitterness.

Anger issues can stem from a variety of factors, including past trauma, stress, unresolved conflicts, or underlying mental health conditions like depression or anxiety.

Effective management typically involves identifying triggers, learning coping strategies, and seeking professional help if necessary, such as therapy or anger management programs.

FREQUENTLY ASKED QUESTIONS AND ANSWERS

WHY DO SO MANY FORMER FAMILY CULT MEMBERS STRUGGLE WITH ANGER MANAGEMENT AFTER LEAVING?

Former family cult members may struggle with anger management after leaving due to the complex and traumatic nature of their experiences. Several factors contribute to this difficulty:

Repressed Emotions: During their time in the family cult, members may have repressed a range of emotions, including anger, as a coping mechanism. Upon leaving, these repressed emotions may surface, leading to intense and uncontrolled expressions of anger.

Betrayal and Deception: Discovering the extent of manipulation, deception, and betrayal within the family cult can evoke profound feelings of anger. Former members may grapple with anger towards the cult leaders, the system, and even themselves for being deceived.

Loss of Control: Family cults often exert extreme control over their members. Upon leaving, individuals may struggle with the sudden freedom and autonomy, leading to a sense of loss of control. This loss can manifest as anger, as they navigate the challenges of making independent choices.

Grieving Process: Leaving a family cult involves a grieving process for the lost relationships, identity, and belief systems. Anger is a common stage of grief, and former cult members may direct their anger at the cult leaders or the organization.

Feelings of Powerlessness: Cults intentionally create a power imbalance, with leaders holding absolute control. After leaving, former members may feel powerless or helpless in the face of their experiences. This sense of powerlessness can contribute to anger as they grapple with regaining a sense of control.

Post-Traumatic Stress: Many former family cult members experience post-traumatic stress disorder (PTSD) or trauma-related symptoms. Anger is a common symptom of PTSD, and triggers or reminders of the cult experience can lead to intense anger reactions.

Difficulty Trusting Others: Betrayal within the cult can lead to difficulty trusting others after leaving. Former members may be wary of forming new relationships, fearing a recurrence of manipulation or deception. This mistrust can contribute to heightened anger responses.

Adjustment Challenges: Transitioning from a controlled cult environment to the outside world presents numerous challenges. Former members may face difficulties adjusting to societal norms, relationships, and expectations, contributing to frustration and anger.

Coping Mechanisms: In the cult, individuals might have learned maladaptive coping mechanisms, such as suppressing emotions or resorting to anger as a way to gain control. Breaking free from these learned behaviors can be a gradual and challenging process.

Shame and Guilt: Former cult members may harbor feelings of shame and guilt for their involvement in the cult or for any perceived compliance with harmful practices. These emotions can manifest as anger directed inward or outward.

Addressing anger management challenges often requires a multifaceted approach, including therapeutic support, counseling, and the development of healthier coping mechanisms. Professional intervention can help individuals explore the root causes of their anger, learn constructive ways to express and manage it, and navigate the process of healing from the complex trauma associated with family cult experiences.

WHY IS IT IMPORTANT TO SEEK ANGER MANAGEMENT COUNSELING IF YOU ARE STRUGGLING AFTER LEAVING YOUR FAMILY CULT?

Seeking anger management counseling is crucial for individuals struggling after leaving a family cult for several reasons:

Understanding Triggers: Anger management counseling helps individuals identify and understand the specific triggers that evoke anger. In the context of leaving a family cult, these triggers may be rooted in past traumatic experiences, manipulation, or feelings of betrayal.

Developing Coping Strategies: Counseling provides a structured environment for developing healthy coping strategies to manage anger. This includes learning effective communication skills, relaxation techniques, and alternative ways to express and process intense emotions.

Addressing Repressed Emotions: Leaving a family cult often involves confronting repressed emotions, including anger. Counseling offers a safe space to explore and address these emotions, facilitating a healthier and more constructive release of pent-up feelings.

Navigating Complex Trauma: Anger stemming from the complex trauma associated with family cult experiences requires specialized attention. Anger management counseling can address the unique challenges of navigating trauma-related anger and guide individuals toward healing.

Preventing Harmful Behaviors: Unmanaged anger can lead to harmful behaviors, both towards oneself and others. Counseling helps individuals recognize and prevent destructive behaviors, fostering a safer environment for personal growth and relationships.

Improving Relationships: Cultivating healthy relationships outside the cult environment is essential for recovery. Anger management counseling equips individuals with the skills needed to build and maintain positive connections, overcoming the interpersonal challenges often associated with cult experiences.

Enhancing Emotional Regulation: Counseling focuses on enhancing emotional regulation, empowering individuals to manage and express their emotions in a balanced and controlled manner. This skill is particularly valuable for those recovering from the intense emotional suppression often experienced in family cults.

Promoting Self-Reflection: Anger management counseling encourages self-reflection, helping individuals explore the root causes of their anger and develop a deeper understanding of themselves. This self-awareness is vital for personal growth and recovery.

Empowering Personal Agency: Cult environments often strip individuals of their personal agency. Anger management counseling empowers individuals to reclaim control over their emotional responses, fostering a sense of autonomy and empowerment.

Integrated Healing: Anger management counseling is part of the holistic healing process. Integrating anger management with other therapeutic approaches ensures a comprehensive and well-rounded recovery from the complex effects of family cult experiences.

It's essential to engage with a qualified mental health professional who specializes in trauma and anger management.

A tailored and supportive approach, coupled with individualized strategies, can significantly contribute to a person's ability to navigate anger and its associated challenges after leaving a family cult.

SELF-MEDICATING

Self-medicating refers to the practice of using substances or behaviors to alleviate symptoms of physical or mental health issues without proper medical supervision or guidance. This could involve using drugs, alcohol, prescription medications, or other substances to cope with symptoms such as anxiety, depression, pain, or stress. Self-medication can be risky and may lead to addiction, worsening of symptoms, and other negative consequences. It's important to seek professional help if you're experiencing health issues rather than attempting to self-medicate.

FREQUENTLY ASKED QUESTIONS AND ANSWERS

WHY DO MANY THAT ESCAPE CHRISTIAN FUNDAMENTALIST FAMILY CULTS TURN TO DRUGS AND ALCOHOL?

It's important to avoid making sweeping generalizations about any group of people, including those recovering from fundamental Christian family cults. Substance abuse, including the use of drugs and alcohol, can be a complex issue influenced by various factors. While some individuals may turn to substances as a way to cope with trauma or the challenges of leaving a cult, it's essential to recognize that not everyone in this situation resorts to such behaviors.

Potential factors contributing to substance use in some individuals recovering from cults might include:

Coping Mechanism: Leaving a family cult can be an emotionally and psychologically challenging experience. Some individuals may turn to drugs or alcohol as a way to cope with the trauma, stress, and emotional pain associated with their past.

Lack of Coping Skills: Cult environments often stifle the development of healthy coping mechanisms. When leaving the cult, individuals may not have acquired the necessary skills to navigate stress and emotional challenges in a constructive way.

Isolation and Loss: Exiting a cult may result in the loss of a tightly knit community. Feelings of isolation and loneliness can contribute to a vulnerability to substance use as individuals seek solace or a sense of belonging.

Emotional Regulation: Cults often manipulate emotions and discourage individual expression. As a result, some individuals may struggle with regulating their emotions after leaving. Substance use might be an attempt to manage intense emotional experiences.

Post-Traumatic Stress: Leaving a family cult can leave individuals with lasting emotional scars. Post-traumatic stress disorder (PTSD) is not uncommon, and some may turn to substances as a way to numb or escape from traumatic memories.

Exploration and Rebellion: Exiting a highly restrictive environment might lead some individuals to experiment with substances as a form of rebellion or as a way to explore newfound freedom.

It's crucial to approach these situations with sensitivity and understanding. If you or someone you know is struggling with substance use after leaving a family cult, seeking professional help is essential. Substance abuse treatment programs, therapy, and support groups can provide the necessary assistance for recovery. It's important to remember that each individual's journey is unique, and support should be tailored to their specific needs and experiences.

HOW CAN YOU SUPPORT SOMEONE THAT IS EXPERIENCING SUBSTANCE ABUSE OR SELF MEDICATING AFTER LEAVING A FUNDAMENTAL CHRISTIAN FAMILY CULT?

Supporting someone who is struggling with self-medicating after leaving a family cult requires compassion, understanding, and a non-judgmental approach. Here are some ways to support them:

Listen without judgment: Create a safe and supportive space for them to express their feelings and experiences without fear of criticism or judgment. Let them know that you're there to listen and support them unconditionally.

Encourage professional help: Suggest seeking professional help from a therapist, counselor, or healthcare provider who can offer guidance, support, and appropriate treatment options for their specific needs.

Offer alternatives: Encourage healthy coping strategies and alternatives to self-medication, such as mindfulness, exercise, creative outlets, or support groups for survivors of cults or addiction.

Provide practical support: Offer practical assistance, such as helping them find resources, attending appointments with them, or assisting with everyday tasks to alleviate stress and support their well-being.

Educate yourself: Take the time to educate yourself about addiction, recovery, and the unique challenges faced by survivors of family cults. Understanding their experiences can help you provide more effective support.

Express empathy and validation: Validate their feelings and experiences, acknowledging the challenges they're facing and expressing empathy for their struggles. Let them know that it's okay to seek help and that they're not alone in their journey.

Set boundaries: Set healthy boundaries with them to protect your own well-being and ensure that your support is sustainable. This might involve being clear about your own limitations and encouraging them to seek professional help when necessary.

Be patient and supportive: Recovery from self-medication and the trauma of leaving a family cult is a complex and challenging process that takes time. Be patient, supportive, and understanding as they navigate their journey towards healing and recovery.

By providing compassionate support, encouraging professional help, and offering alternatives to self-medication, you can help someone struggling after leaving a family cult find healthier ways of coping and moving forward in their recovery journey.

SELF DISCOVERY

Self-discovery is the process of gaining insight into oneself, including one's values, beliefs, strengths, weaknesses, desires, and identity. It involves exploring and understanding one's thoughts, emotions, motivations, and behaviors to develop a deeper understanding of who you are and what is important to you. Self-discovery often involves introspection, reflection, and exploration of new experiences, ideas, and perspectives. It can lead to greater self-awareness, personal growth, and a stronger sense of authenticity and purpose in life.

FREQUENTLY ASKED QUESTIONS AND ANSWERS

WHAT ARE THINGS SOMEONE MIGHT EXPERIENCE WHEN GOING THROUGH SELF DISCOVERY AFTER LEAVING A FAMILY CULT?

Embarking on a journey of self-discovery after leaving a family cult can be both liberating and challenging. Here are some experiences that individuals might encounter during this process:

Identity Exploration: Individuals may question and explore their authentic identity, distinct from the role assigned to them within the cult. This involves rediscovering personal values, interests, and aspirations.

Emotional Rollercoaster: The process of self-discovery often involves a range of emotions, including joy, confusion, sadness, and relief. Navigating these emotions is a natural part of uncovering one's true self.

Reevaluation of Beliefs: Cults often instill rigid belief systems. After leaving, individuals may reevaluate and reshape their beliefs, forming a more nuanced understanding of spirituality, morality, and personal values.

Cognitive Dissonance: As individuals confront conflicting beliefs or information, they may experience cognitive dissonance. This discomfort is a common part of the process of reconciling old beliefs with new insights.

Recovery from Indoctrination: Recovering from the effects of indoctrination involves recognizing and challenging deeply ingrained thought patterns. This process requires a commitment to critical thinking and a willingness to question previously accepted truths.

Rediscovering Passions: Individuals may rediscover interests and passions that were suppressed or overlooked in the cult environment. Exploring these newfound interests contributes to a sense of fulfillment and purpose.

Challenges in Social Relationships: Rebuilding or establishing new social relationships can be challenging. Cult survivors may need to learn healthy relationship dynamics and boundaries while navigating trust and connection.

Developing Autonomy: Cult environments often restrict autonomy. During self-discovery, individuals learn to make independent choices, set personal goals, and take responsibility for their own lives.

Coping with Guilt and Shame: Cults often use guilt and shame as control mechanisms. Individuals may grapple with these emotions during self-discovery, necessitating self-compassion and forgiveness.

Exploring Personal Boundaries: Learning to establish and enforce personal boundaries is crucial. Individuals may need to identify where their comfort zones lie and communicate those boundaries in relationships.

Acceptance of Imperfection: Cults may foster a perfectionist mindset. Embracing the idea that it's okay to be imperfect and make mistakes is an important aspect of self-discovery.

Cultivating Resilience: Overcoming the challenges of leaving a family cult requires resilience. Individuals develop resilience as they face setbacks, learn from experiences, and continue to move forward in their journey.

Embracing Open-Mindedness: Cult environments often discourage questioning or exploration of diverse perspectives. Engaging in self-discovery involves embracing open-mindedness, curiosity, and a willingness to learn from others.

Integration of Past Experiences: Coming to terms with the past and integrating past experiences into one's narrative is a significant part of self-discovery. This involves acknowledging the impact of the cult while focusing on personal growth.

Nurturing a Positive Self-Image: Cults may undermine self-esteem. During self-discovery, individuals work towards building a positive self-image, recognizing their strengths, and fostering self-love.

Navigating the complexities of self-discovery after leaving a family cult is a unique and deeply personal process. Seeking support from mental health professionals, counselors, and support groups can provide valuable guidance and encouragement throughout this transformative journey.

WHY DO MANY PEOPLE EXPLORE THEIR SEXUALITY DURING THEIR SELF DISCOVERY PHASE AFTER LEAVING THEIR FAMILY CULT?

Exploring one's sexuality after leaving a family cult can be a complex and multifaceted process. Several factors contribute to this exploration:

Repression in the Cult: Cult environments often enforce strict sexual norms and may suppress any form of sexual expression outside specific guidelines. Leaving the cult provides individuals with the freedom to explore their sexuality without these constraints.

Sexual Repression and Curiosity: Individuals who have experienced sexual repression in a cult may feel a natural curiosity about their own desires and preferences. Exploring one's sexuality is a way to understand and embrace these aspects of identity.

Developmental Milestones: Cult members may have missed out on typical developmental milestones, including sexual exploration and education. After leaving, individuals may seek to catch up on these experiences and gain a deeper understanding of their sexuality.

Establishing Autonomy: Leaving a family cult often involves reclaiming autonomy over various aspects of life, including personal relationships and sexual choices. Exploring one's sexuality is a way to assert independence and make personal decisions.

Understanding Healthy Relationships: Cult environments may distort or limit individuals' understanding of healthy relationships, including romantic and sexual connections. Exploring one's sexuality can be part of a broader effort to learn about healthy intimacy and connection.

Overcoming Guilt and Shame: Cults often use guilt and shame as control mechanisms, particularly regarding sexuality. Exploring one's sexuality can be a way to confront and overcome these ingrained feelings, promoting a healthier relationship with one's own body and desires.

Recovery from Sexual Trauma: Some individuals leaving family cults may have experienced sexual trauma or abuse within the cult. Exploring sexuality post-cult may involve healing from these traumas and reclaiming agency over one's body.

Building a Positive Body Image: Cult environments may perpetuate unrealistic or harmful ideals about the body. Exploring one's sexuality can contribute to building a positive body image and cultivating self-acceptance.

Understanding Sexual Orientation: Cults may stigmatize or condemn certain sexual orientations. Exploring one's sexuality after leaving allows individuals to better understand and accept their sexual orientation, whether it aligns with the norms enforced in the cult or not.

Educational Gaps: Cult environments may limit access to comprehensive sexual education. Exploring sexuality can involve filling gaps in knowledge and understanding about one's own body, consent, and sexual health.

Connection with Others: Exploring sexuality often involves forming connections with others who share similar interests and desires. Building relationships outside the cult provides an opportunity for emotional and physical intimacy.

It's important to note that everyone's journey is unique, and individuals explore their sexuality for diverse reasons. The process can be liberating but may also come with challenges, and seeking support from professionals or support groups can be beneficial for those navigating this aspect of post-cult life.

HOW TO SUPPORT SOMEONE EXPERIENCING SELF DISCOVERY AFTER LEAVING A CULT?

Supporting someone experiencing self-discovery after leaving a family cult involves providing a safe and nurturing environment for their exploration and growth. Here are some ways to support them:

Encourage exploration: Encourage them to explore their interests, passions, and values without judgment or pressure. Validate their curiosity and encourage them to try new things, meet new people, and engage in activities that resonate with their authentic self.

Listen actively: Be a compassionate listener and provide a non-judgmental space for them to share their thoughts, feelings, and discoveries. Encourage open and honest communication, and validate their experiences and emotions.

Offer reassurance: Offer reassurance and encouragement as they navigate the ups and downs of self-discovery. Remind them that it's okay to feel uncertain or conflicted and that self-discovery is a journey that takes time and patience.

Respect their autonomy: Respect their autonomy and agency in their journey of self-discovery. Avoid imposing your own beliefs or expectations on them and allow them to explore and define their own identity and values.

Provide resources: Offer resources and support to help them in their self-discovery journey, such as books, articles, workshops, or therapy. Connect them with supportive communities or groups of individuals who have also left family cults and are on similar journeys of self-discovery.

Celebrate milestones: Celebrate their achievements and milestones along the way, no matter how small. Acknowledge their progress and growth, and remind them of their strengths and resilience.

Be patient and supportive: Be patient and supportive as they navigate the complexities of self-discovery. Offer unconditional support, understanding, and encouragement, and be there for them through the challenges and triumphs of their journey.

By providing a supportive and nurturing environment, encouraging exploration and growth, and respecting their autonomy and agency, you can help someone experiencing self-discovery after leaving a family cult find greater authenticity, fulfillment, and purpose in their life.

CRITICAL THINKING

Critical thinking is the ability to analyze, evaluate, and synthesize information independently. It involves questioning assumptions, considering multiple perspectives, and reaching well-reasoned conclusions. Critical thinking is a valuable skill that fosters intellectual independence, informed decision-making, and a deeper understanding of various subjects.

In a fundamental Christian family cult, critical thinking may be discouraged for several reasons:

Authority of Interpretation: The cult leader, often a patriarch or central religious figure, claims authority in interpreting religious texts. Critical thinking might be perceived as challenging this authority or deviating from the established interpretations.

Fear of Doubt: Encouraging critical thinking may lead to questioning fundamental beliefs and doctrines. The cult may instill a fear that such questioning could lead to doubt or disbelief, which is often viewed as a threat to the faith.

Preservation of Dogma: Fundamentalist beliefs often rely on strict adherence to a set of doctrines. Critical thinking may be seen as a potential disruptor to these doctrines, and cult leaders may discourage it to maintain the purity of their established dogma.

Control and Obedience: Discouraging critical thinking serves the purpose of maintaining control over followers. By limiting independent analysis, the cult leader ensures that followers adhere unquestioningly to the prescribed beliefs and directives.

Closed Information System: Cults often control the information available to members. Discouraging critical thinking helps to prevent followers from seeking alternative sources of information that might challenge the cult's narrative.

Maintaining Hierarchy: Cult leaders may fear that encouraging critical thinking could lead to questioning of the hierarchical structure within the cult. Followers might begin to question the authority of leaders, challenging the established power dynamics.

Fear of Apostasy: Apostasy, or the abandonment of religious beliefs, is often seen as a grave sin in fundamentalist contexts. Discouraging critical thinking helps to suppress doubts and prevents followers from considering alternative belief systems.

Emphasis on Faith: Fundamentalist religious groups often emphasize faith as a virtue. Critical thinking might be perceived as relying on human reason rather than relying solely on faith in religious teachings.

It's important to note that not all religious groups, including fundamentalist ones, discourage critical thinking. Many religious communities actively encourage thoughtful engagement with beliefs and provide spaces for questioning and exploration. However, in more authoritarian or cult-like contexts, the suppression of critical thinking can be a means of maintaining control and conformity.

FREQUENTLY ASKED QUESTIONS AND ANSWERS

WHY IS IT SO IMPORTANT TO LEARN CRITICAL THINKING DURING FUNDAMENTAL CHRISTIAN FAMILY CULT RECOVERY?

Learning critical thinking during fundamental Christian family cult recovery is essential for several reasons:

Empowerment and Autonomy: Critical thinking empowers individuals to think independently and make informed decisions. Recovering from a family cult involves reclaiming personal autonomy, and critical thinking is a key tool in this process.

Rebuilding Cognitive Skills: Cult environments often suppress critical thinking, and recovery provides an opportunity to rebuild cognitive skills. Learning to analyze information, question assumptions, and consider multiple perspectives is crucial for mental and emotional well-being.

Resilience to Manipulation: Cults often employ manipulative tactics to control followers. Critical thinking acts as a defense mechanism against manipulation, allowing individuals to recognize coercive tactics and resist undue influence.

Coping with Doubt: Leaving a family cult may introduce doubts and uncertainties about previously held beliefs. Critical thinking helps individuals navigate these doubts by providing a framework for evaluating and processing new information.

Engaging with Diverse Perspectives: Critical thinking encourages an openness to diverse perspectives and ideas.

This is vital for individuals who have been isolated within a cult environment, as it allows them to explore a broader range of viewpoints and make more informed choices.

Developing Analytical Skills: The analytical skills fostered by critical thinking contribute to clearer decision-making and problem-solving. This is particularly beneficial as individuals rebuild their lives outside the confines of the family cult.

Facilitating Emotional Healing: Critical thinking can aid in emotional healing by providing a structured approach to understanding and challenging harmful beliefs instilled by the family cult. It promotes a healthier relationship with one's thoughts and emotions.

Building Resilience to Fear Tactics: Cults often use fear tactics to control members. Critical thinking helps individuals recognize and resist fear-based manipulation, fostering resilience and the ability to confront fears associated with leaving the cult.

Encouraging Curiosity and Learning: Recovering individuals can cultivate a sense of curiosity and a love for learning. Critical thinking encourages a lifelong pursuit of knowledge, enabling individuals to explore diverse subjects and develop a more nuanced worldview.

Fostering Open Dialogue: Critical thinking promotes open dialogue and communication. As individuals recover from a family cult, these skills become crucial for healthy relationships, allowing them to engage in constructive conversations with others who may have different perspectives. By embracing critical thinking, individuals in family cult recovery can reclaim their intellectual independence, navigate the complexities of the post-cult experience, and build a foundation for a more fulfilling and authentic life.

HOW IS CRITICAL THINKING WEAPONIZED WITHIN A FUNDAMENTAL CHRISTIAN FAMILY CULT?

In a fundamental Christian family cult, critical thinking can be weaponized through specific tactics aimed at controlling, manipulating, or suppressing independent thought. Here are ways in which critical thinking may be weaponized in such contexts:

Labeling Doubt as Sinful: Critical questioning or doubt may be labeled as a sin against the faith. Cult leaders may manipulate followers into believing that questioning the established beliefs is equivalent to challenging God's authority.

Fear of Consequences: Cult leaders may instill a deep fear of negative consequences for engaging in critical thinking. Followers may be warned of divine punishment, exclusion from the community, or eternal damnation if they question the established doctrines.

Emotional Manipulation: Leaders may use emotional manipulation to discourage critical thinking by associating doubt with feelings of guilt, shame, or betrayal. Followers may fear damaging relationships within the cult if they express independent thoughts.

Isolation from Dissenters: Individuals who openly engage in critical thinking or express doubt may be isolated or shunned within the cult community. This social ostracizing serves as a deterrent for others who might be considering independent thought.

Control of Information: Cult leaders often control the information available to followers. Access to alternative perspectives or critical literature may be restricted, limiting the resources that could encourage independent thinking.

Selective Scriptural Interpretation: Cult leaders may selectively interpret religious texts to suppress critical thinking. They may present a narrow interpretation that discourages questioning or alternative viewpoints, reinforcing a singular narrative.

Intellectual Fear Tactics: Cult leaders may use intellectual fear tactics, suggesting that engaging in critical thinking leads to moral or spiritual decay. Followers may be led to believe that questioning beliefs is a slippery slope to abandoning faith altogether.

Rewarding Conformity: Conformity to established beliefs may be rewarded within the cult, while dissent or critical thinking is punished. This reinforces a culture where individuals are discouraged from questioning the status quo.

Mind Control Techniques: Cults may employ mind control techniques, such as thought-stopping strategies, to suppress critical thinking. Followers may be taught to shut down any thoughts that deviate from the established beliefs.

Us vs. Them Mentality: Cult leaders often foster an "us vs. them" mentality, portraying those outside the cult as enemies or agents of evil. This can discourage followers from engaging with external perspectives that might challenge their beliefs.

It's crucial to recognize these manipulative tactics and understand that healthy religious environments should encourage thoughtful engagement, critical thinking, and open dialogue rather than using fear and control to suppress independent thought.

HOW CAN YOU SUPPORT CRITICAL THINKING IN SOMEONE THAT IS RECOVERING FROM THEIR FAMILY CULT?

Supporting someone in family cult recovery and fostering their critical thinking involves creating a safe and open environment for them to explore and question beliefs. Here are ways to support their critical thinking:

Encourage Open Dialogue: Create a space where the individual feels comfortable expressing their thoughts and doubts. Encourage open conversations without judgment, allowing them to freely share their evolving perspectives.

Validate Their Experience: Acknowledge the challenges of leaving a family cult and validate the individual's experiences. Let them know that it's okay to question beliefs and that their journey is valid.

Provide Access to Information: Share diverse sources of information and encourage exploration beyond the previously limited information they may have been exposed to within the cult. Offer books, articles, documentaries, and resources that present alternative perspectives.

Model Critical Thinking: Demonstrate critical thinking in your own conversations and decision-making. By modeling healthy skepticism, thoughtful analysis, and a willingness to consider various viewpoints, you encourage them to do the same.

Ask Thoughtful Questions: Pose open-ended and thought-provoking questions to stimulate critical thinking. Avoid imposing your views but guide them in questioning assumptions, evaluating evidence, and considering the implications of their beliefs.

Celebrate Growth and Exploration: Acknowledge and celebrate moments of growth and exploration. Recognize their efforts to think critically, even if it leads to challenging or uncomfortable realizations.

Encourage Self-Reflection: Foster self-reflection by encouraging the individual to examine their values, beliefs, and motivations. This introspection is a key aspect of critical thinking and personal development.

Provide Emotional Support: Recognize the emotional challenges associated with questioning deeply ingrained beliefs. Offer emotional support and reassurance as they navigate this process. Be patient and understanding, acknowledging that it's a gradual journey.

Promote Intellectual Curiosity: Encourage a sense of intellectual curiosity by exploring various subjects together. Attend lectures, join discussion groups, or participate in activities that stimulate curiosity and broaden their knowledge base.

Respect Their Pace: Critical thinking and belief exploration are personal processes that unfold at different paces for each individual. Respect their journey and avoid pressuring them to conform to a specific timeline or set of beliefs.

Offer Professional Support: Suggest seeking professional guidance, such as counseling or therapy, to support their emotional and cognitive well-being during the recovery process. A mental health professional can provide additional tools and perspectives.

Remember that supporting critical thinking is an ongoing process, and patience, empathy, and a non-judgmental approach are key components of effective support.

RELIGIOUS DECONSTRUCTION

Religious deconstruction is a process where individuals critically examine and question their beliefs, doctrines, and practices within a religious framework. It involves breaking down, analyzing, and reevaluating one's faith or religious identity, often leading to a reformation of beliefs or departure from organized religion altogether. It can be a deeply personal and challenging journey as individuals confront doubts, inconsistencies, and contradictions within their religious worldview.

Religious deconstruction is a deeply personal and introspective journey that varies greatly from person to person. It often begins with a sense of doubt or discomfort with certain aspects of one's faith or religious tradition. This can be triggered by encountering new ideas, experiences, or evidence that challenges previously held beliefs.

During the process of religious deconstruction, individuals may engage in critical examination of their beliefs, questioning the teachings, doctrines, and practices they were taught. They may delve into theological study, philosophy, psychology, and other disciplines to gain a deeper understanding of their faith and its implications.

As individuals grapple with their beliefs, they may experience a range of emotions, including confusion, fear, anger, sadness, and liberation. They may confront difficult questions about the nature of God, the meaning of life, the existence of evil, and the validity of religious authority.

Religious deconstruction often involves a period of uncertainty and exploration as individuals navigate new perspectives and seek to reconcile their evolving beliefs with their personal values and experiences. This process can be isolating, as individuals may feel alienated from their religious community or fear judgment and rejection from loved ones.

Ultimately, religious deconstruction can lead to a variety of outcomes. Some individuals may undergo a gradual reinterpretation of their faith, integrating new insights and perspectives into their religious worldview. Others may undergo a more radical transformation, rejecting organized religion altogether and embracing a more secular or spiritual approach to life. Regardless of the outcome, religious deconstruction is a profound and transformative process that challenges individuals to confront and reconsider the foundations of their faith.

FREQUENTLY ASKED QUESTIONS AND ANSWERS

WHY IS RELIGIOUS DECONSTRUCTION SO IMPORTANT AFTER LEAVING A FUNDAMENTAL CHRISTIAN FAMILY CULT?

Religious deconstruction is particularly important after leaving a Fundamental Christian Family Cult because it offers individuals the opportunity to critically examine and untangle the deeply ingrained beliefs, practices, and trauma associated with their upbringing. In such environments, adherence to rigid doctrines and unquestioning obedience to authority figures are often paramount, leaving little room for individual exploration or questioning.

After leaving such a context, individuals may experience a range of emotions, including confusion, guilt, fear, and anger. Religious deconstruction provides a framework for processing these emotions and reclaiming agency over one's beliefs and identity. It allows individuals to unravel the layers of indoctrination and control, enabling them to discern their own values, beliefs, and spiritual path.

Moreover, religious deconstruction offers a way to heal from the psychological and emotional wounds inflicted by the cult environment. It provides a space for individuals to confront and make sense of their experiences, to challenge harmful teachings, and to rebuild a sense of self-worth and autonomy.

By engaging in religious deconstruction, individuals who have left Fundamental Christian Family Cults can begin to reclaim their autonomy, agency, and inner sense of truth. It empowers them to chart their own spiritual journey, free from the constraints of coercive control and dogmatic belief systems.

WHAT ARE SOME TYPICAL STEPS SOMEONE TAKES DURING RELIGIOUS DECONSTRUCTION?

During religious deconstruction, individuals often undergo a series of steps as they critically examine and reevaluate their beliefs, practices, and identity within a religious framework. While the process is deeply personal and varies from person to person, some typical steps include:

Questioning beliefs: The process of deconstruction often begins with questioning previously held beliefs and assumptions about religion, spirituality, and faith. Individuals may confront doubts, inconsistencies, or conflicts within their religious worldview, leading them to seek answers and deeper understanding.

Exploring doubts and uncertainties: Deconstruction involves wrestling with doubts, uncertainties, and existential questions about the nature of God, the meaning of life, and the validity of religious teachings.

This phase may involve engaging in theological study, philosophical inquiry, and introspection to grapple with complex theological and existential issues.

Reevaluating religious teachings: Deconstructing individuals critically examine the teachings, doctrines, and practices of their religious tradition. They may reassess interpretations of scripture, reevaluate moral and ethical teachings, and challenge the authority structures within their religious community.

Engaging with diverse perspectives: Deconstructing individuals often seek out diverse perspectives and alternative viewpoints outside of their religious tradition.

This may involve exploring other religious traditions, spiritual practices, or secular philosophies to gain new insights and broaden their understanding of spirituality and faith.

Processing emotions and experiences: Religious deconstruction can evoke a range of emotions, including confusion, anger, grief, and liberation. Individuals may need to process feelings of guilt, shame, or betrayal associated with questioning their faith or leaving their religious community.

This phase often involves seeking support from friends, family members, or mental health professionals to navigate the emotional complexities of deconstruction.

Reconstructing beliefs and identity: As individuals deconstruct their religious worldview, they may undergo a process of reconstruction where they develop new beliefs, values, and identity markers.

This phase involves integrating insights from their deconstruction journey, embracing uncertainty, and forging a more authentic and personally meaningful spiritual path.

Embracing personal autonomy and authenticity: Deconstruction ultimately empowers individuals to reclaim their autonomy and agency over their beliefs, identity, and spiritual journey.

This may involve asserting independence from religious authority figures, setting boundaries with family or community members, and embracing a more flexible and inclusive approach to spirituality.

Continuing growth and reflection: Deconstruction is an ongoing and iterative process that continues to evolve over time. Individuals may find themselves revisiting and reevaluating their beliefs and practices as they encounter new experiences, insights, and challenges in their lives.

While these steps provide a general framework for religious deconstruction, it's important to recognize that the process is nonlinear and may unfold differently for each individual.

WHAT ARE SOME WAYS SOMEONE CAN DECONSTRUCT THEIR FUNDAMENTAL CHRISTIAN FAMILY CULT?

Deconstructing a fundamental Christian family cult is a deeply personal and often challenging process. Here are some steps someone can take to begin this journey:

Recognize and acknowledge the cult dynamics: The first step in deconstructing a fundamental Christian family cult is to recognize and acknowledge the manipulative and controlling dynamics at play within the group. This may involve educating oneself about cult behavior, tactics of manipulation, and the psychological impact of cult indoctrination.

Question beliefs and teachings: Begin questioning the beliefs, doctrines, and teachings that were ingrained within the cult environment. This may involve critically examining scripture, theological teachings, and the authority structures within the group. It's important to approach this process with an open mind and a willingness to challenge previously held beliefs.

Seek outside perspectives: Reach out to trusted friends, family members, or mental health professionals who are outside of the cult environment for support and perspective. Engage in conversations with individuals who hold different beliefs and worldviews to gain new insights and perspectives.

Educate yourself: Take the time to educate yourself about different religious traditions, spiritual practices, and philosophical perspectives. Explore a wide range of sources, including books, articles, podcasts, and documentaries, to gain a deeper understanding of the diversity of human belief and experience.

Process emotions and trauma: Deconstructing a fundamental Christian family cult can be emotionally challenging and may bring up feelings of guilt, fear, anger, and grief. Take the time to process these emotions in a safe and supportive environment, whether through therapy, support groups, or personal reflection.

Reclaim autonomy and agency: Reclaiming autonomy and agency over one's beliefs and identity is a central aspect of deconstructing a cult environment. This may involve setting boundaries with family members or former group members, asserting your right to think and believe for yourself, and making decisions that align with your own values and principles.

Build a supportive community: Surround yourself with a supportive community of friends, family members, or fellow survivors who understand and validate your experiences. Seek out individuals and groups who share similar values and beliefs as you navigate your journey of deconstruction and recovery.

Practice self-care: Prioritize self-care and well-being as you navigate the process of deconstructing a fundamental Christian family cult. Engage in activities that bring you joy, fulfillment, and peace, whether it's spending time in nature, practicing mindfulness, or pursuing creative hobbies.

Deconstructing a fundamental Christian family cult is a challenging but ultimately liberating journey that requires courage, self-reflection, and resilience. By questioning beliefs, seeking support, and reclaiming autonomy, individuals can break free from the grip of cult indoctrination and forge their own path toward healing and personal growth.

WHAT ARE SOME WAYS YOU CAN HELP SOMEONE GOING THROUGH RELIGIOUS DECONSTRUCTION?

Supporting someone going through religious deconstruction requires empathy, patience, and a willingness to listen without judgment. Here are some ways you can help:

Listen with empathy: Be a compassionate listener and allow them to express their thoughts, doubts, and feelings without feeling judged or invalidated. Validate their experiences and emotions, even if you don't fully understand or agree with them.

Provide a safe space: Create a safe and non-judgmental environment where they feel comfortable discussing their journey of deconstruction. Respect their boundaries and allow them to set the pace for their exploration.

Offer emotional support: Religious deconstruction can be emotionally challenging and isolating. Offer your support and reassurance, letting them know they're not alone in their journey. Be available to lend a listening ear or a shoulder to lean on when needed.

Educate yourself: Take the time to educate yourself about religious deconstruction, including its causes, processes, and common challenges. This will help you better understand what they're going through and offer more informed support.

Encourage self-care: Remind them to prioritize self-care and well-being during this challenging time. Encourage healthy coping mechanisms such as exercise, mindfulness, journaling, or seeking professional support if needed.

Respect their autonomy: Respect their right to explore and question their beliefs without pressure or coercion. Avoid imposing your own beliefs or agendas onto them and allow them the freedom to navigate their own spiritual journey.

Offer resources: Provide them with resources such as books, articles, support groups, or therapy options that may be helpful in their deconstruction process. Encourage them to seek out diverse perspectives and engage in constructive dialogue.

Be patient: Remember that religious deconstruction is a complex and deeply personal process that takes time. Be patient and understanding as they navigate their journey, and avoid pressuring them to reach any particular conclusion or outcome.

By offering support, understanding, and empathy, you can help someone going through religious deconstruction feel heard, validated, and supported on their journey of self-discovery and growth.

SUICIDE

"I AM HERE!!!!!" This is what I would scream inside my head as I feel my lungs absorb the scream and sounds to the center of my body. I feel my breathing level and the gentle exhale of the scream that only lived inside my head. "I am here." I say to myself one more time in a low calm tone to reassure my presence of body. I am still inside my body, the screams and noises didn't take me that time, but I feared that one day they would. I would let the silent scream swallow me, and there would be no lungs to absorb the pain. I would imagine the peace of floating off to a place that I will live outside of my body, outside of my pain, and finally outside of my silence.

There are many times I have been asked by people who know my full story, ALWAYS ask me, "How are you still here?" In this section, I will not be giving the clinical lists and breakdowns of this subject matter, as this is a personal topic and one that needs a personal explication of the complete state of being, existing in an environment in which you have no control over your personal autonomy at any given time.

I will be the first to admit, I personally have never attempted suicide. However, they say you need to write about what you know. Here is what I know, I struggled for 39 years, 3 months, and 14 days longing for a death not at my own hands.

That is not to say, I did not struggle with suicidal ideations that sometimes went as far as planning how I would take my own life, and laying out the items to do so. Even now as I sit at my keyboard, it is very easy to feel the same feelings of being trapped inside of a invisible prison, my physical person intruded on both day and night without any control over myself, and seeing no other way out of this life was through death.

The first time I ever planned my own death, I was just over 10 years old and my mother had recently went no contact with her entire family, and my grandparents were trying to force my mother back into their lives by suing for total custody of me, as an unfit mother. It is at this time, my mothers hyper-vigilance became more pronounced over my physical person. All I can describe from that time was complete and total fear of my surroundings and of my mother. Understand, my grandfather was a monster and the idea of living with them terrified me.

My mother, also at this time went through a complete break with reality and I watched her literally shift into a completely different person. A person that no longer felt any love for me; Quote,"I hate you! You have everything I ever wanted as a child! A loving, doting mother! I am so jealous of you!" And then she would beat me, all while screaming and crying at me, "You don't deserve me! You don't appreciate me!". Once she would finish beating me, she would run and lock herself in the bathroom for hours, soaking in the bathtub crying until my father would come home. He was the only one that could console her.

I never knew what I would do wrong or what would set these rages off. That year felt like a lifetime of walking on eggshells, eggshells I didn't break, and I didn't know how to avoid. At one point, I created a safe space deep inside the back corner of my closet full of pillows, blankets, snacks, and a few things to help keep myself comfortable. I would spend the hours after each beating in that space, weeping and praying to the god I was taught to pray to, to save my mom. To help her overcome whatever this monster feeding on her was, to help me to be a better more obedient child. The answer to those prayers never came.

Closer to the end of that year my mother began to "hear the voice of god". It was December 1993 when I just had turned 11, the beatings, and my mothers jealousy had started to subside slightly, but by this time she had become a divine mouth piece for god, and her views of sin started to broaden. I was held to such an incredible scale of perfection and indoctrination, that I believed for quite sometime that the beatings and the rituals (some sexually abusive), was for my best interest and that I needed to fight the duality that lived within me that screamed "THIS IS WRONG! NO! STOP!". Simply, I wanted to die. I yearned for death during that period. I wanted, no, needed the abuse to stop.

I came to a harsh reality, I didn't want to die. I didn't, and I still don't. I wanted the pain to stop and I wanted to be free. Instead of taking my own life, I let the life drain out of me metaphorically. I became a robot, an automaton at best.
I am only learning to live again, to speak my thoughts and feelings without fear of reproach. I am discovering my voice for the first time in my life, and allowing the world to see my true self without the fear of daily retribution.

It is in these beautiful moments of my life now, I often wonder why I was able to make it out and have all of these wonderful freedoms? Typically, in these cases, children, and adult children do not live to tell their stories. Unfortunately, there is limited options for those people:

1. Conform/Submit to the demands of the Fundamental Christian Family Cult at all cost to yourself
2. Continue the process of indoctrination by marriage and procreation
3. Stop submitting and become an apostate or shunned
4. Escape on your terms
5. Suicide

Suicide is by far the most common choice among children and adult children raised within these situations. This is the reason our stories are so rarely heard, is because we by and large, do NOT make it out. It is why I am personally giving a voice to all of those who no longer have a voice, for the ones that will be forever hushed.

CHAPTER 8

PROCESSING TRAUMA AND THERAPY

Trigger Warning: Sensitive Content

This content may contain information or discussions that could be distressing or triggering for some individuals. Topics may include but are not limited to trauma, abuse, violence, or other potentially upsetting subject matter. Reader discretion is advised. If you find that you are emotionally impacted by such content, it is recommended to seek support or refrain from reading further. Your well-being is important.

Processing family cult trauma is critically important for several reasons:

Emotional Healing: Family cult experiences often involve emotional manipulation, abuse, and control. Processing the trauma allows individuals to confront and understand their emotions, paving the way for healing and emotional well-being.

Reclaiming Personal Narrative: Family cults often control members' narratives, shaping their beliefs and identities. Processing trauma enables individuals to reclaim their personal narrative, allowing them to define themselves outside the confines of the cult's influence.

Breaking the Cycle: Understanding and processing family cult trauma is crucial for breaking the cycle of generational trauma. By addressing the impact of the cult experience, individuals can strive to create healthier patterns and prevent the perpetuation of harmful behaviors in their own lives and relationships.

Reconnecting with Authentic Self: Family cults often force individuals to suppress or alter their true selves to fit the cult's narrative. Processing trauma enables individuals to reconnect with their authentic selves, fostering a sense of self-discovery and personal authenticity.

Rebuilding Trust: Cult experiences can erode trust in oneself and others. Processing trauma allows individuals to rebuild trust in their own judgments, perceptions, and in forming healthy connections with others.

Mitigating Mental Health Effects: Cult trauma can lead to various mental health challenges, including anxiety, depression, and post-traumatic stress disorder (PTSD). Processing the trauma is crucial for mitigating these effects and promoting mental well-being.

Establishing Boundaries: Family cults often blur or violate personal boundaries. Processing trauma involves recognizing and establishing healthy boundaries, enabling individuals to protect themselves from potential harm and manipulation.

Gaining Closure: Processing family cult trauma is an essential step toward achieving closure. It allows individuals to acknowledge the impact of their experiences, make sense of their emotions, and work toward closure on their own terms.

Empowerment and Autonomy: Family cults thrive on disempowering and controlling their members. Processing trauma is a journey toward reclaiming personal empowerment and autonomy, enabling individuals to make choices aligned with their values and desires.

Preventing Future Manipulation: Understanding the mechanisms of manipulation and control within a family cult is crucial for preventing future susceptibility to similar tactics. Processing trauma provides the tools to recognize and resist manipulative influences.

Connecting with Support Systems: Processing trauma often involves reaching out to support systems, whether through therapy, support groups, or trusted friends. Establishing connections with understanding individuals helps create a strong foundation for healing.

Facilitating Personal Growth: The process of processing family cult trauma can be transformative, fostering personal growth and resilience. It provides an opportunity for individuals to learn from their experiences, cultivate resilience, and build a more fulfilling life outside the influence of the cult.

While processing family cult trauma is a challenging journey, seeking professional support, such as therapy or counseling, can provide valuable guidance and assistance in navigating this process. It is a crucial step toward reclaiming one's life and building a future free from the lingering effects of cult experiences.

GENERATIONAL TRAUMA

Generational trauma, also known as intergenerational trauma, refers to the transmission of trauma from one generation to the next. It occurs when the emotional or psychological effects of a traumatic experience are passed down within a family or community. This transmission can influence the beliefs, behaviors, and mental health of subsequent generations. Key aspects of generational trauma include:

Transmission Mechanisms: Trauma can be transmitted through various mechanisms, including family dynamics, cultural practices, communication patterns, and learned behaviors.

Inherited Stress Response: Individuals may inherit not only the traumatic experiences themselves but also altered stress response systems. This can lead to heightened sensitivity to stressors and an increased risk of mental health issues.

Impact on Identity: Generational trauma can influence how individuals perceive themselves, their families, and their cultural identity. It may shape a collective sense of belonging or result in a fragmented identity.

Cultural and Social Context: Historical events, such as war, displacement, colonization, or systemic oppression, can contribute to generational trauma. The effects may be felt within specific cultural or social groups.

Repetition of Patterns: Unresolved trauma may lead to the repetition of destructive patterns within families. This can include dysfunctional relationships, substance abuse, or abusive behaviors.

Healing and Breakthrough: Recognizing and addressing generational trauma is crucial for breaking the cycle. Healing often involves acknowledging the impact of trauma, seeking therapy, and fostering resilience within individuals and communities.

Generational trauma is a complex phenomenon, and its effects can manifest in various ways. Acknowledging and understanding this concept can be an essential step in addressing the mental health and well-being of individuals and communities affected by historical or systemic trauma. Professional therapeutic interventions, cultural practices, and community support play vital roles in the healing process.

FREQUENTLY ASKED QUESTIONS AND ANSWERS

HOW DOES GENERATIONAL TRAUMA RELATE TO FAMILY CULTS?

Generational trauma can be closely intertwined with the dynamics within family cults. Here's how generational trauma may relate to family cults:

Transference of Beliefs and Practices: Family cults often involve the transmission of specific beliefs, ideologies, and practices from one generation to the next. These can become ingrained and perpetuate over time, contributing to a cycle of generational trauma.

Control and Manipulation: Family cults typically have a hierarchical structure with a charismatic leader exerting control. The dynamics of control and manipulation within these groups can lead to trauma that is passed down through generations.

Isolation and Dependence: Generations within a family cult may experience isolation from external influences, fostering a dependency on the cult's belief system.

This isolation can contribute to the perpetuation of trauma as individuals are cut off from alternative perspectives.

Cultural and Identity Impact: Family cults often have their own unique culture and identity. This distinct identity, shaped by the cult's beliefs, rituals, and practices, can influence how generational trauma is experienced and transmitted within the group.

Repetition of Abusive Patterns: Unresolved trauma within a family cult may lead to the repetition of abusive patterns across generations. Individuals who grow up in such an environment may perpetuate harmful behaviors learned from the cult leader or within the cult community.

Fear and Coercion: Fear and coercion are common elements within family cults. The trauma associated with these experiences can impact individuals psychologically, making it more likely for them to pass on similar patterns to their own children.

Breakdown of Family Bonds: Family cults often manipulate familial bonds to maintain control. The breakdown of healthy family relationships can contribute to the transmission of generational trauma as individuals struggle to form and maintain healthy connections outside the cult.

Cultural Isolation: Some family cults isolate themselves culturally, rejecting societal norms and influencing how trauma is perceived and addressed. This isolation can further embed generational trauma within the group.

Recognizing the interplay between generational trauma and family cult dynamics is crucial for understanding the complexities of individuals trying to break free from such environments. Breaking the cycle often involves seeking therapy, finding support networks outside the cult, and fostering resilience to overcome the long-lasting effects of trauma within the family cult context.

WHY IS IT IMPORTANT TO BREAK GENERATIONAL TRAUMA AFTER LEAVING YOUR FAMILY CULT?

Breaking generational trauma after leaving a family cult is crucial for several reasons:

Promoting Mental Health: Generational trauma can have severe impacts on mental health, leading to conditions like anxiety, depression, and post-traumatic stress disorder (PTSD). Breaking the cycle is essential for fostering mental well-being and preventing the transmission of trauma to future generations.

Creating Healthy Relationships: Family cults often foster unhealthy dynamics and relationships. Breaking generational trauma allows individuals to establish and maintain healthy connections with others, free from the patterns of control and manipulation seen in the cult.

Empowering Future Generations: Breaking the cycle of generational trauma empowers individuals to create a healthier environment for future generations. It involves making conscious choices to provide a better foundation for children and breaking away from harmful practices learned within the family cult.

Cultivating Independence: Family cults often suppress individuality and independence. Breaking generational trauma involves reclaiming autonomy, making independent choices, and fostering personal growth outside the restrictive environment of the cult.

Preventing Abusive Patterns: Individuals who have experienced trauma within a family cult may unknowingly perpetuate abusive patterns if the cycle is not broken. By addressing and healing from generational trauma, there is a better chance of preventing the continuation of harmful behaviors.

Building Resilience: Breaking generational trauma requires developing resilience. It involves learning healthier coping mechanisms, addressing past traumas, and cultivating emotional strength to navigate life outside the cult.

Seeking Professional Help: Breaking the cycle often involves seeking professional therapeutic help. Mental health professionals can assist in processing trauma, developing coping strategies, and creating a path towards healing and recovery.

Establishing Healthy Boundaries: Family cults often blur boundaries, making it challenging for individuals to establish and maintain healthy personal boundaries. Breaking generational trauma involves learning to set boundaries that protect one's well-being and autonomy.

Encouraging Open Communication: Breaking generational trauma requires open communication about past experiences. Sharing one's story with trusted individuals, such as friends or mental health professionals, can be a crucial step in the healing process.

Rebuilding Identity: Family cults often dictate identity and self-worth. Breaking generational trauma involves a process of self-discovery and rebuilding one's identity outside the confines of the cult.

Breaking generational trauma is a complex but essential journey toward healing and creating a more positive legacy for oneself and future generations. It involves a combination of self-reflection, therapy, support networks, and a commitment to breaking free from the harmful patterns learned within the family cult.

ONE ON ONE THERAPY

One-on-one therapy, also known as individual therapy or 1-on-1 therapy, is a form of psychotherapy where a therapist works directly with an individual client in a private and confidential setting.

In one-on-one therapy, the therapist and client engage in a collaborative and therapeutic relationship, focusing on the client's unique concerns, experiences, and goals. The therapist provides support, guidance, and expertise to help the client explore their thoughts, feelings, and behaviors, identify patterns and challenges, gain insight into underlying issues, and develop coping strategies and skills to address them.

One-on-one therapy sessions typically last around 45 to 60 minutes and occur on a regular basis, usually weekly or biweekly, although the frequency may vary depending on the client's needs and the therapist's recommendations.

One-on-one therapy can be conducted using various therapeutic approaches and techniques, such as cognitive-behavioral therapy (CBT), psychodynamic therapy, humanistic therapy, mindfulness-based therapy, or interpersonal therapy, tailored to the client's specific needs and preferences.

Overall, one-on-one therapy provides a supportive and confidential environment for individuals to explore and address their mental health concerns, improve their emotional well-being, and work towards personal growth and positive change.

FREQUENTLY ASKED QUESTIONS AND ANSWERS

WHY IS IT IMPORTANT TO DO ONE ON ONE THERAPY AFTER LEAVING A FAMILY CULT?

One-on-one therapy is crucial for individuals who have left a family cult for several reasons:

Personalized Support: Individual therapy allows for personalized and focused support tailored to the specific needs and experiences of the individual. This level of customization is essential for addressing the unique challenges associated with leaving a family cult.

Safe and Confidential Space: Trauma therapy provides a safe and confidential space where individuals can openly discuss their experiences without fear of judgment. This privacy is especially important when sharing sensitive information about life within the cult.

Trauma-Informed Approach: One-on-one therapy allows for a trauma-informed approach, acknowledging the impact of past traumatic experiences on mental health. Therapists can tailor interventions to address the complex trauma associated with cult involvement.

Building Trust: Establishing trust is a crucial aspect of recovery, and individual therapy facilitates a strong therapeutic alliance between the survivor and therapist. This trust is foundational for exploring difficult emotions, thoughts, and memories related to cult experiences.

Processing Traumatic Memories: Trauma therapy provides a structured environment for processing traumatic memories at a pace that feels manageable for the individual. Therapists use evidence-based techniques to help survivors navigate and make sense of their past experiences.

Exploring Identity and Belief Systems: Leaving a family cult often involves a process of rediscovering one's identity and questioning deeply ingrained belief systems. Individual therapy provides a supportive space to explore these existential and identity-related challenges.

Coping Strategies and Skills: Therapists in individual sessions can collaboratively develop coping strategies and skills tailored to the survivor's specific needs. This includes addressing anxiety, managing triggers, and developing healthy ways to navigate emotions.

Addressing Shame and Guilt: Survivors of family cults often carry a burden of shame and guilt. Individual therapy allows for the exploration and processing of these emotions, promoting self-compassion and helping individuals detach from undeserved feelings of responsibility.

Navigating Life Transitions: Leaving a family cult involves significant life transitions. Individual therapy assists in navigating these transitions, providing emotional support and practical guidance as individuals establish themselves in a new and independent life.

Empowerment and Autonomy: Individual therapy empowers survivors to reclaim autonomy and make decisions that align with their values and aspirations. Therapists can guide the individual in rebuilding a sense of agency over their life after leaving the controlling environment of the cult.

Preventing Re-victimization: Cult survivors may be vulnerable to re-victimization or exploitation due to their past experiences. Individual therapy helps survivors develop a strong sense of self and set boundaries, reducing the risk of falling into harmful situations.

Integrated Approach: Trauma therapy can be integrated with other therapeutic modalities, offering a comprehensive approach to addressing not only trauma, but also related mental health concerns such as anxiety, depression, and PTSD.

Overall, one-on-one trauma therapy provides a personalized and comprehensive approach to healing, supporting individuals in their journey of recovery after leaving a family cult. It allows survivors to process trauma, regain a sense of self, and build the resilience needed to navigate the challenges of post-cult life.

COGNITIVE BEHAVIORAL THERAPY

Cognitive Behavioral Therapy (CBT) is a widely used therapeutic approach that focuses on the relationship between thoughts, feelings, and behaviors. It is based on the premise that our thoughts influence our emotions and behaviors, and by identifying and changing negative thought patterns, individuals can bring about positive changes in their feelings and actions. Key components of Cognitive Behavioral Therapy include:

Cognitive Restructuring: This involves identifying and challenging negative thought patterns or cognitive distortions. Clients work with the therapist to reframe negative thoughts and develop more balanced and realistic perspectives.

Behavioral Activation: Behavioral activation involves modifying behavior patterns that contribute to emotional distress. Clients learn to engage in activities that bring a sense of accomplishment and pleasure, counteracting negative emotions.

Exposure Therapy: Particularly used for anxiety disorders, exposure therapy encourages individuals to confront and gradually overcome their fears or anxieties. It involves controlled and systematic exposure to feared stimuli.

Problem-Solving: CBT often incorporates problem-solving strategies. Clients learn to break down overwhelming issues into manageable parts, identify potential solutions, and implement effective problem-solving techniques.

Homework Assignments: Therapists may assign homework to clients, encouraging them to practice and apply the skills learned in therapy to real-life situations. This helps reinforce the therapeutic process and promotes ongoing skill development.

Mindfulness and Relaxation Techniques: Mindfulness and relaxation exercises are often integrated into CBT to help individuals become more aware of their thoughts and emotions, promoting a non-judgmental acceptance of the present moment.

Collaborative Approach: CBT is a collaborative and goal-oriented therapy. Therapists work closely with clients to set specific, measurable, and achievable goals, fostering a sense of empowerment and active participation in the therapeutic process.

Time-Limited and Structured: CBT is typically time-limited and structured, with a focus on achieving specific treatment goals within a defined timeframe. This makes it a practical and effective option for many individuals.

CBT has demonstrated effectiveness in treating a wide range of mental health issues, including anxiety disorders, depression, phobias, and stress-related disorders. It is often used in individual or group therapy settings and has been adapted for various populations and age groups. The collaborative and practical nature of CBT makes it a popular and evidence-based approach in the field of psychotherapy.

FREQUENTLY ASKED QUESTIONS AND ANSWERS

WHAT ARE DIDACTICS WITHIN COGNITIVE BEHAVIORAL THERAPY AND WHY IS IT IMPORTANT TO USE TO HELP SUPPORT SOMEONE RECOVERING FROM A FAMILY CULT?

Didactics refer to the methods and techniques used in teaching or instructing. In the context of supporting someone recovering from a family cult, didactics play a crucial role in providing structured and informative assistance. Here's why didactics are important in this context:

Education and Awareness: Didactics provide a means of educating individuals about the dynamics of cults, the psychological impact of cult experiences, and the process of recovery. This knowledge is empowering and helps survivors understand their own experiences.

Understanding Manipulation Tactics: Through didactic approaches, individuals can learn to recognize the manipulation tactics commonly employed by cults.
This understanding is fundamental to breaking free from the influence of coercive control.

Promoting Critical Thinking: Didactic methods encourage critical thinking and independent reasoning. Survivors can learn to question beliefs, analyze information, and develop a more discerning mindset as they navigate their recovery.

Validation of Experiences: Learning about the common characteristics of family cults through didactics can validate survivors' experiences. This validation is essential for individuals who may have felt isolated or doubted the legitimacy of their concerns.

Building a Supportive Community: Didactics contribute to building a supportive community of survivors who share similar experiences. Workshops, seminars, or group sessions provide opportunities for survivors to connect, share insights, and offer mutual support.

Skill Development: Didactic approaches can focus on skill development, such as communication skills, boundary-setting, and coping strategies. These skills are crucial for survivors as they navigate relationships and situations outside the cult environment.

Navigating Emotional Challenges: Understanding the psychological impact of cult experiences through didactics helps survivors navigate the emotional challenges associated with recovery. It provides insights into trauma recovery and self-care strategies.

Empowering Decision-Making: Didactics empower survivors to make informed decisions about their lives. This includes decisions about relationships, education, career choices, and personal beliefs.

Preventing Recidivism: Through education and didactics, individuals can develop resilience against potential relapses into cult-like environments. Knowledge about manipulation tactics serves as a protective factor against falling into similar patterns of coercion.

Fostering Independence: Didactics support the development of independence by providing survivors with the tools to think critically, make autonomous decisions, and shape their own belief systems outside the influence of the cult.

Addressing Cognitive Dissonance: Didactic methods help survivors address cognitive dissonance by providing a framework for understanding conflicting beliefs. This assists in resolving internal conflicts and promoting a more cohesive worldview.

Cultivating a Positive Identity: Didactics contribute to the cultivation of a positive and authentic identity. Survivors can redefine themselves outside the constraints imposed by the cult, fostering a sense of self-acceptance and self-worth.

In supporting someone recovering from a family cult, a combination of didactic approaches, therapeutic interventions, and community support creates a comprehensive framework for healing and empowerment. The educational component of recovery is vital in helping survivors reclaim their lives and build a foundation for a healthier, more autonomous future.

WHY CAN COGNITIVE BEHAVIORAL THERAPY BE USED WHEN ESTABLISHING YOURSELF AFTER LEAVING A FAMILY CULT?

Cognitive Behavioral Therapy (CBT) can be highly beneficial for individuals establishing themselves after leaving a family cult for several reasons:

Addressing Distorted Thought Patterns: CBT focuses on identifying and challenging distorted thought patterns. After leaving a family cult, individuals may carry ingrained beliefs and cognitive distortions. CBT helps to recognize and reframe these thoughts, fostering a healthier mindset.

Coping with Change: Leaving a family cult often involves significant life changes. CBT equips individuals with effective coping strategies, helping them manage stress, anxiety, and the challenges associated with transitioning to a new and independent life.

Building Self-Esteem: Cult environments can erode self-esteem. CBT works on improving self-esteem by challenging negative self-perceptions and fostering a more positive and realistic self-image, crucial for rebuilding one's identity after leaving a cult.

Developing Healthy Relationships: Cult dynamics can distort individuals' understanding of relationships. CBT provides tools to recognize and change unhealthy relationship patterns, promoting the development of positive and fulfilling connections with others.

Managing Emotional Responses: Individuals leaving a family cult may grapple with intense emotions. CBT helps in understanding and managing these emotions, providing practical skills to regulate mood and respond to challenging situations in a more adaptive way.

Setting and Achieving Goals: Establishing personal goals is a crucial aspect of building a new life outside the cult. CBT is goal-oriented, assisting individuals in setting realistic and achievable objectives, and providing strategies to work towards them.

Overcoming Fear and Anxiety: Cult experiences often leave individuals with lingering fear and anxiety. CBT, including exposure therapy, helps individuals confront and gradually overcome these fears, promoting a sense of empowerment and control over their lives.

Empowering Autonomy: CBT reinforces the concept of personal agency and autonomy. It helps individuals assert themselves, make independent decisions, and develop a stronger sense of self outside the constraints of the family cult.

Resolving Cognitive Dissonance: Leaving a family cult may introduce cognitive dissonance as individuals reconcile their past beliefs with their newfound independence. CBT assists in navigating this cognitive dissonance, providing a framework for understanding and resolving conflicting thoughts.

Building Resilience: Cult survivors often face unique challenges that require resilience. CBT builds resilience by teaching adaptive coping mechanisms, problem-solving skills, and a more flexible mindset, fostering the ability to navigate uncertainties.

Overall, CBT offers practical tools and a structured approach that aligns well with the challenges individuals may face after leaving a family cult.

It provides a supportive framework for rebuilding one's life, fostering emotional well-being, and promoting a positive transition to autonomy and independence.

INTENSIVE INPATIENT AND OUTPATIENT THERAPY

Outpatient Intensive Therapy:

Outpatient intensive therapy, also known as intensive outpatient therapy (IOP), is a structured and comprehensive mental health treatment program that is conducted on an outpatient basis, meaning the individual attends sessions at a clinic or treatment center but does not reside there.

Intensive outpatient therapy typically involves more frequent and longer therapy sessions than traditional outpatient therapy, often ranging from several hours to full-day programs, several days per week. It is designed to provide intensive support and treatment for individuals who require more intensive care than traditional outpatient therapy can offer but do not require round-the-clock supervision or inpatient hospitalization.

Outpatient intensive therapy programs may include a combination of individual therapy, group therapy, family therapy, medication management, psycho-education, and other therapeutic modalities tailored to the individual's needs. These programs are often used to address a wide range of mental health issues, including depression, anxiety, trauma, substance abuse, eating disorders, and more.

The goal of outpatient intensive therapy is to provide comprehensive and focused treatment while allowing individuals to maintain their daily routines, responsibilities, and connections with their support systems outside of the treatment setting. It can be an effective option for individuals who require more structured and intensive support than traditional outpatient therapy but do not require the level of care provided in inpatient or residential treatment settings.

Inpatient Intensive Therapy:

Inpatient intensive therapy, also known as inpatient intensive treatment or residential intensive treatment, is a comprehensive and structured mental health treatment program that takes place in a residential facility or hospital setting.

Inpatient intensive therapy involves round-the-clock care and supervision, with individuals residing at the treatment facility for the duration of the program.
It is typically recommended for individuals who require intensive support and treatment due to severe mental health issues or acute crises that cannot be adequately addressed on an outpatient basis.

Inpatient intensive therapy programs offer a wide range of therapeutic interventions and services, including individual therapy, group therapy, medication management, psycho-education, medical monitoring, and support with daily living activities. The focus is on stabilizing the individual's mental health, addressing immediate concerns or crises, and providing a safe and supportive environment for recovery.

Inpatient intensive therapy programs vary in length, ranging from a few days to several weeks or longer, depending on the individual's needs and progress. The goal of inpatient intensive therapy is to provide intensive and focused treatment in a controlled environment while addressing the individual's immediate mental health needs and preparing them for transition to less intensive levels of care, such as outpatient therapy or step-down programs.

FREQUENTLY ASKED QUESTIONS AND ANSWERS

WHAT ARE SOME REASONS SOMEONE MIGHT NEED INPATIENT OR OUTPATIENT INTENSIVE THERAPY?

Leaving a family cult can be an extremely challenging and traumatic experience, and individuals who have left cults may face a wide range of complex psychological and emotional issues that require intensive support and treatment. Here are some reasons why someone leaving a family cult might need intensive outpatient or inpatient therapy:

Trauma and Post-Traumatic Stress: Many individuals leaving family cults have experienced psychological, emotional, and sometimes physical trauma as a result of their experiences within the cult. They may have been subjected to manipulation, control, abuse, or exploitation, which can lead to symptoms of post-traumatic stress disorder (PTSD) or other trauma-related disorders.

Identity and Belief Confusion: Leaving a family cult often involves questioning deeply ingrained beliefs, values, and identities that were instilled by the cult. Individuals may struggle with feelings of confusion, guilt, shame, and existential crisis as they navigate their beliefs and sense of self outside of the cult environment.

Loss of Social Support: Leaving a family cult often entails leaving behind one's entire social support network, including family members, friends, and community members who remain in the cult. This loss of social support can exacerbate feelings of isolation, loneliness, and disconnection, making it difficult for individuals to cope with the challenges of transitioning to life outside of the cult.

Cognitive and Emotional Distress: Individuals leaving family cults may experience a wide range of cognitive and emotional distress, including anxiety, depression, panic attacks, intrusive thoughts, nightmares, and difficulty regulating emotions. These symptoms can significantly impair functioning and quality of life, necessitating intensive therapeutic intervention.

Reintegration Challenges: Reintegrating into mainstream society after leaving a family cult can be a daunting and overwhelming process. Individuals may struggle with basic life skills, social interactions, educational or vocational pursuits, and establishing a sense of identity and purpose outside of the cult environment.

Intensive outpatient or inpatient therapy provides a structured and supportive environment for individuals leaving family cults to address these complex issues and work towards healing, recovery, and reintegration. These programs offer intensive therapeutic interventions, including individual therapy, group therapy, family therapy, psycho-education, and support with daily living activities, tailored to the specific needs and challenges of survivors of family cults. Additionally, the round-the-clock support and supervision provided in inpatient settings can help ensure safety and stability during the early stages of recovery.

EMDR THERAPY
(EYE MOVEMENT DESENSITIZATION AND REPROCESSING)

EMDR stands for Eye Movement Desensitization and Reprocessing. It is a psychotherapy approach that is used to help individuals process and heal from traumatic experiences and distressing memories.

During EMDR therapy sessions, the individual is asked to recall distressing memories while simultaneously engaging in bilateral stimulation, which can involve following the therapist's hand movements with their eyes, listening to alternating sounds or tones, or feeling tapping or vibrations on their hands. The bilateral stimulation is believed to facilitate the processing of traumatic memories by activating the brain's natural healing mechanisms.

EMDR therapy involves a structured eight-phase approach, which includes assessment, preparation, desensitization, installation of positive beliefs, and closure. The goal of EMDR therapy is to help individuals reprocess traumatic memories and reduce the emotional distress associated with them, leading to resolution and healing.

EMDR therapy has been found to be effective in treating post-traumatic stress disorder (PTSD) and other trauma-related disorders, as well as a range of other mental health conditions, including anxiety, depression, and phobias. It is considered a safe and evidence-based treatment approach when conducted by trained and certified therapists.

FREQUENTLY ASKED QUESTIONS AND ANSWERS

WHAT ARE THE BENEFITS OF EMDR AFTER LEAVING A FAMILY CULT?

EMDR (Eye Movement Desensitization and Reprocessing) therapy can be beneficial for someone recovering from a family cult for several reasons:

Trauma Processing: Leaving a family cult often involves traumatic experiences, including psychological, emotional, and sometimes physical abuse or manipulation. EMDR therapy is specifically designed to help individuals process and heal from traumatic memories, reducing the emotional distress associated with them and promoting resolution and recovery.

Addressing Core Beliefs: Family cults often instill rigid and harmful beliefs in their members, which can persist even after leaving the cult.
EMDR therapy can help individuals identify and reprocess these core beliefs, challenging their validity and promoting more adaptive and healthy beliefs and perspectives.

Managing Triggers and Flashbacks: Individuals recovering from a family cult may experience triggers and flashbacks related to their cult experiences, which can be distressing and disruptive to daily functioning. EMDR therapy can help individuals learn to manage these triggers and reduce the frequency and intensity of flashbacks, allowing for greater stability and emotional regulation.

Reprocessing Attachment and Relationship Issues: Family cults often foster unhealthy attachment patterns and relationship dynamics, which can impact individuals' ability to form healthy relationships outside of the cult. EMDR therapy can help individuals reprocess attachment-related traumas and develop more secure and functional relationship patterns.

Empowerment and Self-Identity: Leaving a family cult can be a profound and transformative experience, but it can also be disorienting and challenging as individuals navigate their identity and sense of self outside of the cult environment. EMDR therapy can help individuals reclaim their sense of agency, autonomy, and self-identity, empowering them to live authentically and confidently.

Overall, EMDR therapy can be a valuable tool in the recovery process for individuals leaving family cults, providing a structured and evidence-based approach to healing from trauma, reprocessing core beliefs, managing triggers and flashbacks, reprocessing attachment issues, and promoting empowerment and self-identity. It is important for individuals considering EMDR therapy to work with a qualified and experienced therapist who can provide appropriate support and guidance throughout the process.

CAN EMDR CREATE FALSE MEMORIES ?

EMDR (Eye Movement Desensitization and Reprocessing) therapy has been subject to some criticism and concerns about the potential for creating false memories, although research and clinical evidence do not support this reputation. Here are some factors that have contributed to this perception:

Misunderstanding of the Therapy: EMDR therapy involves recalling and processing traumatic memories while engaging in bilateral stimulation, such as eye movements, hand tapping, or auditory stimulation. Some individuals may misunderstand or misinterpret this process as a form of suggestion or manipulation, leading to concerns about the potential for creating false memories.

Controversial History of Memory Recovery Therapies: EMDR therapy emerged in the 1980s and 1990s, a period when there was heightened interest in memory recovery therapies for trauma, including techniques like hypnosis and guided imagery. Some of these therapies were later found to be associated with the unintentional creation of false memories, leading to skepticism and caution about new therapies like EMDR.

Skepticism and Criticism: EMDR therapy has faced skepticism and criticism from some practitioners and researchers within the mental health field, who have questioned its mechanisms of action and effectiveness. Concerns about the potential for creating false memories may be fueled by these broader debates about the validity and efficacy of EMDR therapy.

It's important to note that there is no empirical evidence to support the idea that EMDR therapy creates false memories. In fact, research studies have consistently demonstrated the safety and effectiveness of EMDR therapy for trauma-related disorders, including post-traumatic stress disorder (PTSD), without any indication of false memory creation.

However, as with any therapeutic approach, it's essential for therapists to adhere to ethical guidelines and best practices when using EMDR therapy, including obtaining informed consent, ensuring the accuracy of information, and providing appropriate support and monitoring throughout the treatment process.

WHY DOES EMDR RECEIVE CRITICISM FOR THE TREATMENT OF PTSD?

While Eye Movement Desensitization and Reprocessing (EMDR) is considered an effective treatment for post-traumatic stress disorder (PTSD) by many mental health professionals, there are some concerns and criticisms associated with its use. Some of these concerns include:

Lack of Understanding: EMDR's mechanisms of action are not fully understood, leading to skepticism from some practitioners and researchers about its efficacy. While there is evidence supporting its effectiveness, there are also questions about how it works and whether its effects are significantly different from other forms of therapy.

Need for Skilled Practitioners: EMDR requires specialized training and certification to administer effectively. Concerns arise when therapists without proper training attempt to use EMDR, as this could potentially lead to inadequate treatment or even harm to clients. Such as creating false memories.

Overemphasis on Eye Movement: Some critics argue that the emphasis on eye movement in EMDR is unnecessary and that other forms of bilateral stimulation, such as hand tapping or auditory stimulation, may be equally effective. This raises questions about whether eye movement is a critical component of EMDR's effectiveness.

Potential for Re-traumatization: EMDR involves revisiting traumatic memories, which can be distressing for some individuals and may lead to re-traumatization if not handled carefully. Therapists need to ensure that clients are adequately prepared and supported throughout the process to minimize the risk of worsening symptoms.

Limited Evidence for Long-Term Effects: While EMDR has been shown to be effective in reducing PTSD symptoms in the short term, there is limited evidence on its long-term effects. Some critics argue that more research is needed to determine whether the benefits of EMDR are sustained over time.

Overall, while EMDR is a widely used and respected treatment for PTSD, it is important for practitioners and researchers to continue to critically evaluate its efficacy, safety, and mechanisms of action. Additionally, clients considering EMDR should seek out trained and experienced therapists to ensure they receive high-quality care.

SUPPORTING SOMEONE IN THERAPY

Supporting someone going through therapy after leaving a family cult involves providing them with empathy, validation, and practical assistance. Here are some best practices:

Listen without judgment: Create a safe and non-judgmental space for the individual to express their feelings, experiences, and concerns about therapy. Validate their emotions and experiences, and offer support and encouragement as they navigate the therapeutic process.

Educate yourself: Take the time to educate yourself about the dynamics of family cults, the challenges faced by survivors, and the therapeutic approaches commonly used in their recovery. This will help you better understand the individual's experiences and provide more effective support.

Respect their autonomy: Respect the individual's autonomy and agency in their therapy process. Avoid imposing your own beliefs or expectations on them, and support their decisions and choices regarding their treatment.

Offer practical assistance: Offer practical assistance to help alleviate the individual's stress and facilitate their participation in therapy. This could include helping them find a therapist, scheduling appointments, providing transportation, or assisting with childcare or other responsibilities.

Encourage self-care: Encourage the individual to prioritize self-care and engage in activities that promote their physical, emotional, and mental well-being. This could include exercise, relaxation techniques, hobbies, or spending time with supportive friends and family members.

Be patient and supportive: Recovery from leaving a family cult and undergoing therapy is a complex and challenging process that takes time. Be patient, supportive, and understanding as the individual navigates their journey towards healing and self-discovery.

Respect confidentiality: Respect the individual's confidentiality and privacy regarding their therapy process. Avoid sharing sensitive information or discussing their therapy without their explicit consent.

Provide validation and encouragement: Validate the individual's progress and achievements in therapy, no matter how small. Offer encouragement and support to help them stay motivated and committed to their healing journey.

By implementing these best practices, you can provide valuable support and encouragement to someone going through therapy after leaving a family cult, helping them navigate their recovery journey with compassion and resilience.

CHAPTER 9

HEALING AND FORGIVENESS

Dear Reader,

Healing and forgiveness is an incredible journey of heartache, pain, loss, and rediscovery of self. It is during this journey that many people begin to question the true meaning of forgiveness and healing. Like most things that are listed in this book, healing and forgiveness is a completely individual experience and no two people can experience this journey in the same way. I can only convey to you what this tapestry of healing has looked like, one thread at a time.

Forgiveness is defined by the following: An intentional decision to let go of resentment, anger, and grudges held against someone, or someones, who have wronged you.

This statement has held a social belief that forgiveness can and should be given to someone even if they do not ask for forgiveness, or apologize for any wrong they might have inflicted.

While most would believe this is the journey to forgive my family for the multiple wrongs and abuses they have inflicted upon me, and find healing in that way, it is not. Surprisingly, it was at the heart of this journey that I learned that the most important person to forgive, was myself. Through much therapy, deconstruction, education, and forcing myself to look in the mirror of my life, and see the truth of my existence; I am both the victim and survivor.

I, the survivor, was able to break free of the bonds of an indoctrinated past, abusive parents, religious trauma, sexual abuse, and face the truth that I was born into a cult. The victim in me, however, was left small with a big voice to mask the deep fear I lived daily. I learned the delicate dance to keep the body safe, and mother pacified.

I was never loved, or comforted. I was forced to normalize behaviors that no human should ever have to suffer. I was never allowed to grow up, and most sadly, I never allowed myself to think I could. I hated and loathed this part of me, the part that I always thought was submissive and pathetic. Always unable to break-free or escape. I blamed myself, I beheld myself a grudge.

In my path to understanding forgiveness, I owe the following deepest apology to myself:

I am so sorry you had to endure what you did. I am so sorry you were ever unsafe, and never given the hand of safety or trust. I am so sorry how she hurt you and how you could not fight back. I am so sorry that your body was violated without your consent.

I am so sorry you were never loved or seen, and forced to sob into your pillow so you couldn't be heard. I am so sorry you had to find refuge inside of your closet for nearly a year to hide from her wrath. I am so sorry about how she broke your spirit and never allowed you autonomy. I am so sorry you ever felt like your existence was ever a burden…for all of this and more, I am sorry.

In my sorrow, I take full accountability for the weight of the apology towards myself and no longer hold a grudge. I offer myself full and complete forgiveness. I offer myself healing and growth. I free myself of the guilt and hate that was thrust on me by the actions of others. I will no longer hold myself accountable for other's actions perpetuated upon me. I will allow myself healthy boundaries, autonomy, and consent in all aspects of my life. I will strive for balance and self-care. I will allow my inner victim as much time and grace as needed to heal. I will be held accountable for all of my past actions, and future ones.

In all that I have learned over the past few years since escaping, forgiveness is very key for healing. Being unable to forgive yourself, clouds all clear vision and perspectives of your life. It is in the forgiveness of myself, I am learning my value and who does or does not deserve a seat at my table.

The remaining question is, have I forgiven my parents for all of their actions? The answer is very simply, yes. That is to say, I do not hold a grudge towards them, nor do I hold any ill will.

However, it is not forgiving my parents that has brought healing, but it was the forgiveness of myself. When I made the conscious decision to truly forgive myself, I understood that I now had to protect myself, and look at my parents for who and what they really are. I will never allow myself to be their victim ever again. I love myself too much for that now.

My parents have failed, and continued to fail, at acknowledging any wrong doing or abuses against me, offer apologies for any wrong doing, nor have they made any valid attempts towards change. The consistent lack of self reflection or emotional maturity on their part, has now and forever changed their seating at my table.

"When Jesus had received the sour wine, He said, 'It is finished,' and He bowed his head and gave up His spirit" (John 19:30)

www.ingramcontent.com/pod-product-compliance
Lightning Source LLC
Chambersburg PA
CBHW080517030426
42337CB00023B/4547